Gender Equity

Gender Equity

Global Policies and Perspectives on Advancing Social Justice

Edited by Elena V. Shabliy, Kimarie Engerman, and Dmitry Kurochkin

LEXINGTON BOOKS
Lanham • Boulder • New York • London

Published by Lexington Books
An imprint of The Rowman & Littlefield Publishing Group, Inc.
4501 Forbes Boulevard, Suite 200, Lanham, Maryland 20706
www.rowman.com
86-90 Paul Street, London EC2A 4NE

British Library Cataloguing in Publication Information Available

Library of Congress Cataloging-in-Publication Data
ISBN 978-1-66691-447-4 (cloth: alk. paper)
ISBN 978-1-66691-448-1 (electronic)

♾™ The paper used in this publication meets the minimum requirements of American National Standard for Information Sciences—Permanence of Paper for Printed Library Materials, ANSI/NISO Z39.48-1992.

Contents

List of Figures and Tables

FIGURES

TABLES

Introduction

Gender Equity and Social Justice

Elena V. Shabliy

Gender equity and equality promotion became a priority for the current political structure of the United States and other countries. The United States has issued the Gender Equity Report on October 22, 2021; and gender equity became an integral part of advancing gender and public policy. Integrating gender equity became an important dimension to human well-being and global flourishing. The concept of gender equity displays different semantic connotations and is loaded with other meanings in contrast to equality. The World Health Organization (WHO) defines gender equality as the absence of discrimination on the basis of a person's gender in opportunities, in the allocation of resources and benefits or in access to services. At the same time, according to the WHO, gender equity refers to justice in the distribution of benefits and responsibilities between women and men.[1] This concept recognizes that they have different needs and power and that these differences should be addressed in a manner that rectifies the social imbalance.[2] Gender equity presupposes fairness to both men and women and ultimately leads to gender equality.[3] Equity is the "consistent and systematic fair, just, and impartial treatment of all individuals, including those who belong to underserved communities that have been denied such treatment, such as women and girls. . ."[4] Both—gender equity and gender equality—promote equal opportunity to all people regardless gender. Gender equ(al)ity remains the timely research issue requiring an in-depth analysis in all economies; promoting and advancing gender equity is a key pillar to fostering not only future political development, but also achieving the overall societal balanced development nationally and worldwide. Comprehensive social and public policies allow narrowing the present gender gap and advancing the role of women in world economies. A complex and multidimensional approach is needed when assessing women's political and economic participation, their leadership, and decision-making opportunities. When analyzing gender equity, the current political structures should be considered and thoroughly examined. This book offers an analysis of gender equity and political development, as well as looks at the participation of women in the economy and decision-making process, and their impact on shaping public and social policies. Profeta (2020) supports the idea that "women's empowerment follows the principle that government should intervene in the economy for equity and efficiency reasons."[5] Universities and research organizations may offer a changing paradigm for gender equity development being organizational leaders in the gender dialogue and offering an effective platform for women's rights discussion. Substantial gender gap problems also persist because of system-based issues, the current political structure, business and economics paradigm: "We see this in the established and deeply entrenched structural and cultural hindrances, treasured hierarchies, existing power differentials, and prevailing stereotypes and biases that have historically been protected to preserve this unacceptable *status quo*."[6] Depending on whether or not we consider women's rights as part of *international human legal rights* (IHLR), there are two approaches in the study of human rights—*political* and *moral*. The *political* approach to human rights gives the reason for sovereign state interference in cases of human rights violations.[7] The *moral approach* presupposes a preexisting philosophical concept of *moral* human rights.[8]

The government's efforts to advance women's position facilitate women's active involvement in the country's economy and political affairs. Not so long ago, women were almost excluded from the economy with limited legal rights across the world and a lack of the right to vote. The Industrial Revolution and women's rights movements across the globe partially changed women's lot. The political opportunity structure is changing gradually, allowing women leaders to participate in public affairs and pave the way to the political leadership. Gender quotas, for example, may facilitate progress toward economic and political gender equality and to promote women's leadership.[9] Women's empowerment directly affects public policy.[10] There are exceptions, of course, such as a famous example when Margaret Thatcher did not always wholeheartedly support women's issues. It sometimes happens that when women leaders achieve a leading position, some might distance themselves from the "woman question."

The style of male and female leadership, which emerges as a combination of different individual psychological attributes, may differ, as some scholars suggest.[11] There is a need to instruct leaders throughout sectors to achieve better results in representing diversity: "Leaders are the stewards of an organization's culture; their behaviors and mindsets reverberate throughout the organization. Hence to dismantle systems of discrimination and subordination, leaders must undergo the same shifts of heart, mind, and behavior that they want for the organization as a whole and then translate those personal shifts into real, lasting change in their companies."[12] Diversity, as it is known, offers a positive angle of view, especially during the crisis time, such as COVID-19. Banks, for instance, with a diverse board have better performances and gender diversity plays a crucial role during crisis times.[13]

Reforms and policies that empower women's advancement boost economic growth.[14] Whereas specifically women suffer during the pandemic crisis, losing their jobs and having so-called double-burden—home and work chores simultaneously—there might be positive trends in the digital revolution in the developed countries, such as the United States, European Union, Australia, New Zealand, etc. More than 90% of companies in Sweden allow flexible working options; and new technology is making it easier to redesign work in all sorts of family-friendly ways.[15] In Germany, some companies (with more than 500 employees) must publish reports on promotion equal pay.[16]

THE PANDEMIC CRISIS: CHALLENGES AND NEW OPPORTUNITIES

During the COVID-19 crisis, particularly women have been negatively impacted.[17] As a result, approximately one in four women are downshifting their careers or leaving the workforce completely.[18] Women in the Workplace 2020 McKinsey report states that companies risk losing women in leadership positions—and future women leaders—and years of progress toward gender diversity.[19] The Report underlines that three groups are especially vulnerable during the pandemic: senior-level women, women of color, mothers.[20] This report shows that when women are well represented at the top, companies are 50 percent more likely to outperform their peers.[21] Also, many companies adjust their policies to support their employees during the pandemic—offering more paid time off and providing resources for homeschooling.[22] Following the Black Swan principle, current challenges also present opportunities if "companies make significant investments in building a more flexible and empathetic workplace . . . they can retain the employees most affected by today's crises and nurture a culture in which women have equal opportunity to achieve their potential over the long term."[23] Women in the Workplace 2020 McKinsey report points out that between 2015 and 2020, there was slow but steady progress in women's representation: "Between 2015 and 2020, the share of women grew from 23 to 28 percent in SVP roles—and from 17 to 21 percent in the C-suite. Women remained dramatically underrepresented, particularly women of color, but the numbers were slowly improving."[24] However, the COVID-19 crisis threatens women's recent achievements.[25] Goldin (2021) examines the current situation and comes to a conclusion that modern women, especially during the ongoing COVID-19 crisis, are anxious: "Despite their travels along this road that was paved by their great-grandmothers, grandmothers, and mothers (most of whom were anxious, too), they are still caught between devoting themselves to a career and devoting themselves to a family."[26]

Another comprehensive report—"Women, Business and the Law 2020" examines 190 economies and women's economic rights measuring gender discrimination over the last decade and tracks how the gender policy advancement impacts women across economies.[27] Female economic participation is higher, where are the effective legislative tools ensuring gender equity and supporting the adequate economic opportunity structure.[28] According to this report, the equal participation of stakeholders will give every economy a chance to achieve its potential.[29] Existing global inequality (with a rare exceptions such as Scandinavian counties), harm and impede potential economic growth and development.[30] Belgium, Canada, Denmark, France, Latvia, Luxembourg, and Sweden—score 100, according to the report, "meaning that women are on an equal legal standing with men . . ." Around ninety economies have at least one restriction on the jobs for women.[31] Some countries reduced the list of jobs prohibited from women's participation—among these countries are the Russian Federation, Kazakhstan, and Uzbekistan.[32] Moldova, on the contrary, lifted legal restrictions on women's employment and women's ability to get jobs that are considered "dangerous."[33] In the recent past, around forty economies implemented reforms toward equality and opportunity; Nepal, for example, introduced a labor law favoring women's entry into the labor market and prohibiting discrimination employment.[34] Moreover, Nepal introduced 15 days of paid paternity leave.[35] In the Indian state of Maharashtra, there were eliminated restrictions on women's ability to work in "dangerous" jobs.[36] Pakistan, Sri Lanka, and Zambia increased the period of paid maternity leave.[37] The latter extended the duration of paid maternity leave from 84 to 98 days.[38] Armenia introduced the law protecting women from domestic violence.[39] Georgia made access to financial services to women.[40] The United States, Canada, Cyprus, Czech Republic, Fiji, Jordan, Nepal, South Sudan introduced paid paternity leave.[41] In New York State, there was introduced paid family leave that currently entitles each parent to 70 days of leave for the birth of a child; and it will gradually increase to 84 days.[42]

GLOBAL DEVELOPMENT GOALS
AND THE 2030 AGENDA

The 2030 Agenda was developed in Europe in 2015 as a way to encourage positive changes and equity advancement across societies; this Agenda aims at solving fundamental problems, such as ending global poverty, reducing gender inequality, and achieving positive results and progress in Sustainable Development by 2030 around the world.[43] Universities establish formal offices for diversity, equity, and inclusion, demonstrating that gender equity is an institutional priority.[44] Gender equity should be achieved not in separate fields, such as political, economic, and business, but across disciplinary boundaries; "it is time to achieve gender equity in science and medicine, not just for the sake of everyone's health, but also for our collective human dignity and value."[45] The goal of this book is to describe barriers to gender equity and to illustrate how some women have worked against those barriers to make important contributions. The book also focuses on *transformational*, generational, and educational women's leadership. Furthermore, the chapters offer up-to-date ideas and examples of women's moral leadership. The term *intersectionality* is widely used in social sciences and legal research. It was coined by an American legal scholar Kimberlé Crenshaw more than two decades ago.[46] This term helps explain the oppression of all women and is widely in social sciences. This book focuses not only on gender equity and policy development, but also on social, cultural, and economic barriers to women worldwide. The chapters provide novel ideas, puzzles, controversies, and debates offering the vehicles for making readers think critically about feminist perspectives on women and politics. These contributions question the structural conditions of gender (in)equality and the conditions under which women's collective action for gender equality succeeds. Chapters present different disciplinary lenses (i.e., psychology, law, sociology, economics, education, management, and political science) touching on issues of interest to academics and practitioners that help reveal women's struggles. The volume covers different regions of the world synthesizing available research and commentary providing examples and tying research findings with real-world events and outcomes also showing why it is important to be aware of these topics. The covered topics include women in peacemaking and conflict resolution, as well as an overview of unconscious biases. This book represents the multiple connections between the political representation of women and the broader political processes, as well as broader gender equity issues. The book is organized as follows. Chapter 1 of this book concentrates on societal effects on women in STEM and well explains the origins of gender gaps in educational fields. Women, for example, in OECD (Organization for Economic

Co-operation and Development) countries constitute the low percentage of women in STEM (Science, Technology, Engineering, Mathematics) fields and still prefer to study humanities.[47] Profeta in her groundbreaking study *Gender Equality and Public Policy Measuring Progress in Europe* points out that there is an urgent need to fill the gap, as these disciplines offer better labor market opportunities providing access to more rewarding jobs, leadership career, and empowerment.[48] In Europe, only 8% of full professors in engineering and technology are women.[49] There are more women receiving higher education than men in all European countries.[50] Women represent 47% of Ph.D. students, 45% of assistant professors, 37% of associate professors, and only 21% of full professors.[51] Although women have surpassed men in the Educational Attainment dimension globally, still only 40.6% of young women and 35.6% of young men graduate from high school and attend university.[52] In the United States, almost 45% of twenty-five-year-old women have graduated or will graduate with a bachelor's equivalent degree; the level for men is 36%.[53] Since 1980s, more women than men graduated from four-year institutions.[54]

Chapter 2 deals with cultural policy economic instruments and their analysis in Serbia, as a case study. It provides a new reflection on economic instruments and measures in culture analyzing their character, structure and effects in Serbia from the female perspective and their perception of fairness and justice. It defines cultural policy economic instruments and measures, types, classification framework and formulation principles of fair practices. The methodology is presented and 38 economic instruments and 103 measures of cultural policies are analyzed. Evidence demonstrates large pay gaps between men and women in the creative sector and a low level of *fair practices* for female cultural producers. Chapter 3 argues that in order to achieve peace and security's goals, it is essential to increase political empowerment for women and engagement at all levels of the decision-making processes, generating a more effective and credible justice and security environment for women and girls after conflicts and economic resources to support them in recovery processes. A peace process raises new opportunities for women to have their concerns and experiences of conflict heard and to play a part in their country's peace building. If successful, women can influence the entire political and legal structures of the country. Women are usually also excluded from negotiating tables, peacemaking and peacebuilding processes despite their significant contributions to preventing and resolving conflicts. It has been demonstrated by the United Nations that women's participation in conflict prevention and resolution can improve the existing state of affairs—before, during and after conflict, but their representation in peace processes (negotiations and agreements) has lagged all around the world. However, the structural gender-based discrimination that women experience in conflict-affected and post-conflict contexts is deep and prevent them participating in political, social and economic decision-making processes on equal terms as men. Chapter 4 presents a case study of Professor Alice Shalvi and her leadership. This chapter describes and defines her leadership in educational and feminist context through her public activism and leadership. Professor Alice Shalvi held a leading position of the unique religious high school for girl, Pelech, and the women's organization, the Israel Women's Network (IWN) that was an organization for political and social policy change to benefit the advancement of the status of the Israeli woman. During the decades when Professor Shalvi was active, there have been far-reaching changes in the status of women in Israel. Professor Shalvi's leadership biography is a real-life example of women's outstanding leadership that served as a catalyst for changes in the status of women in many ways with a profound impact on advancing public and social policy. Chapter 5 provides a biographical account of the Holocaust survivor—Zofia Rozensztrauch, née Naomi Judkowski. Her paintings and leadership beyond imaginable present an inter-generational memory mapping. Her paintings were provided as evidence, in addition to witnesses' testimonies. Her courage and courage of other women, who took such a great risk keeping these documents, make inter-generational justice and "never again" imperative possible. Remembering and keeping this collective trauma is humanity's duty. Eufrosinia Antonovna Kersnovskaya (1908–1994) is also an example of an exceptional woman who spent many years in GULAG camps, wrote her memoirs, and left many paintings documenting history and presenting collective memory mapping. Chapter 6 describes women's collective action in West Africa. Women's organizations helped advance public and social policy in the Gambia. Chapter 7 attempts to define the principles of inclusive education and the challenges families and girls face to access inclusive education (e.g., broadband access, accommodations, modifications due to disabilities) during the pandemic.

Chapter 8 discusses Arab women's political participation. Arab women are subject to political underrepresentation and marginalization. Many variables have their impact on the efforts made to attain their political inclusion. Strategies that are implemented to foster it deliver better results if they are incorporated in the process of democratization, embedding the latter's values in institutional mechanisms addressing Arab women's political representation and participation. The Arab world is witnessing extensive gender political inequality, extending over long periods. The chapter examines the figures published by international development organizations, and the literature produced by scholars, regarding the status of Arab women's political rights. Chapter 9 offers a comparative analysis of women's political representation in India and Bangladesh. This chapter examines the correlation of gender quotas and gender equality. This chapter evaluates how gender quotas reduced gender inequality in the decision-making process in India and Bangladesh. Furthermore, this volume considers current public gender policies and gender dynamics worldwide. Despite continuous steady progress and "quiet revolution," the gender gap is wide open across various economies.[55] Goldin (2021) writes in her book *Career and Family: Women's Century-long Journey Toward Equity* about the "quiet revolution" that radically changed the happiness formula for American women.[56] This Revolution transformed women's lives, according to Goldin (2021):

> The Quiet Revolution was amazingly swift in its transformation of women's lives. But the transformation didn't come out of nowhere. Its members were in training from the time they were young. They had observed a succession of generations and seen how theirs would be different. They formed more accurate expectations of their future labor force participation and had ambitions that were consistent with it. . . . They began to prepare themselves early. They took more science and math courses in high school and increased their scores on standardized tests.[57]

The participants members of this revolution set new gender equ(al)ity goals. As Goldin argues, women had to restructure their lives delaying marriage and motherhood to achieve this goal.[58] After the "quite revolution," female graduates prefer the career tracks, but "their earnings and promotions—relative to those of the men they graduated with—continue to make them look like they've been sideswiped."[59] To date, there is still a 31.4% average gender gap that remains to be closed globally.[60] To eliminate this persisting gap, multiple programs and policies are being introduced; public policies are continuously being readjusted as governments are taking new course of action to meet the needs and sometimes change accordingly.[61] "Thus, affirmative action, . . . quota system, or reservations for special groups have become policy instruments with which gender equity is introduced in economic institutions, social structures and education schemes."[62] European countries gradually introduce gender quotas that lead to positive outcomes and a better women's representation across the economy. Iceland is one of the most gender-equal countries in the world.[63] It is followed by Norway which is one of the first countries that implemented gender quotas, with the 2003 requirement threshold of 40 percent of each gender on the boards of companies listed on its stock market.[64] The Norwegian law "imposed a dramatic and rapid transformation of the composition of boards of directors . . . with an increase in women and young members as well as an increase in female directors with multiple positions (the so-called golden-skirt phenomenon)."[65] In two other Scandinavian countries—Finland and Sweden—gender parity has been almost achieved.[66] France also adopted gender quotas in 2011 and introduced board gender quotas in industry.[67] After France, Italy and Belgium followed this example in 2011.[68] Germany joined the quota system in 2015 and Portugal—in 2018.[69] Goldin point out that rising inequality in earning may be one of the reasons why the gender gap among college graduates persists, despite some visible improvements in women's lot; it may be the reason why the gender earnings gap for college graduates became larger than that between men and women in the entire population in the 1990s.[70]

CONCLUSION

Advancing gender equity and global policy is a timely theme representing interconnections between social justice and the broader philosophical issues at the global, national, or local level. Unconscious biases have a great impact on women's careers. According to the *Harvard Business Review*, the very words that society uses to describe men and women may significantly impact their careers.[71] Goldin (2021) convincingly argues: "Women continue to feel shortchanged. They fall behind in their careers while earning less than their husbands and male colleagues . . . They are taken advantage of, discriminated against, harassed, and excluded from the boys' club."[72] Chapters 1 and 2 of this book well describe these biases. This book brings together leading scholars working on gender equ(al)ity issues to explore key sources of female empowerment and discuss the current challenges and opportunities for the future. The volume adopts a multi-disciplinary approach to present different angles from gender-focused economics and social research addressing the topics of gender asymmetries and cultural stereotypes that prevail in the political and business contexts, and hinder the progress of humanity. The book tackles many contemporary and historic(al) issues, supported by a wide variety of chapters, creating a space for a critical thought and by presenting a diversity of voices and experiences. To date, no country has yet achieved full gender parity; the top advanced economies have closed at least 80% of their gaps, and the best performer, Iceland, has closed 82% of its gap so far.[73] This book considers both—developed and developing economies. Sustainable societal development is one of the major goals of the near future.[74] Equity, inclusion, and diversity are those flagships that will foster the near future political and societal development. Gender quotas may be useful in reducing the glass ceiling.[75] Despite recent positive changes for the women's representation in the political arena, "[e]vidence on women in politics generally shows that they are underrepresented compared to men at all levels and that they are more represented in local politics than at the national level. This seems, again, to support the evidence that a career for women in politics is difficult."[76] Promoting gender equality and advancing gender global policy are ways to fully realize talents that are essential for growth and a globally competitive world.[77] Advancing family and parental policy help support the female labor supply, and gender quotas may be useful in reducing the glass ceiling.[78] According to the *Economist*, "Women's economic empowerment is arguably the biggest social change of our times."[79] Projecting current trends and predicting the future sustainable development, the overall global gender gap will close in around 100 years, on average, across the 107 countries.[80] At a slow speed, taking into account also the pandemic crisis, which will impact sustainable development worldwide—to close this gap will take even more than twice longer.[81] Gender gaps can be closed in 50–60 years in Western Europe, the Caribbean, and Latin America, in around 70 years in South Asia, and around 100 years—in Sub-Saharan Africa, Eastern Europe, and Central Asia, around 140 years—in the Middle East and North Africa.[82] Policy-makers and other stakeholders need to develop gender policies, in order to accelerate future progress.[83] According to the Global Gender Gap Report, the gap remains wide open in Political Empowerment worldwide.[84] The Economic Participation and Opportunity in the second dimension where women are extremely underrepresented: economic opportunities for women are extremely limited in India (35.4%), Pakistan (32.7%), Yemen (27.3%), Syria (24.9%), and Iraq (22.7%).[85] In the dimension of Educational Attainment, some countries achieved full parity and there was significant progress across the world: nine are in Western Europe, nine are in Latin America, eight are in the Eastern Europe and Central Asia region, three in Sub-Saharan Africa, two in East Asia and the Pacific, two in North America, and one each in South Asia and the Middle East and North Africa.[86] Braking cultural barriers as well as introducing and promoting public policies regarding gender equ(al)ity are essential steps for the future gender equity goals achievement.

BIBLIOGRAPHY

Acosta, David, D. M. Lautenberger, L. Castillo-Page & D. J. Skorton. 2020. "Achieving Gender Equity Is Our Responsibility: Leadership Matters." *Academic Medicine* 95 (10): 1468–1471.

Barling, J. 2014. "Gender and Leadership." In *The Science of Leadership*, chapter 8. Oxford: Oxford University Press. DOI: 10.1093/acprof: oso/9780199757015.003.0008

Burns, James MacGregor. 1979. *Leadership*. New York: Harper & Row.

"COVID-19 Impact on Women and Gender Equality." McKinsey & Company. https://www.mckinsey.com/featured-insights/future-of-work/covid-19-and-gender -equality-countering-the-regressive-effects (Last accessed 09/07/2021).

"COVID-19's Impact on Women's Employment." McKinsey & Company. https://www.mckinsey.com/featured-insights/diversity-and-inclusion/seven-charts-that-show-covid-19s-impact-on-womens-employment#:~:text=The%20pandemic%20had%20a%20near,versus%20one%20in%20five%20men (Last accessed 09/07/2021).

De Beauvoir, Simone. 1957. *The Second Sex*. New York: Knopf.

Ely, Robin J., and David A. Thomas. 2020. "Getting Serious About Diversity: Enough Already with the Business Case." *Harvard Business Review* 98 (6)(November): 114–22.

Gheaus, Anca. 2011. "Gender Justice." *Journal of Ethics & Social Philosophy* 6: 1–25.

Goldin, Claudia. 2021. *Career and Family: Women's Century-long Journey toward Equity*. Princeton: Princeton University Press.

Maliks, R. and J. K. Schaffer (eds.). 2017. Moral and Political Conceptions of Human Rights: Implications for Theory and Practice. Cambridge: Cambridge University Press.

Matland, Richard E. *Women in Parliament: Beyond Numbers*. Stockholm: International IDEA, 2006.

O'Brien Diana Z. and Johanna Rickne. "Gender Quotas and Women's Political Leadership." *The American Political Science Review* 110 (1): 112–26.

Profeta, Paola. 2020. *Gender Equality and Public Policy: Measuring Progress in Europe*. Cambridge, United Kingdom; New York, NY: Cambridge University Press.

Rawls, John. 2001. *The Law of Peoples.* Cambridge: Harvard University Press.

Ryan, Michelle and Alex Haslam. 2006. "What Lies Beyond the Glass Ceiling?" *Human Resource Management International Digest* 14 (3): 3–5.

Shabliy E., Kurochkin D., and Gloria Ayee (eds.). 2020. *Global Perspectives on Women's Leadership and Gender (In)Equality.* London: Palgrave Macmillan.

Schüssel Fiorenza, Elisabeth. 2007. *The Power of the Word: Scripture and the Rhetoric of Empire*. Minneapolis: Fortress Press, 2007.

Sutton, Robert. "True Leaders Are Also Managers." *Harvard Business Review.* https://hbr.org/2010/08/true-leaders-are-also-managers (Last Accessed 09/07/2021).

The Inter-Parliamentary Union. 2020. https://www.unwomen.org/en/digital-library/publications/2020/03/women-in-politics-map-2020 (Last accessed 09/07/2021).

The Inter-Parliamentary Union. 2021. https://www.unwomen.org/en/digital-library/publications/2021/03/women-in-politics-map-2021 (Last accessed 09/07/2021).

The Sustainable Development Agenda. "17 Goals for People, for Planet." https://www.un.org/sustainabledevelopment/development-agenda/ (Last Accessed 09/07/2021).

"Women, Business, and the Law 2020." World Bank Group. https://openknowledge.worldbank.org/bitstream/handle/10986/32639/9781464815324.pdf (Last accessed 09/07/2021).

"Women in the Workplace 2020." Corporate America Is at a Critical Crossroads, https://www.mckinsey.com/featured-insights/diversity-and-inclusion/women-in-the-workplace McKinsey & Company (Last accessed 09/07/2021).

World Economic Forum. 2020. *Global Gender Gap Report 2020: Insight Report*. http://www3.weforum.org/docs/WEF_GGGR_2020.pdf (Last accessed 09/07/2021).
World Economic Forum. 2021. *Global Gender Gap Report 2021: Insight Report.* http://www3.weforum.org/docs/WEF_GGGR_2021.pdf (Last accessed 09/07/2021).

NOTES

1. "Integrating Gender Perspectives in the Work of WHO," https://apps.who.int/iris/handle/10665/67649 (last accessed 11/20/2021).

2. Ibid.

3. UNFPA, "What Is Meant by Gender?" https://www.unfpa.org/resources/frequently-asked-questions-about-gender-equality (last accessed 11/19/2021).

4. "National Strategy on Gender Equity and Equality," https://www.whitehouse.gov/wp-content/uploads/2021/10/National-Strategy-on-Gender-Equity-and-Equality.pdf (last accessed 11/19/2021).

5. Paola Profeta, *Gender Equality and Public Policy: Measuring Progress in Europe* (Cambridge: Cambridge University Press, 2020), xv.

6. On a system-based gender problem please see David A. Acosta, Diana M. Lautenberger, Laura Castillo-Page, and David J. Skorton, "Achieving Gender Equity Is Our Responsibility: Leadership Matters," *Academic Medicine 95,* no. 10 (2020): 1468–1471 (my emphasis).

7. *Moral and Political Conceptions of Human Rights: Implications for Theory and Practice* by Reidar Maliks and Johan Karlsson Schaffer (eds.) (Cambridge: Cambridge University Press, 2017).

8. Ibid., 16. Griffin, for example, rejects the idea that collective rights could be human rights; human rights are individual. John Rawls's *Law of Peoples* (1999), for example, is a contribution to the *political approach* in the field of human rights.

9. Paola Profeta, *Gender Equality and Public Policy*, 55.

10. Ibid., 82.

11. Ibid., 83–84.

12. Robin J.. Ely and David A. Thomas. "Getting Serious About Diversity: Enough Already with the Business Case," *Harvard Business Review* 98, no. 6 (November 2020): 119.

13. Paola Profeta, *Gender Equality and Public Policy,* 87.

14. Ibid.; "Women, Business, and the Law 2020," https://openknowledge.worldbank.org/bitstream/handle/10986/32639/9781464815324.pdf?sequence=10&isAllowed=y (last accessed 1/31/2021).

15. "We Did It," *The* Economist, January 2, 2010.

16. "Women, Business, and the Law 2020," https://openknowledge.worldbank.org/bitstream/handle/10986/32639/9781464815324.pdf (last accessed 1/31/2021), 14. In Iceland, companies with 25 or more workers are required to obtain equal pay certification from the government.

17. "Women in the Workplace 2020," Corporate America Is at a Critical Cross-roads, https://www.mckinsey.com/featured-insights/diversity-and-inclusion/women -in-the-workplace (last accessed 1/31/2021).

18. Ibid.

19. Ibid.

20. "Women in the Workplace 2020," https://wiw-report.s3.amazonaws.com/ Women_in_the_Workplace_2020.pdf, 9. (last accessed 1/31/2021).

21. Ibid., 25.

22. Ibid., 42.

23. Ibid.

24. Ibid., 6, 8.

25. Ibid., 7.

26. Claudia Goldin, *Career and Family: Women's Century-long Journey Toward Equity* (Princeton: Princeton University Press, 2021), 15.

27. "Women, Business, and the Law 2020," https://openknowledge.worldbank.org /bitstream/handle/10986/32639/9781464815324.pdf (last accessed 1/31/2021). This report is offered in three languages—English, French, and Spanish.

28. Ibid., 4.

29. Ibid.

30. Ibid., 5.

31. Ibid., 9.

32. Ibid., 9.

33. Ibid., 9, 39.

34. Ibid., 9,12.

35. Ibid., 12.

36. Ibid.

37. Ibid., 12–13, 43.

38. Ibid.

39. Ibid., 14.

40. Ibid.

41. Ibid.

42. Ibid., 43. Parents receive paid parental leave benefits through their employer's insurance benefits.

43. *Global Perspectives on Women's Leadership and Gender (In)Equality,* Elena V. Shabliy, Dmitry Kurochkin, and Gloria Ayee (eds.) (London: Palgrave Macmillan, 2020), 6, 44.

44. Acosta, Lautenberger, Castillo-Page, Skorton, "Achieving Gender Equity Is Our Responsibility," 1469.

45. Ibid.,1470.

46. "Kimberlé Crenshaw on Intersectionality, More Than Two Decades Later," https: //www.law.columbia.edu/pt-br/news/2017/06/kimberle-crenshaw-intersectionality (last accessed 1/24/2021).

47. Paola Profeta, *Gender Equality and Public Policy*, 10.

48. Ibid., 10–11.

49. Ibid., 14.

50. Ibid., 14.

51. Ibid., 14.

52. "Global Gender Gap," http://www3.weforum.org/docs/WEF_GGGR_2020 .pdf, p.14 (last accessed 1/31/2021).

53. Claudia Goldin, *Career and Family*, 5.

54. Ibid.

55. "Global Gender Gap," p. 1 (last accessed 1/31/2021).

56. Claudia Goldin, *Career and Family*, 112.

57. Ibid., 119.

58. Ibid., 120.

59. Ibid., 1.

60. "Global Gender Gap," http://www3.weforum.org/docs/WEF_GGGR_2020 .pdf, p.1 (last accessed 1/31/2021).

61. Ibid.

62. Krishna Ahooja-Patel and Gujarat Vidyapith, *Gender Equity in the Third Millenium*, 1st ed. (Ahmedabad: Gujarat Vidyapith, Institute on Equity and Development, 1999).

63. "Global Gender Gap," http://www3.weforum.org/docs/WEF_GGGR_2020 .pdf., 6. Other economies in the top ten are Nicaragua (5th, 80.4%), New Zealand (6th, 79.9%), Ireland (7th, 79.8%), Spain (8th, 79.5%), Rwanda (9th, 79.1%), and Germany (10th, 78.7%).

64. Paola Profeta, *Gender Equality and Public Policy*, 101.

65. Ibid., 100.

66. "Global Gender Gap," http://www3.weforum.org/docs/WEF_GGGR_2020 .pdf., p. 6 (last accessed 1/31/2021).

67. Paola Profeta, *Gender Equality and Public Policy*, 101.

68. Ibid., 101.

69. Ibid., 102.

70. Claudia Goldin, *Career and Family*, 10.

71. Mikki Hebl, Christine L. Nittrouer, and Abigail R. Corrin, "How We Describe Male and Female Job Applicants Differently," *Harvard Business Review*, https:// hbr.org/2018/09/how-we-describe-male-and-female-job-applicants-differently?ab=at _art_art_1x1 (last accessed 1/24/2021).

72. Claudia Goldin, *Career and Family*, 2.

73. "Global Gender Gap," http://www3.weforum.org/docs/WEF_GGGR_2020 .pdf., p. 8 (last accessed 1/31/2021).

74. Paola Profeta, *Gender Equality and Public Policy*, 161.

75. Ibid., 31.

76. Ibid., 34.

77. Ibid., 138.

78. Ibid., 37.

79. "Women and work—We Did It!" https://www.economist.com/leaders/2009/12 /30/we-did-it, The *Economist*, December 30, 2009.

80. "Global Gender Gap," http://www3.weforum.org/docs/WEF_GGGR_2020.pdf (last accessed 1/31/2021).

81. Ibid.
82. Ibid.
83. Ibid.
84. Ibid., 10.
85. Ibid, 10–11.
86. Ibid., 11.

Chapter 1

Societal Effects on Women in Science, Technology, Engineering, and Mathematics (STEM) Fields

Eman Tadros and Melanie Barbini

From birth, children are taught gender roles and socialized to differentiate between what is acceptable for little boys and girls to what is acceptable for men and women. These teachings are carried with them throughout their lives and each of these individuals shapes society's view as a whole. Some argue that sex differences are responsible for the underrepresentation of women in science, technology, engineering, and math (STEM) fields while others disagree and say the "math is for boys" attitude is to blame. Despite all the academic and intellectual advancements women have made over the years since the feminist movement, women are still lacking in representation and equity in STEM fields due to some biological factors, yet much more societal and sociological forces.

The notion that men are better than women at excelling in math/science courses due to biological differences is supported by very few studies (Ecklund, 2012). There are some biological differences, such as there's a "tendency of females to use more language-based counting strategies to solve arithmetic problems and for males to have a small advantage on estimation tasks, sex differences are not typically found for these basic numerical domains" (Halpern, 2007, p. 6). This "small advantage" males have seemed to be hyperbolized and dramatically overstated. Males are better at spatial and rotation abilities (Ceci, 2010)—this does not imply that males are remarkably advantageous at math and science in its entirety, these differences are smaller than one may think:

It should be noted that despite the significant sex difference in spatial performance, most women in R.C. Gur et al.'s (1999) study performed comparably to
the men on the spatial tests. As suggested in several sections of this monograph,
it is possible that (some) females may achieve high levels of spatial performance
using different strategies than males and possibly by using different regions of
the brain. Haier et al. (2005) also found that males and females may solve some
complex problems, such as items on IQ tests, differently, with females showing
a greater use of language-related brain regions and males showing greater use
of spatial-related brain regions. (Halpern, 2007, p. 6)

Females using distinct methods to come to the same conclusion is not a
handicap; this simply translates that there are distinct ways of doing the same
task yet reaching the same conclusion. Especially if both genders are attaining
similar solutions, the technique utilized is simply a preference.

It is vital to be mindful that "the environment also shapes the brain"
(Halpern, 2007, p. 30). Biological and societal forces working together corre-
sponds to the ongoing nature vs nurture debate; both rely on one another and
in most cases, they go hand in hand. "Early experience, biological constraints,
educational policy, and cultural context each have effects, and these effects
add and interact in complex and sometimes unpredictable ways" (Halpern,
2007, p. 41) Thus, there are multiple explanations for this and when these
variables are mixed the reaction would be that the results vary from individual to individual.

Socialization is the lifelong process by which, through social interaction, one learns culture, develops a sense of self, and becomes a functioning
member of society. The socialized behavior for the unfair treatment toward
women in STEM fields begins at an impeccably early age. An experiment
was conducted where children at age six were asked to draw mathematicians
and scientists; most of them drew them as male (Betz, 2012). This experiment
displays how at such an early age, children acknowledge the gender biases
in our culture.

Being brought up in today's society, many girls at some point in their academic careers were told some variation of the statement, "you are not good at
math"; perhaps consequently many female students have stayed away from
classes such as calculus and physics (Betz, 2012). Such statements are nothing more than stereotypical assumptions because the performance of female
and male students is comparable in high school math and science classes
(Betz, 2012). In addition, teachers' treatment towards male students differs
from their treatment toward female students in these subject areas (Halpern,
2007). Their schemas of what is appropriate in society at times triumphs their
duty as educators to supply an equal and supportive academic environment
to both genders. When comparing the advice high school counselors gave to

their students, the National Science Foundation found that boys were encouraged more than girls to take electives and advanced math/science courses (Farmer, 2012). This supports normative gender roles, expected for male students to take such classes, while it is sparser for female students to.

"Academic choice is shaped by two kinds of stereotypes: those about students' own identities and those about given fields" (Betz, 2012, p. 744). Stereotype threat is when one fears they will fulfill their negative stereotype of their group and thus perform poorly (Halpern, 207). Society's gender biases should be held accountable for the anxiety women face due to the doubt in place for women's achievement in such fields. Divisions between academic subjects are made to make them more specifically appropriate for gender (Ecklund, 2012). For example, dividing science into physical science—more appropriate for men—and life and social science, more appropriate for women. Therefore, it is socially acceptable for a woman to become a scientist so long as she is a part of a more gender suitable category of the subject, such as a sociologist, psychologist, or biologist. Society has created gender roles that make certain criteria more suitable for one gender than the other, in this case, academic subject matters. The discrepancy of PHDs earned by women in the STEM fields is mindboggling. In 2009, over 70% of PHDs in Psychology were earned by women, compared to fewer than 25% in Engineering and under 20% in Physics (Wade, 2011). Similarly, in 2006, only 12% of women worked as an academic scientist in the physical sciences or engineering compared to 81% of women who worked in psychology, social sciences, and life sciences (Ecklund, 2012). This mentality displays that if women do happen to attain a degree in the sciences that is most likely a life/social science. This additionally exhibits the fact that as a society we have advanced, however, not nearly enough to be even considered to have equal standards.

Traditional romantic scripts state that men should show attributes such as "dominance, competence, and assertiveness" (hegemonic masculinity) while women are expected to be passive, admiring, and accommodating (emphasized femininity) (Park, 2011). Social constructionism argues that history and culture are central to the construction of gendered behavior. It is a socially constructed notion that hegemonic masculinity and emphasized femininity are the ideal forms of men and women; inevitably women who go against these norms are negatively sanctioned. There is an assumption that if a woman excels in a field, which predominantly consists of males, that they lack femininity—this assumption would be a prime example of the negative sanction. When a woman is deemed to be unfeminine it is seen as negative because it does not fit society's ideal view of women (Betz, 2012).

A daily-diary study was conducted on fifty-four women who were enrolled in college math courses (twenty-eight in relationships and twenty-four not).

The participants were given PDAs to document their daily responses and they also took nightly surveys (Park, 2011). The study's results displayed that women who were "striving to be romantically desirable" engaged in more romantic activities and felt more desirable but engaged in fewer math activities. In contrast, on days when women were striving to do well academically, they engaged in more math activities. Thus, the results reinstate the idea that women who focus more on being romantically available are less motivated to excel at STEM subjects and women who are more focused on STEM subjects make it less of a priority to be romantically desirable. If it was more acceptable and normative in today's society to be equally concentrated on both pursuing a relationship and being intelligent then women would not have to feel as if they are settling for one of the other. These traditional scripts suggest that men can excel in the STEM field and still be able to commit to a relationship. However, women are posed with the struggle of the ever-swinging pendulum between having a successful romantic relationship while also managing being a well-rounded intellectual (Park, 2011).

Due to the fact that women are stereotyped to be the more nurturing gender, they are generally the ones who take on the role of caring for the family. If they do happen to have a career, they are more inclined to pursue one that will be accommodating to their responsibilities of a caregiver (Ecklund, 2012, p. 709). This coincides with women routinely lacking entitlement because they are expected to do the work without being praised or acknowledged for having extra responsibilities in the home that the men do not. It is a general norm for women to have to balance both regardless of their career choice. Women make up 48% of all jobs, but only hold 24% of all STEM jobs; these statistics display a considerable large gender gap (Sharp, 2011). When women do happen to hold such jobs, specifically women of color, they are made unavoidably aware of their differences, reinforcing the idea that they are not welcome in the male-dominated STEM field (Ong, 2005).

Over the years, advancements have been made to make starting salaries equal for men and women; however, particularly in STEM fields, the distinctions in salaries form ranks. These ranks suggest that men are the superior gender in such fields and that is the explanation for their unfair, higher salaries (Bystydzienski, 2006). This coincides with the discouragement women receive entering these fields and is also the feeling of discomfort and criticism they receive from the men (Ecklund, 2012). Research on sex biases during the hiring process explains that when a job was sex-typed as male, the employers would rate the women lower than the men. When the job was sex-typed as female, then the women would be rated higher than the men (Halpern, 2007).

Schemas are unconscious evaluations that make it troublesome to notice our involvement in creating them. Schemas make it difficult for others to view women as leaders (Bystydzienski, 2006). An experiment was performed where individuals of both genders were asked to pick out which person seated at a table, man or woman, was the leader of the group. The results showed that most picked a man regardless of the position they had at the table, even if the woman was seated at the head of the table (Bystydzienski, 2006). This experiment enforces that even women have a hard time viewing other women as leaders.

Women of color are usually the most discriminated against because not only do they fit into the marked categories of females in the STEM field, but also the racial minorities category. *Intersectionality* is a theory that seeks to examine how various socially and culturally constructed categories (gender, race, religion, socioeconomic status) interact on multiple and simultaneous levels, contributing to systematic social inequality. "Minority women's experience at the intersection of gender, race, ethnicity, nation of origin, and class can amount to much more than the sum of racism and sexism" (Ong, 2005, p. 611).

Women of color often experience a "double bind" of race and gender marginalization because of the compounded biases they face as women with dual minority identities (Ong et al., 2015). This idea reflects the reality of programs that serve to encourage more women or women of color to join the STEM field, but in actuality disproportionately benefiting white women or minority males, respectively (Liu et al., 2019; Ong et al., 2015). According to the National Center for Science and Engineering Statistics (2017), 30.11% of white women compared to an 11.96% of women of color were awarded a Ph.D. degree within the United States in 2014 (Liu et al., 2019; National Center for Science and Engineering Statistics, 2017). There are myths to suggest that women of color are underrepresented in the STEM fields because they are not interested in pursuing scientific careers. However, compared to their white peers, underrepresented minority women were just as likely to pursue an undergraduate STEM degree (Eaton et al., 2019; Liu et al., 2019; Ong et al., 2015).

Even with a degree, women and underrepresented minorities are less likely to graduate with the highest paying STEM degrees and earn significantly less than white men as full-time workers four years after graduation (Russell, 2017). This pattern even holds for the most accomplished female and minority students at the most elite four-year institutions in the country (Russell, 2017). When comparing the 2015 unemployment rates for all scientists and engineers combined, the unemployment rates for women of color were found to be higher than any other racial and gender group (Flores, 2018). Women of color are outnumbered in the STEM workforce and make up less than 4% of it. This statistic holds even though underrepresented minority women earn a higher percentage of STEM degrees than underrepresented men at each degree level (Flores, 2018).

Stereotypes are one of the major determinants in the gender and racial disparity women of color face in the STEM fields. Studies have shown that underrepresented minority women face additional challenges because of both their race and gender (Flores, 2018; Williams et al., 2014). For example, Asian-American female scientists are more likely to report being perceived as hyperaggressive for being assertive and self-promoting compared to white female scientists (Berdahl & Min, 2012; Flores, 2018; Liu et al., 2019). In addition, compared to their white female colleagues, Asian-Americans women are more likely to be frequently pressured into traditionally feminine roles. On the other hand, when Latina scientists behave assertively, they are perceived as angry or emotional and are expected by their colleagues to take on more office housework. Black women were reported to have more leeway to behave in dominant ways but were often perceived as the "angry Black woman" (Flores, 2018; Williams et al., 2014). Often, women who actively resist incivility or bullying are treated negatively (Babcock et al., 2003; Liu et al., 2019; Sandberg, 2013). This leads women of color to report feelings of inadequacy and isolation as they feel more socially excluded and have less social support than their peers at work. (Clancy et al., 2017; Flores, 2018; Williams et al., 2014).

Unfortunately, these gender and racial stereotypes impact the advancement of women of color who try to pursue post-doctoral and faculty positions, even more so than white women and minority men (Eaton et al., 2019). In studies examining how faculty evaluated CVs, it was found that both men and women science faculty rated women as less competent than men and were less likely to hire a woman candidate compared to an identical man for a laboratory manager or even a post-doctoral position (Eaton et al., 2019; Moss-Racusin et al., 2012). Faculty members also showed racial biases when hiring for STEM departments. Asian and white candidates were seen as more competent than Black candidates. In addition, Black and Latina women were rated significantly lower than all other candidates on the measure of hireability (Eaton et al., 2019).

As demonstrated above, women of color tend to not only face the discrimination faced by white women, but also tend to face compounded discrimination due to their dual minority status as both female and non-whites (Eaton et al., 2019; Williams et al., 2014). This may explain why women of color make up only 5.1% of non-tenure-track faculty and 2.3% of tenure-track or tenured faculty, compared to 38.5% and 23.4% respectively for white women (Ginther et al., 2013; Liu et al., 2019). Furthermore, women of color tend to be employed in less prestigious settings, compared to white women and men of color (Ginther et al., 2013; Liu et al., 2019). However, women of color perform equally as well as white women and rise through the ranks at a similar pace if they are able to attain a tenure-tracked position (Ginther et al., 2013; Liu et al., 2019).

Some of the reasons why women and more specifically women of color are found less at the forefront of STEM fields can be attributed to a "leaky pipeline" that often deters them from advancing in their careers (Liu et al., 2019; Shapiro et al., 2011; Tellhed et al., 2016). One of the primary barriers to promotion is institutional housekeeping. This may include ordering lab supplies, organizing lab space, managing lab personnel, and training new hires. Women of color are often tasked with additional service obligations and overburdened by committee work, which hold less value in promotion cases, especially at research-intensive universities (Britton, 2017; Liu et al., 2019; Miller & Roksa, 2019). Even when men and women held the same job classifications, women's tasks tended to be restrained to daily procedures while men's tasks were more diversified (Miller & Roksa, 2019). Therefore, women had fewer opportunities to take on developmental challenges in the workplace and acquired less networks, skills, and experiences than men, making them less eligible for promotions (Miller & Roksa, 2019). In a study comparing the experiences of both minority men and women and white men and women, it was found that men of color had more advantages than women of color but were disadvantaged compared to white men (Miller & Roksa, 2019). White women also had more privileges than women of color because their advisors often protected their time and integrated research projects along with their service work. On the other hand, women of color often reported being given service tasks that extended beyond their time in the lab and the academic year (Miller & Roksa, 2019).

In addition to housekeeping, publication rates also largely determine a student's competitiveness for new jobs in academia. One study found that program structure and promotions of inclusivity greatly affected the rate at which students published. In the study, structure referred to as "the degree to which students perceived clear expectations and clear performance standards in their respective departments" (Fisher et al., 2019, p. 3). On the other hand, belonging was operationalized as "the degree to which students felt accepted (positive valence) or insignificant (negative valence) in STEM settings" (Fisher et al., 2019, p. 3). Results showed that women of color and white women were more likely to feel levels of distress in their programs. However, with clearly articulated expectations given by STEM departments, a sense of preparedness for graduate-level courses, and a sense of acceptance by their colleagues, the negative factors affecting both white women and women of color were mitigated (Fisher et al., 2019). These factors contributed to women publishing at rates comparable to white men (Fisher et al., 2019).

Having the opportunity to share, network, and form collaborative relationships with other researchers also contributes to the ability of women to progress in their careers. However, women continue to be underrepresented at events such as conferences and symposiums. For example, over 15 years, the Society for Conservation Biology (SCB) conferences, had only 36.4% and 31.7% of their symposia organizers and presenters be women, respectively. And this included students of which more than 50% were women (Sardelis & Drew, 2016; Sardelis et al., 2017). Similarly, the 15th International Congress of Quantum Chemistry was boycotted by 1,500 scientists in response to the conference's list of exclusively male speakers, chairs, and honorary chairs (Arnold, 2015; Sardelis et al., 2017). More needs to be done to address the persistent social problems women and people of color face as they try to advance in their STEM careers.

Currently, the NIH offers training opportunities for Underrepresented Minorities through the Minority Opportunity in Research Division of the National Institute of General Medical Sciences. In the last decade, the NIH attributed approximately $650 million to fund 15,000 trainees per year (Committee for the Assessment of NIH Minority Research Training Programs, 2005; Syed & Chemers, 2011). However, more needs to be done to address the barriers women of color face with dual minority statuses. Kimberlé Crenshaw alluded to the idea that "ignoring difference within groups contributes to tension among groups" (Crenshaw, 1991, p. 1242). She goes on further to say, "Feminist efforts to politicize experiences of women and antiracist efforts to politicize experiences of people of color have frequently proceeded as though the issues and experiences they each detail occur on mutually exclusive terrains. Although racism and sexism readily intersect in the lives of real people, they seldom do in feminist and antiracist practices. And so, when the practices expound identity as woman or person of color as an either/or proposition, they relegate the identity of women of color to a location that resists telling" (Crenshaw, 1991, p. 1242). Therefore, when women of color try to identify with one group or the other, they are marginal-ized within each one and become more powerless to the issues both groups are trying to challenge. Hence, it is important to encourage women and minorities to come together rather than pitting themselves against each other.

In order to encourage and protect the jobs of women of color, various stud-ies have complied with recommendations to increase the representation of women with dual minority identities. One way is for STEM organizations, including graduate programs, school departments, and conference com-mittees, to clarify their expectations and standards in an effort to equalize access to teachers and resources (Fisher et al., 2019; Teo, 2014). We live in a society that believes in hard work and the promises of social mobility through a meritocratic system. However, hard work should be protected with the development of civic literacies that are sensitive to communities with people of diverse races, ethnicities, and cultures (Teo, 2014). "It is important to understand the difference between equality—where everyone is treated exactly the same—and equity—where differences in social position and privilege are recognized and addressed. Treating all delegates exactly the same and ignoring individual circumstances can amplify discrimination" (Sardelis et al., 2017, p. 2). This is especially important because research has shown that "ethnic minority or female leaders who engage in diversity valuing behavior are penalized with worse performance ratings, whereas white or male leaders who engage in diversity valuing behavior are not penalized for doing so" (Hekman et al., 2017, p. 771). One study came up with ten guidelines to reduce gender inequity at conferences. However, many of these guidelines can be applied to policies enacted by STEM organizations. These policies include, "adopting community principles and a Code of Conduct," "appointing a Safety Officer," "offering a mentorship program," "organizing focus groups," "giving benefits for participating in diversity programming," "assisting with child care," "proffering travel grants," and "randomizing the conference program" (Sardelis et al., 2017, p. 1). In much the same light, it is important to remove implicit biases that affect the hiring of all women. One way is for STEM job candidates to submit material that does not include their full names in hopes of fairly evaluating candidates (Eaton et al., 2019). In addition, checks and balances can be added to the hiring process so that hiring committees are composed of people with diverse perspectives and backgrounds (Eaton et al., 2019).

Likewise, although many anti-discrimination trainings exist, many of them only focus on one form of bias, such as sexism or racism. Creating trainings that promote awareness of the unique and intersecting forms of different minorities may help address the specific issues faced by women of color (Eaton et al., 2019). For example, perspective-taking exercises that emphasize the importance of acknowledging one's own bias have been successful at reducing implicit biases. (Carnes et al., 2012; Todd et al., 2011) Many implemented search committee implicit bias training programs have resulted in more diverse faculty in STEM departments (Smith et al., 2015). These efforts may lead to more equality and equity, that is desperately needed throughout all stages of the STEM pipeline for women of color.

Overall, the issue of underrepresentation of women in STEM fields is in need for immediate remedy. Perhaps, we can start with parents, teachers, and guidance counselors doing their bests to treat students equally academically and not foster stereotype threat for female students. Having role models can lessen the stereotype threat against them and be a powerful source in motivating female students, "exposure to successful women in science and engineering boosts female STEM students'" (Betz, 2012, p. 738). Other suggestions: "reform hiring policies," "sustain support structures," "change traditional patterns of interaction within the community," and "create a more hospitable environment for all students" (Ong, 2005, p. 613). As a society the more knowledgeable we are on this issue, the better the chances are to lessen the disparities for future generations.

BIBLIOGRAPHY

Arnold, C. (2015). Countering gender bias at conferences. Science, American Association for The Advancement of Science. Available online at: www.sciencem ag.org/careers/2015/07/countering-gender-bias-conferences

Babcock, L., LaSchever, S., Gelfand, M., & Small, D. (2003). Nice girls don't ask. *Harvard Business Review*, 81, 14–16.

Berdahl, J. L., & Min, J. A. (2012). Prescriptive stereotypes and workplace conse-quences for East Asians in North America. *Cultural Diversity and Ethnic Minority Psychology*, 18, 141–152. dx.doi.org/10.1037/a0027692

Betz, D. (2012). My fair physicist? Feminine math and science role models demo-tivate young girls. *Social Psychological and Personality Science*, 3 (6), 738–746.

Britton, Dana M. 2017. Beyond the chilly climate: The salience of gender in women's academic careers. *Gender & Society*, 31 (1), 5–27.

Bystydzienski, J. (2006). *Removing barriers: Women in academic science, technol-ogy, engineering, and mathematics*. Bloomington: Indiana University Press, 2006.

Carnes, M., Devine, P. G., Isaac, C., Manwell, L. B., Ford, C. E., Byars-Winston, A., . . . Sheridan, J. (2012). Promoting institutional change through bias lit-eracy. *Journal of Diversity in Higher Education*, 5 (2), 63–77. doi: 10.1037/a0028128

Ceci, S. (2010). Sex differences in math-intensive fields. *Current Directions in Psychological Science*, 19 (5), 275–279.

Clancy, K. B., Lee, K., Rodgers, E. M., & Richey, C. (2017). Double jeopardy in astronomy and planetary science: Women of Color face greater risks of gen-dered and racial harassment. *Journal of Geophysical Research: Planets*, 122 (7), 1610–1623.

Committee for the Assessment of NIH Minority Research Training Programs (2005). Assessment of NIH Minority Research and Training Programs, Phase 3. The National Academies Press: Washington, DC.

Crenshaw, K. (1991). Mapping the margins: Intersectionality, identity politics, and violence against women of color. *Stanford Law Review*, 43 (6), 1241–1299. doi: 10.2307/1229039

Eaton, A. A., Saunders, J. F., Jacobson, R. K., & West, K. (2019). How gender and race stereotypes impact the advancement of scholars in STEM: Professors' biased evaluations of physics and biology post-doctoral candidates. *Sex Roles*, 82 (3–4), 127–141. doi: 10.1007/s11199-019-01052-w

Ecklund, E. (2012). Gender segregation in elite academic science. *Gender & Society*, 26 (5), 693–717.

Farmer, H. (2012). Antecedent factors differentiating women and men in science/nonscience. *Psychology of Women Quarterly*, 23 (4), 763–780.

Fisher, A. J., Mendoza-Denton, R., Patt, C., Young, I., Eppig, A., Garrell, R. L., . . . Richards, M. A. (2019). Structure and belonging: Pathways to success for underrepresented minority and women PhD students in STEM fields. *Plos One*, 14 (1). doi: 10.1371/journal.pone.0209279

Flores, C. (2018). Spotlight on women of color in STEM. *Industrial and Organizational Psychology*, 11 (2), 291–296. doi: 10.1017/iop.2018.17

Ginther, D. K., & Kahn, S. (2013). Education and academic career outcomes for women of color in science and engineering. In K. Matchett (Ed.), *Seeking solutions: Maximizing American talent by advancing Women of Color in academia* (pp. 71–92). Washington, DC: National Academies Press.

Halpern, D. (2007). The science of sex differences in science and mathematics. *Psychological Science in the Public Interest*, 8 (1), 1–51.

Hekman, D. R., Johnson, S. K., Foo, M. D., and Yang, W. (2017). Does diversity valuing behavior result in diminished performance ratings for non-white and female leaders? *Academy of Management Journal*, 60, 771–797. doi: 10.5465/amj.2014.0538

Liu, S.-N. C., Brown, S. E. V., & Sabat, I. E. (2019). Patching the "leaky pipeline": Interventions for Women of Color faculty in STEM academia. *Archives of Scientific Psychology*, 7 (1), 32–39. doi: 10.1037/arc0000062

Moss-Racusin, C. A., Dovidio, J. F., Brescoll, V. L., Graham, M. J., & Handelsman, J. (2012). Science faculty's subtle gender biases favor male students. *PNAS Proceedings of the National Academy of Sciences of the United States of America*, 109 (41), 16474–16479. doi.org/10.1073/pnas.1211286109.

Miller, C., & Roksa, J. (2019). Balancing research and service in academia: Gender, race, and laboratory tasks. *Gender & Society*, 34 (1), 131–152. doi: 10.1177/0891243219867917

National Center for Science and Engineering Statistics. (2017). Women, minorities, and persons with disabilities in science and engineering [Data files]. Retrieved from National Science Foundation website: www.nsf.gov/statistics/2017/nsf17310/data.cfm

Ong, M. (2005). Body projects of young women of color in physics: Intersections of gender, race, and science. Cambridge, MA: Harvard University.

Ong, M., Wright, C., Espinosa, L., & Orfield, G. (2011). Inside the double bind: A synthesis of empirical research on undergraduate and graduate women of color in science, technology, engineering, and mathematics. *Harvard Educational Review*, 81 (2), 172–209. doi: 10.17763/haer.81.2.t022245n7x4752v2

Park, L. (2011). Effects of everyday romantic goal pursuit on women's attitudes toward math and science. *Personality and Social Psychology Bulletin*, 37 (9), 1259–1273.

Russell, L. (2017). Can learning communities boost success of women and minorities in STEM? Evidence from the Massachusetts Institute of Technology. *Economics of Education Review*, 61, 98–111. doi: 10.1016/j.econedurev.2017.10.008

Sandberg, S. (2013). *Lean in: Women, work, and the will to lead.* New York, NY: Knopf.

Sardelis, S., and Drew, J. (2016). Not "pulling up the ladder": Women who organize conference symposia provide greater opportunities for women to speak at conservation conferences. *PLoS ONE* 11:e0160015. doi: 10.1371/journal.pone.0160015

Sardelis, S., Oester, S., & Liboiron, M. (2017). Ten strategies to reduce gender inequality at scientific conferences. *Frontiers in Marine Science*, 4. doi: 10.3389/fmars.2017.00231

Shapiro, C. A., & Sax, L. J. (2011). Major selection and persistence for women in STEM. *New Directions for Institutional Research*, 2011 (152), 5–18. doi: 10.1002/ir.404

Sharp, G. (2011). *Gender Gap in Science and Tech Jobs.* https://www.tampabay.com/archive/2011/08/16/gender-gap-in-science-tech/

Smith, J. L., Handley, I. M., Zale, A. V., Rushing, S., & Potvin, M. A. (2015). Now hiring! Empirically testing a three-step intervention to increase faculty gender diversity in STEM. *Bioscience*, 65, 1084–1087. dx.doi.org/10.1093/biosci/biv138

Syed, M., & Chemers, M. M. (2011). Ethnic minorities and women in STEM: Casting a wide net to address a persistent social problem. *Journal of Social Issues*, 67 (3), 435-441. doi: 10.1111/j.1540-4560.2011.01708.x

Tellhed, U., Bäckström, M., & Björklund, F. (2016). Will I fit in and do well? The importance of social belongingness and self-efficacy for explaining gender differences in interest in STEM and HEED majors. *Sex Roles*, 77 (1–2), 86–96. doi: 10.1007/s11199-016-0694-y

Teo, T. W. (2014). Hidden Currents in the STEM Pipeline: Insights from the dyschronous life episodes of a minority female STEM teacher. *Theory Into Practice*, 53 (1), 48–54. doi: 10.1080/00405841.2014.862122

Todd, A. R., Bodenhausen, G. V., Richeson, J. A., & Galinsky, A. D. (2011). Perspective taking combats automatic expressions of racial bias. Journal of Personality and Social Psychology, 100, 1027–1042. dx.doi.org/10.1037/a0022308

Wade, L. (2011). *Gender composition of academic disciplines: PHDs in 2009.* Sociological Images. https://thesocietypages.org/socimages/2011/05/05/gender-composition-of-academic-disciplines-phds-in-2009/

Williams, J. C., Phillips, K. W., & Hall, E. V. (2014). Double jeopardy? Gender bias against Women of Color in science. San Francisco, CA: University of California Hastings College of Law. Retrieved from https://worklifelaw.org/publications/Double-Jeopardy-Report_v6_full_web-sm.pdf

Chapter 2

Economic Instruments and Measures of Cultural Policy and Fair Practice

Case of Female Artists and Creative Entrepreneurs in Serbia

Hristina Mikić

For a long time, cultural policy economic instruments have not been given much importance. This situation was changed in the second half of the last century, when cultural policy become the central concern of governments.[1] This arose a need for designing various policy instruments (especially economic ones) that could be used to achieve its goals. There are different opinions of scholars as to whether it should deal with economic issues or not. Representatives of critical cultural studies generally reject the economic foundations of cultural policy, believing that it should deal with identity, cultural rights of citizens and social change.[2] Proponents of cultural policy organizational theory have a different opinion. They believe that cultural policy is a type of practical public policy aimed at encouraging the creation, production and dissemination of cultural goods and services, which uses various instruments (including economic ones) to achieve its goals.[3]

Various UNESCO reports on a cultural policy published in the 1960s and 1970s show that economic instruments were not particularly affirmed in this public policy domain.[4] If they were a topic of discussion, they mostly emphasized the public funds for financing culture. Throsby states that a greater influence of economics in the field of cultural policy occurred in the early 1980s, and globalization and broader interpretations of culture as a way of life contributed to this. The former influenced the acceptance of economic principles in the creation of national and international policies; while the latter contributed to expanding the definition of culture beyond the field of "high culture" and increasing the scope of cultural policy.[5] The emergence of new actors and the increasing complexity of the cultural sector imposed a need for various economic mechanisms that can be used in this domain. On the other hand, the crisis of the welfare state raised questions about the scope of state interventions in all areas, including the creative sector. All these accelerated the processes of "economization of cultural policy"[6] and contributed to the growing importance of economic instruments in culture. Accordingly, in a new cultural ecosystem "conducting cultural policy requires a better understanding of complex interrelation between culture and economy."[7]

Cultural policy economic instruments are legal acts and decisions that affect economic behavior or produce certain economic consequences in culture. They can be broadly divided into: fiscal, credit, foreign trade, and state regulation instruments (see table 2.1).[8]

Broadly speaking, cultural policy economic instruments should encourage, protect and enable a diversity of cultural expressions and cultural well-being of all members of society.[9] The cultural policy model very often influences the choice of economic instruments. In liberal cultural policies, the priority will be given to indirect economic instruments that contribute to better resource efficiency, the promotion of private initiative in the creative sector and encouragement of social and economic rights and freedoms. On the other hand, more conservative cultural policies will give priority to direct economic instruments that can ensure the protection of jobs in the public cultural sector, social security and state "programming" of cultural development.

Cultural policy economic measures represent different mechanisms by which a concrete application of the chosen economic instrument is realized. They should contribute to the achievement of cultural policy goals that cannot be achieved spontaneously. They can be aimed at users of cultural content or creators/producers of cultural programs.[10]

Economic measures of cultural policy can be classified in different ways. From the aspect of their action, they can be stabilization and development of economic measures. Economic stabilization measures aim to secure some conditions or eliminate a critical situation (e.g., COVID-19 economic measures packages in the cultural sector), while economic development measures aim to encourage positive structural changes in the creative sector and ensure a higher quality of cultural development. From the direction of their action, they can be stimulative (which have a driving effect) and destimulative (which have a discouraging effect). In relation to the time, cultural policy economic measures can be short-term and long-term. Short-term measures should eliminate some consequences in the creative sector in short term, while long-term measures should contribute to the stability of the creative

Table 2.1. A framework of cultural policy economic instruments and measures

Group of instruments	Type of instruments	Typical measures
Fiscal instruments	Taxes	Tax rate reduction/increase
		Deferral of tax liability
		Tax exemptions
		Tax credits
		Special regimes of taxation
		Accelerated depreciation of business properties and equipment
		Tax base reduction for qualified expenditures
	Public finance	Subsidies
		Grants
		Budgetary transfers
		Donations
		State aid
		State purchasing of art works
		Public procurements
		Capital investments in culture
		Right of first refusal
		Stimulations
	Duties	Public goods duties
		Special copyrights duties
		Heritage duty of care
		Duties for commercial use of heritage
Credit instruments	Credits and interests, guarantees, concessions	Interest free credits
		Credits with noncommercial interests
		Grace period credits
		State guarantees for cultural events
		Concessions for commercial use of heritage
Foreign trade instruments	Duty rate, import duties, export licenses, free trade agreements, double taxation avoidance agreements	Reduced or zero duty rate for cultural goods
		Favorable import duty rates for cultural goods
		Duty exemptions for cultural goods
		Temporary admissions for cultural goods
		Special taxation regimes for international trade incomes
		Preferential treatment of cultural goods
State regulation instruments	Penalties, quotas, certificates, licenses	Penalties
		Licenses for certain cultural activities (archeological excavation, museum . . .)
		Certifications (e.g., crafts, musicians . . .)
		Audio-visual quotas (e.g., for domestic, educational, art program)

Source: authors' elaboration.

sector and balanced satisfaction of cultural needs. From the aspect of their
action, they can be general (when they refer to all actors), or sectoral when
they refer exclusively to the creative sector or its individual areas. From a
gender perspective, economic measures can be gender-neutral (when their
implementation does not affect gender inequality in the creative sector) and
transformative (when their implementation creates opportunities for actively
changing gender inequality in the creative sector).

In order for cultural policy economic measures to be successful, they need
to be contextualized in relation to the social and economic system, institutions' development level, and specificity of cultural actors. They need to be
harmonized with other cultural policy instruments, but also with a strategic
vision of cultural development. An important factor for their success is to be
familiar with their effect on a specified cultural policy goal. In addition, costs
and benefits of their introduction (cost-benefit analysis) need to be estimated,
and to what extent their application is administratively simple and economi-
cal, as well as whether they meet the principles of fair practice. *Fair practice*
in culture is a set of norms that regulate economic relations between different
stakeholders involved in the culture (creation, production, dissemination and
distribution of cultural products and services).[11] It identifies the standards,
guidelines and recommendations that are accepted as the desired models
of stakeholder's behavior in certain cultural value chains. The purpose of
these principles is to establish sustainable and equitable economic relations
between different actors in the creative sector for their mutual benefit, but
also for the broader cultural well-being of the community. Fair practices can
be applied on a micro and macro level. Usually, *fair practice* is formulated
and applied at the guild level, in the form of a codex (for music, visual arts,
design, radio and TV programming, craft fair trade, etc.). At the cultural
policy level, *fair practice* is still an emerging concept and it appeared recently
in the new Dutch cultural policy.[12] The Dutch government made a proposal
for mandatory Fair Practice Code in public finance measures by requesting
each organization that receives government subsidies have to comply with
fair compensation to artists.[13]

In the last several years, gender issues in the creative sector become an
important topic in cultural policy discussions. Several international organizations (Council of Europe, UNESCO, and International Labour Organization)
emphasize gender equality in their activities and policy papers as an important topic for public policy measures. Recently conducted studies show that in
many creative sectors men are present much more on higher leadership functions as well as competitive and more commercial job positions.[14] Women
have a lack of access to the different resources necessary for advance in
creative sectors. This is very often a reason why they are facing higher carrier

difficulties and barriers in individual professional development in the labor and art market. Evidence shows also large pay gaps between men and women in the creative sector and a low level of fair remuneration for female cultural producers or artists.[15]

METHODOLOGY OF RESEARCH AND DATA COLLECTION

In this chapter, we use a framework of *fair practice* as a tool to more deeply understand economic instruments of cultural policy in Serbia and their impacts on gender equality and equity. We use *fair practice* as the innovative benchmarks for the ex-post evaluation of economic instruments and measures of cultural policy as well as the framework for the understanding interrelation between the economics of cultural policy and gender equality.

We have defined *fair practice* through six dimensions (see table 2.2) that contribute to establishing sustainable and fair economic behavior of different stakeholders in the creative sector, with a special focus on female cultural producers, artists and entrepreneurs. The proposed framework does not have the ambition to offer final solutions, but its goal is to provide a broader picture of the structure and characteristics of cultural policy economics in Serbia as well as the level of its fairness and impact on gender equality.

The analysis covered only cultural policy economic instruments and measures at the national level in the period 2010–2020. For these purposes, an inventory of these instruments and measures was formed. They were identified on the basis of two criteria: to influence economic behavior and/or to produce economic consequences in the creative sector. Definition of the creative sector is based on the UNESCO model (narrow definition) which covers core domains—13 economic activities at the 3-digit level of ISIC rev. 4.[16]

This study combines mixed methods of research. In the first stage of the research data on economic instruments and measures are systematized and descriptive statistics are used to provide data on the structure, type and frequency. For each measure, legal acts were collected by which it was regulated, as well as official explanations and opinions on its application. The quantitative analysis covers the investigation of economic instruments and measure's content, analysis of their effects as well as to what extent they are grounded on *fair practice* principles and contributed to the equality. Each dimension is evaluated descriptively by using the assessment scale (High, Medium and Low) and short justification. Explanations, interpretations and conclusions were made by data and methodological triangulation to capture

Table 2.2. A framework for analysis of cultural policy economic instruments and measures based on gender equality perspective and the principles of fair practice

Dimension	Description
Relevance	Does the measure meet to a great extent the economic needs of the target stakeholders to which it refers and how they impacted gender equality in the creative sector?
Efficiency	Does the measure achieve high-quality results in the field of cultural development at reasonable costs?
Equity	Is the economic burden of the measure evenly distributed in relation to the economic strength of the stakeholder by gender?
	Do the measures improve economic conditions for the protection, promotion and access to cultural expressions of women and men?
	Do the measures have a transformative effect on gender inequality in the creative sector?
Transparency	Have economic measures been adopted with equal stakeholder participation by gender in their planning and decision-making?
	Are the criteria on which the measures are implemented clear?
Participative governance	Did creative sector stakeholders have the opportunity to comment on economic measures? Are stakeholders' comments taken into account?
Sustainability	Do the measures have long-term effects/benefits on the development of gender equality in the creative sector and/or cultural well-being of citizens?

the fairness of the economic instruments and measures of cultural policy and their effects on gender equality.

We identified thirty-eight instruments and 103 measures that are included in the analysis. The additional material consisted of the expressions related to the cultural policy economic instruments collected through semi-structural interviews with ten female stakeholders (four artists, five creative entrepreneurs and one representative of public cultural institutions). In-depth interviews were conducted from April 2020 to July 2021.

The analysis presented in this chapter has several limitations. First, the coverage of respondents—beneficiaries of cultural policy economic measures and their representativeness is small, and in the future research, the sample should be expanded; the analysis did not include qualitative research of policymakers, as well as the instruments at provincial and local levels; the instruments are insufficiently sectoral differentiated, nor stratified in relation to the type of user and other specific characteristics that could affect their assessment. However, as this is the first research on cultural policy economic instruments in Serbia, it can serve as an explanatory research in this area, and these limitations can be an inspiration for the future and more detailed research on this topic.

ECONOMICS OF CULTURAL POLICY IN SERBIA

In the structure of cultural policy economic instruments, the largest number refers to fiscal (85%), 3% of credit, 7% of foreign trade and 5% of regulation instruments (figure 2.1). Within the most numerous groups of instruments, more than 72% of the measures are direct financial support. This finding indicates a certain imbalance of instruments and the decision-makers' choice for the model of "programming" cultural development. This model implies that decisions regarding size, composition and cultural forms of direct support are made by policymakers.[17] In the long run, this model is unsustainable. Namely, the existing measures do not provide a basis for diversification of culture funding sources, nor a broader framework for fostering diversity of cultural expressions. This creates a great risk, because the limitations in the state budget directly determine the continuity and quality of cultural development. It is also questionable that public funds for culture in the amount of 0.7% of the national budget are distributed through almost forty measures. This obscures the fact that the amount of support is actually symbolic (for example, in some competitions, co-financing is around 1000 euros) and to a low extent meet the economic needs of cultural stakeholders, especially female producers and artists.

> Fundraising for art and culture projects is at high risk. There is no diversification of funding resources available for female creative entrepreneurs. We are mostly dependent on the market. Some unemployed entrepreneurs can get subsidies for starting an entrepreneurial venture, but the selection is rigorous. Priority is given to those businesses that are much more commercial. Creative entrepreneurship business and cultural ventures are on the margin of this kind of supports. (A female creative entrepreneur, 37 years old)

The structure of economic instruments by cultural policy objectives shows a high level of concentration (figure 2.2). Public finance appears as the main group of economic instruments formulating in the "Architect" manner. Chartrand and McCaughey describe this approach as bureaucratic where the direct government funding very often leads to creative stagnation,[18] while Grampp emphasizes the inefficiency of this kind of measure due to

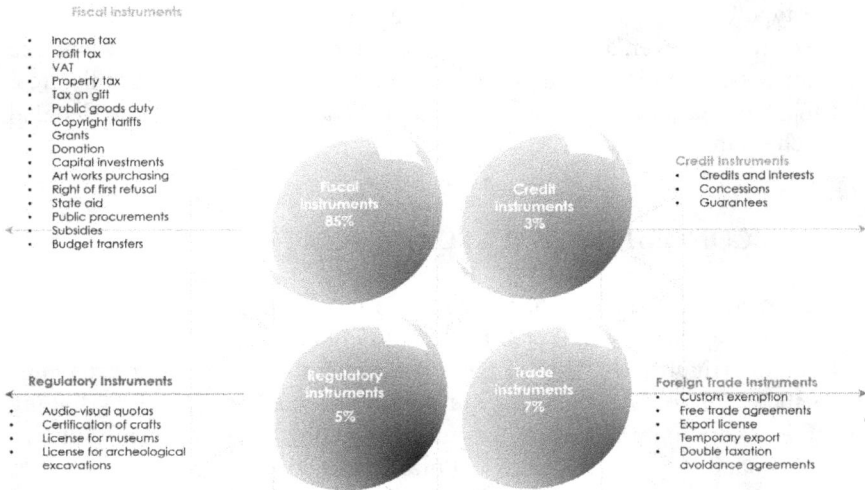

Fiscal instruments
- Income tax
- Profit tax
- VAT
- Property tax
- Tax on gift
- Public goods duty
- Copyright tariffs
- Grants
- Donation
- Capital investments
- Art works purchasing
- Right of first refusal
- State aid
- Public procurements
- Subsidies
- Budget transfers

Credit Instruments
- Credits and interests
- Concessions
- Guarantees

Fiscal instruments 85%
Credit instruments 3%
Regulatory instruments 5%
Trade instruments 7%

Regulatory Instruments
- Audio-visual quotas
- Certification of crafts
- License for museums
- License for archeological excavations

Foreign Trade Instruments
- Custom exemption
- Free trade agreements
- Export license
- Temporary export
- Double taxation avoidance agreements

Figure 2.1. Structure of economic instruments of cultural policy in Serbia, 2020.

Cultural Policy Objectives	Tax Instruments	Public Finance	Duty	Credit Instruments	Trade Instruments
Promotion of Diversity of Cultural Expressions	✴	✴	✴	✴	
Cultural Production	✴	✴			
Access to Culture	✴				✴
Cultural Activities of Diaspora		✴			
International Cultural Relations		✴			✴
Research in Culture					
Cultural Education		✴			
Digitalization	✴	✴			
Youth Talents in Culture		✴			
Cultural Amateurism		✴			
Culture For Children		✴			
Development of Cultural Market		✴			

Figure 2.2. Structure of economic instruments by cultural policy objectives (%). *Author's calculation. Specified by article 6. Law on Culture.*

government subsidies only serving the interest of a member of the minority group.[19]

From the aspect of time, about 66% of the measures are short-term. Short-term measures are mainly a feature of public finances, while foreign trade measures have the greatest long-term characteristic. Short-term measures are not the result of a planning decision, but are often the result of instability in the economic environment. Many female respondents believe that therefore economic measures cannot be purposeful in achieving cultural policy goals.

> Changes in the taxation of entrepreneurs are to a great extent detrimental to small creative entrepreneurs. No one cared about the consequences they would have on our work. For the last 10 years, we have been living in uncertainty about how our work will be taxed and how much our tax obligations will be. Our sustainability depends on it. Economic measures of cultural policy, especially those related to taxation, must be sensitive to the cultural values that we create with our work and should enable us to have a stable job, and not the other way around. (A female creative entrepreneur, 45 years old)

Female artists and creative entrepreneurs often see economic measures as a result of lobbying and some major interests, rather than as a tool of protecting and promoting diversity of cultural expressions.

> Until now, I have never participated in the planning of cultural policy economic measures, because it is necessary to be close to state structures. Various economic measures are adopted to protect the interests of some major market players, we artists are marginal when it comes to such things and no one attaches importance to our work to improve the cultural well-being of the nation. (A female artist, 35 years old)

A significant number of economic measures are of a general nature, and about 40% of them are sectorally differentiated. Tax and credit instruments are the least sectoral differentiated, while the measures within public finances show the greatest differentiation (see figure 2.3).

As a result, female respondents believe that a lot of economic measures are dysfunctional and difficult to implement in practice. Namely, the fiscal administration cannot properly perceive all the circumstances that are important for the adequate tax treatment of culture, and they are often inclined to propose rigid solutions in order to avoid abuses.[20] Therefore, it happens that implementation of these measures mainly depends on how much individuals in the government administration understand arts and cultural production, and how much they are willing to contextualize this knowledge in everyday work.

As far as equity is concerned, the effects of measures are mostly weak, as it is shown in figure 2.4. This dimension was evaluated through the four pillars. Those multiple perspectives includes: economic fairness (how economic burdens and opportunities are shared between men and women), economic well-being (the ability of women to make economic choices and access to economic resources), social fairness (level of women's access to wealth and social

Taxes	L	Export duties	M
Public finance	H	Double taxation avoidance agreements	L
Duties	M	Export licenses	M
Credits and interests	L	Quotas	H
Guarantees	L	Certificates	H
Concessions	L	Licenses	H
Fee trade agreements	L		

Figure 2.3. Structure of economic instruments by the level of sectoral differentiation, 2020. *The assessment scale of the level of sectoral differentiation of economic measures is: High (H), Medium (M) and Low (L). HIGH: economic measures are formulated to respect all the specifics of the creative sector; MEDIUM: economic measures are sectorial differentiated to some specifics of the creative sector and targets only key needs of creative subjects; LOW: low level or lack of any kind of sectorial differentiation of economic measures.*

Figure 2.4. Level of equity of economic measures of cultural policy in Serbia, 2020. *Level of harmonization of economic measures with equity principles. The assessment scale is: High (H), Medium (M) and Low (L). HIGH: high level of harmonization economic measures with a concrete dimension of equity; MEDIUM: medium level of harmonization between economic measures and the concrete dimension of equity; LOW: low level or lack of harmonization.*

privileges within a society) and transformative power (the ability to provoke structural changes in creative sector from the perspective of gender equality).

Tax measures are insufficiently fair, because their tax burden is not evenly distributed in relation to the economic strength of taxpayers in culture. Thus, for example, the tax burden on income is up to 6 times higher, depending on whether artistic work is conducted as an independent occupation or by an entrepreneur. Other taxes (e.g., value-added tax, gift tax, tax incentives for the artwork purchase, etc.) are not more adequate, which worsens the economic conditions for the protection and promotion of the cultural expressions diversity and gender equality in the creative sector.

> After several years, I managed to find a financier for my art project. However, when we got to the point to be funded, we realized that over 40% of these funds would go to taxes and contributions. The legal team of my financier studied the regulations and advised him not to finance my project, because there are a lot of legal ambiguities. So, in the end, it turned out that my project could not be financed by anyone from the private sector, because I have to register my enterprise in order to be legal and economically viable. (A female artist, 52 years old)

A similar situation exists also with other measures, such as grants for self-employment. Examples like this one, show that in most cases, economic measures do not improve economic conditions for the protection and promotion of the diversity of cultural expressions of female entrepreneurs.

> I was granted in the amount of 180.000 dinars as an unemployed person. With this grant, I have obligation to work for the last 12 months and to pay taxes and social security contributions during this period. On the other side, as a registered creative entrepreneur, I am obliged to pay the yearly amount of taxes and social contribution from 240.000 to 350.000 dinars which means I will return grant to the state through fiscal payments in the first 4 months of my work. (A female creative entrepreneur, 46 years old)

Cultural policy economics is gender-neutral, because 95% of measures do not take into account this aspect. Some analyses of the creative sector have shown that better gender mainstreaming of cultural policy economic instruments is necessary, as well as the introduction of new measures to encourage women's creativity and entrepreneurship.[21] Similar views have been confirmed in this research, as well. Respondents pointed out that it was paradoxical that the gender perspective was not respected in those artistic fields where gender inequality is very pronounced, such as digital arts, design, film and music.

> Grants for female digital artists are very poor. Fundraising pressures very often impacted the balance between work and my private life as well as the quality of my work. The cultural expression of female artists is at risk, but there are no effective policy measures that will decrease them. (A female digital artist, 28 years old)

About 5% of the analyzed measures are stabilization, 30% development, whereas almost 65% of the measures are neutral. These measures do not have a large impact on the sustainability of the creative sector, so they can be characterized as "pseudo" economic measures. Their main feature is that they are legally regulated, but that they do not have an effect in practice. Respondents add that even measures of a development character do not lead to the desired results. Some respondents see the reason for this in the situation that they are not connected with other cultural policy instruments, while others believe that there is a conflict between the normative and real system in culture.

Transparency and participation in the creation of cultural policy economic measures haven't reached an enviable level. The measures are generally not adopted with the participation of stakeholders, which reflects on their quality. Although there is no legal obligation for them to hold public hearings and consultations (unless they are integrated into public policy or a draft legal act), this does not mean that they should not be organized.[22] The need for participative governance is evident in the artist' community.

> Artists must become active participants in the decision-making process on cultural policy instruments that affect their field of work and not just their passive users. (A female artist, 46 years old)

Regarding the hierarchy in the creation and implementation of economic instruments and measures, there are also some ambiguities. The overlap of the same and similar tasks between several bodies (2 advisory bodies—Council for Cultural Affairs and Council of Creative Industries, 1 government body—Ministry of culture and 1 public administration body—E-government office) speaks of the institutional imbalance in the creation of creative sector development policy and economic measures. It is actually about certain institutions which entered in the competence of the Ministry of Culture and the absence of co-determination principle, which in this case would have to be legally regulated. All these things lead to the conclusion that the process of bureaucratization and growth of discretionary decision-making scope in the creative sector is currently underway.[23] Actors in culture often complain about this situation that it is not clear who creates cultural policy and its economic instruments nowadays and from which centers of power it is directed.[24] For example, members of the Association Independent Culture Scene protested against the Prime Minister Council and the "Serbia Creates" platform. They paid attention to the disruptive effects of government creative industries promotion (especially in the field of contemporary art practices) and the introduction of non-transparent decisions making in the creative sector.[25] This situation is complicated by the fact that in communication with the public, newly established bodies and their competencies are presented vaguely and non-transparently—as part of the activities of the "Serbia Creates" Office[26] (which does not legally exist), then as the "Serbia Creates" Platform which initiates and includes systemic measures for creative industries development[27] (which is legal without merits) or as an executive body of the Creative Industries Council[28] (which is not legally possible). Therefore, it is not surprising that the public can often hear the views that these are, in fact, para-governmental institutions, which "moved the center of political decision-making outside the domain of public control"[29] and transparency.

CONCLUSIONS

Our analysis shows that economic measures of cultural policy mostly are not harmonized with principles of *fair practice*. They are not sensitive to gender equality in the creative sector. The structure of economic instruments is not balanced, and it mainly comprises fiscal instruments. Prevalence of measures within public finances (most notably in the form of direct state interventions), gives reasons to argue that economic instruments are geared toward "programming" cultural development rather than encouraging it through indirect policy measures and incentives. In the long run, this model is unsustainable. Namely, the existing measures do not provide a basis for diversification of culture funding sources, nor a broader framework for fostering diversity of cultural expressions, especially of female cultural creators. This creates a great risk, because the limitations in the state budget directly determine the continuity and quality of cultural development as well as access to the different resources necessary for advance in creative sectors. In addition, the sheer quantity of measures is counter proportional to their quality. The confusion in the economics of cultural policy is further exacerbated by various "para-governmental" bodies whose work is non-transparent and based on principles of political voluntarism (such as "Serbia Creates"). In this way, the center of political decision-making is removed from the reach of public control, while the cultural policy's economic instruments are put in the service of personal wish lists instead of public interests in culture such as diversity of cultural expression, especially for a female artist and creative entrepreneurs. This situation starts to change with the appointment of the new Ministry of culture and media staff at the end of 2020 and the passivation of the Creative Industries Council's role in the policy-making decision, but still, there are no visible consequences of those changes.

BIBLIOGRAPHY

Bennett, T. (1992) "Putting Policy into Cultural Policy Studies" in: L. Grossber, C. Nelson and P. Treicher (eds.) *Cultural Studies*, London: Routledge, pp. 23–37.
Bennett, T. (2001) "Cultural Policy," in: Neil J. Smelser and Paul B. Baltes, *International Encyclopedia of the Social & Behavioral Sciences*, Amsterdam: Elsevier, pp. 3092–3097.

Blic (2019) "Nezavisna kulturna scena Srbije protiv premijerkinog Saveta za kreativne industrije (Serbia's Independent Cultural Scene against the Prime Minister's Council for Creative Industries)," *Blic* 13. www.blic.rs/kultura/vesti/nezavisna -kulturna-scena-srbije-protiv-premijerkinog-saveta-za-kreativne-industrije/4phm93g

Chartrand, H. H. and C. McCaughey (1989) "The Arm's Length Principle and the Arts: An International Perspective—Past, Present, and Future" In: M. Cummings and J. Schuster (eds.) *Who's to Pay for the Arts?: The International Search for Models of Arts Support*, New York: ACA.

Demirović, D. (2014) "Poresko-pravni aspekt saradnje privrednog i kulturnog sektora (Tax Perspective on Cooperation Between Business and Cultural Sector)," in: G. Rikalović and H. Mikić (eds.) *Biz&Art: ka održivim partnerstvima privrede i kulture* (*Biz&Art: Towards Sustainable Partnership Between Business and Culture*), Belgrade: Creative Economy Group.

Dimić, R. (2018) "Paravladine jedinice (Para-governmental Units)," *Peščanik*, 17. December 2018. pescanik.net/paravladine-jedinice/

Dutch Government (2019) Cultural Policy Principles 2021–2024. July 10, 2020. www.rijksoverheid.nl/documenten/beleidsnota-s/2019/06/11/uitgangspunten -cultuurbeleid-2021-2024

EU (2021) *Towards Gender Equality in the Cultural and Creative Sectors*, Report of the OMC Working Group of member states' experts, Brussels: European Union.

Gamble, A. (2001) Neo-Liberalism, *Capital and Class 71*, autumn, pp. 127–34.

Grampp, W.D. (1989) *Pricing the Priceless—Art, Artists and Economics*, New York: Basic Books.

Hesmondhalgh, D. and A. Pratt (2005) "Cultural Industries and Cultural Policy," *International Journal of Cultural Policy*, 11 (1), pp. 1–14.

Klamer, A. et al. (2013) "Cultural Heritage Policies: A Comparative Perspective," in: R. IIdle and A. Mignosa (eds.) *Handbook on the Economics of Cultural Heritage*, Cheltenham, UK: Edward Elgar Publishing, p. 37.

Knežević, V. (2019) "Vanredno stanje u kulturi: Muzej savremene, javni konkurs i izložba Marine Abramović (State Emergency in Culture: Museum of Contemporary Arts, Public Competitions and Marina Abramovic Exhibition)," *Mašina*, September 20. www.masina.rs/?p=10831

Kovačević, N. (2019) "Korupcijski performans oko Čistača (Corruption Performance around 'Cleaner')," *Danas*, 17. September. www.danas.rs/kultura/ korupcijski-performans-oko-cistaca

Lewis, J. and T. Miller (2003) *Critical Cultural Policy Studies,* Oxford: Blackwell.

Marković, T. (2019) "Kreativni industrijalci Ane Brnabić (Creative Industrialists of Ana Brnabić)," *Antena M*, 6. January. www.antenam.net/stav/106206-kreativni-industrijalci-ane-brnabic?fbclid=IwAR0OATnavrERudX5KNwAHMOpZVlgFa2aAPb9Nf0z3o5A CuvsCC0nPomIxiQ

Mikić, H. (2020) "Gender (In)Equality in the Creative Industries: Insights from Serbia," In: D. Kurochkin, E. Shabliy and G. Y. A. Ayee (eds.) *Global Perspectives on Women's Leadership and Gender (In)Equality*, Basingstoke: Palgrave Macmillan.

Mikić, Hristina (2012) *Measuring Economic Contribution of Cultural Industries: Review and Assessment of Methodological Approaches*, Montreal: UNESCO-Institute for Statistics.

Mikić, Hristina (2015) *Measuring Economic Contribution of Cultural Industries: Case Study Serbia*, Montreal: UNESCO-Institute for statistics, 2015.

Ministry of Culture and Heritage of New Zealand (2010) "Cultural Well-Being and Local Government," Wellington, July 2020. mch.govt.nz/

Pujar, S. (2016) *Gender Inequalities in the Cultural Sector*. Culture Action Europe, 2016. cultureactioneurope.org/files/2016/05/Gender-Inequalities-in-the-Cultural-Sector.pdf

Srbija Stvara. (2020). "O nama," July 20, www.serbiacreates.rs/

Stojkov, V. (2019) "Paušal je morao da ode—šta treba uraditi da svi ne odu? (The Lump Sum Taxation Had to Go—What Needs to Be Done So That Everyone Doesn't Leave?)," *Startit Dnevnik*, 30. September. startit.rs/pausal-je-morao-da-ode-sta-treba-uraditi-da-svi-ne-odu.

Throsby, David. (2010) *Economics of Cultural Policy*. Cambridge: Cambridge UniversityPress.

UNESCO (1969) *Cultural Policy: A Preliminary Study*, Paris: UNESCO.

UNESCO (1970) *Intergovernmental Conference on Institutional, Administrative and Financial Aspects of Cultural Policies*. Final Report. Paris: UNESCO.

UNESCO (1983) *Cultural Development: Documentary Dossier*. No. 1, Paris: UNESCO.

UNESCO (2014) *Gender Equality, Heritage and Creativity*, Paris: UNESCO.

UNESCO Institute for Statistics [UIS] (2009) *The UNESCO Framework for Cultural Statistics*, Montreal: UIS.

Vatić, S. (2018) "'Srbija stvara' je nova kampanja za promociju Srbije i njenih kreatora i inovatora u svetu ('Serbia Creates' Is a New Campaign for Promotion of Serbia and Its Creators and Innovators in the World)," *Startit Dnevnik*, 12. December. startit.rs/srbija-stvara-kampanja-za-promociju-srbije-kreatora-i-inovatora-u-svetu

VOICE (2019) "Vlada priprema mere za prevremeno penzionisanje baletskih igrača (Government is Preparing Measures for Temporary Retirement of Ballet Dancers)," 23. September. voice.org.rs/voice-vlada-priprema-mere-za-prevremeno-penzionisanje-baletskih-igraca

Winden, J. (2019) Retort#21 Fair practice according to the government and the client. https://www.platformbk.nl/en/rt21-fair-practice-according-to-the-government-and-according-to-the-client/

NOTES

1. See: T. Bennett (2001) "Cultural Policy" in: Neil J. Smelser and Paul B. Baltes, *International Encyclopedia of the Social & Behavioral Sciences*, Amsterdam: Elsevier, pp. 3092–3097.

2. For more see: Bennett, T. (1992) "Putting Policy into Cultural Policy Studies" in: L. Grossber, C. Nelson and P. Treicher (eds.) *Cultural Studies,* London: Routledge,

pp. 23–37; Gamble, A. (2001) Neo-Liberalism, *Capital and Class 71*, Autumn, pp. 127–34; Lewis, J. and T. Miller (2003) *Critical Cultural Policy Studies,* Oxford: Blackwell.

3. See: D. Hesmondhalgh and A. Pratt (2005) "Cultural Industries and Cultural Policy," *International Journal of Cultural Policy*, 11 (1), pp. 1–14; Throsby, D. (2010) *Economics of Cultural Policy*, Cambridge: Cambridge University Press.

4. See: UNESCO (1969) *Cultural Policy: A Preliminary Study*, Paris: UNESCO; UNESCO (1970) *Intergovernmental Conference on Institutional, Administrative and Financial Aspects of Cultural Policies*. Final Report. Paris: UNESCO; UNESCO (1983) *Cultural Development: Documentary Dossier*, No. 1, Paris: Unesco.

5. D. Throsby. (2010) *Economics of Cultural Policy.* Cambridge: Cambridge University Press, pp. 2–3.

6. In this chapter, the term "economization of cultural policy" refers to growing importance of the processes of shaping economic instruments and measures by which the cultural sector is governed economically rationally and sustainably.

7. A. Klamer et al. (2013) "Cultural Heritage Policies: A Comparative Perspective" in: R. Ildle and A. Mignosa (eds.) *Handbook on the Economics of Cultural Heritage*, Cheltenham, UK: Edward Elgar Publishing, p. 37.

8. In the case of state regulation instruments, it should be borne in mind that their economic character results from the consequences of their application (higher costs of conducting an administrative procedure, higher costs due to changes in production processes to comply with a standard, etc.), unlike legal instruments that have a legislative role and legal consequences.

9. Cultural well-being is defined as a vitality that communities and individuals enjoy through participation in creative activities and freedom of creating and expressing their arts, history and tradition. See: Ministry of culture and heritage of New Zealand (2010) "Cultural Well-Being and Local Government," Wellington, July 2020, mch.govt.nz/.

10. NGOs, private companies, entrepreneurs, artists and all other entities involved in creation, production, collection and dissemination of cultural goods and services.

11. In the creative sector, such rules appeared in the seventies and eighties of the last century, in the form of various trade customs (customs on book sales, customs on the sale of artwork, fair trade of handicrafts and artwork, etc.). Later, this model spread to other areas and gained wider coverage, e.g., codex of fair practice in visual art, codex of fair practice in music, design, radio and TV programming, etc.

12. Dutch Government (2019) Cultural Policy Principals 2021–2024, July 10, www.rijksoverheid.nl/documenten/beleidsnota-s/2019/06/11/uitgangspunten-cultuurbeleid-2021-2024.

13. J. Winden (2019) Retort#21 Fair practice according to the government and the client, https://www.platformbk.nl/en/rt21-fair-practice-according-to-the-government-and-according-to-the-client/.

14. S. Pujar (2016) *Gender Inequalities in the Cultural Sector*. Culture Action Europe, cultureactioneurope.org/files/2016/05/Gender-Inequalities-in-the-Cultural-Sector.pdf; UNESCO (2014) Gender equality, heritage and creativity, Paris: UNESCO.

15. EU (2021) *Towards Gender Equality in the Cultural and Creative Sectors*, Report of the OMC Working Group of member states' experts, Brussels: European Union.

16. For more see: H. Mikić (2012) *Measuring Economic Contribution of Cultural Industries: Review and Assessment of Methodological Approaches*, Montreal: UNESCO-Institute for statistics; Hristina Mikić (2015) *Measuring Economic Contribution of Cultural Industries: Case Study Serbia*, Montreal: UNESCO-Institute for statistics, 2015; [UIS] UNESCO Institute for Statistics (2009), *The UNESCO Framework for Cultural Statistics*, Montreal: UIS.

17. The opposite of this model is the one that "encouraging" cultural development. In this model funding decisions are made private and stimulated mostly by indirect policy measures or by combination direct and indirect measures.

18. H. Chartrand and C. McCaughey (1989) "The arm's length principle and the arts: An international perspective—Past, present, and future," in: M. Cummings and J. Schuster (eds) *Who's to Pay for the Arts?: The International Search for Models of Arts Support*, New York: ACA.

19. W. D. Grampp (1989) *Pricing the Priceless—Art, Artists and Economics*, New York: Basic Books.

20. D. Demirović (2014) "Poresko-pravni aspekt saradnje privrednog i kulturnog sektora," in G. Rikalović and H. Mikić (eds.), *Biz&Art: ka održivim partnerstvima privrede i kulture*, Beograd: Grupa za kreativnu ekonomiju, p. 40.

21. For more see: H. Mikić (2020) "Gender (In)Equality in the Creative Industries: Insights from Serbia" in: D. Kurochkin, E. Shabliy and G. Y. A. Ayee (eds.) *Global Perspectives on Women's Leadership and Gender (In)Equality*, Basingstoke: Palgrave Macmillan.

22. The law on planning policy framework offers the possibility for public hearings and consultations to be organized, based on decrees, decisions and other legal acts, and the methodology prescribed for public policies management can be applied to cultural policy economic measures.

23. For example, there are examples of discretionary decision-making by the Prime Minister's Office, such as the non-transparent financing of the opening of the Museum of Contemporary Art in Belgrade (Knežević, V. [2019] "Vanredno stanje u kulturi: Muzej savremene, javni konkurs i izložba Marine Abramović," *Mašina*, September 20, https://www.masina.rs/?p=10831), exhibition "Cleaner" (Kovačević, N. [2019] "Korupcijski performans oko Čistača," *Danas*, September 17, www .danas.rs/kultura/korupcijski-performans-oko-cistaca), a non-transparent draft of the Decree on the engagement of ballet dancers (VOICE [2019] "Vlada priprema mere za prevremeno penzionisanje baletskih igrača," September 23, voice.org.rs/ voice-vlada-priprema-mere-za-prevremeno-penzionisanje-baletskih-igraca), as well as amendments to the taxation of entrepreneurs (Stojkov, V. [2019] "Paušal je morao da ode—šta treba uraditi da svi ne odu?" *Startit Dnevnik*, September 30, startit.rs/ pausal-je-morao-da-ode-sta-treba-uraditi-da-svi-ne-odu).

24. For more see: T. Marković (2019) "Kreativni industrijalci Ane Brnabić," *Antena*, January 6, www.antenam.net/stav/106206-kreativni-industrijalci-ane-brnabic

?fbclid=IwAR0OATnavrERudX5KNwAHMOpZVlgFa2aAPb9Nf0z3o5ACuvsCC0 nPomIxiQ.

25. For more see: Blic (2019) "Nezavisna kulturna scena Srbije protiv premijerkinog Saveta za kreativne industrije," *Blic* December 13,www.blic.rs/kultura/vesti /nezavisna-kulturna-scena-srbije-protiv-premijerkinog-saveta-za-kreativne-industrije /4phm93g.

26. "Serbia creates" promotional publication, July 2019, en.serbiacreates.rs/publications/, p. 4.

27. S. Vatić (2018) "'Srbija stvara' je nova kampanja za promociju Srbije i njenih kreatora i inovatora u svetu," December 12, startit.rs/ srbija-stvara-kampanja-za-promociju-srbije-kreatora-i-inovatora-u-svetu/.

28. Srbija stvara, "O nama," July 20, www.serbiacreates.rs/.

29. Rastislav Dimić (2018) "Paravladine jedinice," *Peščanik,* December 17, pescanik.net/paravladine-jedinice/.

Chapter 3

Women's Participation in Peace Processes

State of the Art and Global Challenges

Ana Belén Perianes Bermúdez

All the countries around the world face a persistent gender gap in decision-making and access to opportunities. This is also the case for women's participation in peace processes, in which despite their important contributions to preventing and resolving conflicts, they are generally excluded from negotiating tables and agreements, peacemaking and peacebuilding (Council on Foreign Relations). Gender equality and peace are very closely linked. In this regard, gender inequality is particularly severe in conflict-affected and post-conflict contexts. The inequality that women suffer in conflict-affected and post-conflict contexts increased several times because they must face the structural discrimination they experience (as problems to access to education, health care, decent works and lack of representation in political and economic decision-making processes) added to their situation as victims of armed violence. Thus, armed conflicts use to take place in countries that are not considered as good places to be a woman or girl due to their high rates of gender inequality, gender-based violence, human rights violations or endemic poverty (United Nations Development Program, 2010), so the discrimination that women face in conflict-affected situations, in post-conflict and when they are on the move is deep.

The aim of this chapter is to provide a global perspective of women's participation in peace process and to make recommendations for improvement. Although women are highly represented in informal roles and groups that work for peace and mobilize communities and society to demand to the parties to the conflict to lay down their arms and negotiate a peace agreement, they are notably underrepresented at peace negotiations in official roles, as negotiators, mediators, signatories, or witnesses (UN Women, 2019). Their credible and significant involvement at the peace tables is essential for gender equality due to this is the place where key decisions about armed conflicts, post-conflict and governance are made. In this sense, until the present date, women's participation in peace processes remains one of the most unachieved goals of the Women, Peace and Security Agenda (Council on Foreign Relations). Women's structural exclusion from peace talks has crucial consequences relating to the issues that concern them (such as Violence against Women [VAW] or other violations of their human rights; women's social, economic and political empowerment or, their right to a credible justice and reparation) and how these matters are addressed in the peace processes.

In order to achieve gender equality and the Women, Peace and Security goals (Sustainable Development Goals Development Platform), it is essential to increase effective women's social, political and economic empowerment at all levels of the decision-making processes, a more credible justice and security environment for women during and after armed conflicts and resources to support them in recovery processes. It is noteworthy that the quality of women's participation in this kind of processes and social, economic and the nature of institutions will be essential tools for gender equality in post-conflict settings, the future of the country and the sustainability of the peace processes (Azarbaijani-Moghaddam, 2019, 50).

The author has used primary and secondary sources to design and develop this chapter. On one hand, primary sources are related to documentary resources, legal documents, official strategies and political statements from international organizations such as the United Nations. Secondary sources are composed of articles, policy briefs, op-eds and reports from international organizations such as the North Atlantic Treaty Organization and outstanding think tanks such as the Centre for Women, Peace and Security from the London School of Economics; PeaceWomen (Women's International League for Peace and Freedom); the International Peace Institute; The Georgetown Institute for Women, Peace and Security, The World Economic Forum or, the Institute for Democracy and Electoral Assistance.

This chapter is structured as follows: after the introduction, the chapter analyzes the background of the research question (the structural gender-based discrimination that women and girls caught in armed conflicts suffer, which is exacerbated by VAW); the next section is dedicated to the Women, Peace and Security Agenda and its significance for this study; the following part explores the state of the art of women's participation in peace processes, the role of civil society and international organizations and the global challenges concerning this issue; afterward, the case study of Afghanistan points out the main issues raised in this country related to women's participation in the peace process before the Taliban return to power, the final section provides conclusions for recommendations, further analysis and discussions. It should be noted that this research question is limited by the fact that many aspects of the Women, Peace and Security Agenda and peace and conflict, in general, lack systematic data. This is particularly significant because it prevents broader inclusion in mainstream research. Furthermore, any data collected on conflict-affected and post-conflict contexts may be incomplete and politically motivated, which means that the use of such data and related statistical findings needs to be considered cautiously (Ulrich, 2019, 18–19).

WOMEN AND GIRLS CAUGHT IN ARMED CONFLICTS: STRUCTURAL GENDER-BASED DISCRIMINATION EXACERBATED BY THE ARMED VIOLENCE

The achievement of gender equality is crucial for women's security and sustainable peace. In conflict-affected settings, women and girls must face exacerbated forms of violence and additional suffering due to the structural discrimination they experience (as problems to access to education, healthcare, decent work and lack of representation in political and economic decision-making processes) added to their situation as victims of armed violence. Armed conflicts used to take place in countries with high rates of gender inequality, gender-based violence, human rights violations or endemic poverty (United Nations Development Program, 2010).

Conflicts have different impacts on women and men. Because of that, it is indispensable that multiple actors such as international organizations, donors, states, programmers or advocates working in conflict-affected settings differentiate between root causes and contributing factors in their long-term efforts to reduce gender inequality in conflict-affected contexts. To that end, they must address these two kinds of factors toward long-term social, political, economic and cultural change (UN Women. Virtual Knowledge Centre to End Violence Against Women and Girls).

Conflict-related violence is one of the worst violations of their human rights that especially women and girls suffer in conflict-affected settings. In this respect, parties to the conflict have regarded VAW as legitimate spoils of war throughout history and VAW was tacitly considered as unavoidable through the early twentieth century. Nevertheless, successive legal ruling in recent decades has recognized VAW as a crime against humanity and war crime (Bigio and Vogelstein, 2017, 2).[1] At present, VAW in conflict-affected settings constitutes a war crime, crime against humanity, or act of genocide. Violence can be perpetrated against women, men, girls or boys by uniformed members of any army, members of a non-state armed group or terrorist organization or civilians. But perpetrators are mainly male and victims of violence in conflict-affected and post-conflict contexts including displacement situations are at large women and girls (United Nations, 2019). Nevertheless, it should be noted that data shows examples from the DRC, Rwanda and elsewhere that prove that women have also played active roles in aspects of armed conflicts. Conflict-related violence use to be committed by the above-mentioned groups or individuals for reasons including this crime as a deliberate tactic of war to target vulnerable populations inflicting traumatization, humiliation, displacements, etc.; as an act of opportunism before, during and after conflict; a form of payment to soldiers; to build group cohesion or, as a tool of ethnic destruction or modification. Other factors such as ideology, state failure, the prevalence of contraband funding, and abduction of fighting forces are also predictors of VAW (Bigio and Vogelstein, 2017, 3).

WOMEN, PEACE AND SECURITY AGENDA

The United Nations Security Council Resolution 1325[2] on Women, Peace and Security (UNSCR 1325) (United Nations Security Council, 2000) was adopted in October 2000 as a landmark Resolution recognizing the additional suffering of women and girls caught in conflict-affected and post-conflict contexts and stating the essential role of women in the prevention and resolution of conflicts, peace negotiations, peacebuilding, peacekeeping, humanitarian response and post-conflict reconstruction. This is a key Resolution for this study because it marked the beginning of the Women, Peace and Security Agenda, fully interconnected with the 2030 Agenda[3] and particularly, with SDG 5 (achievement of gender equality and empowerment of all women and girls) and SDG 16 (peace, justice and strong institutions) (Sustainable Development Goals Development Platform). UNSCR 1325 was the result of sustained and collective advocacy and campaigning carried out by women activists, peacebuilders and civil society around the world. With this respect, women in civil society organizations continue to strive to advance on the implementation, monitoring, and accountability for achieving Women, Peace and Security Goals (Allen, 2019, 8–11).

Since the adoption of UNSCR 1325, only marginal progress has been made with respect not only to the number of women in formal peace processes and the design and conduct of peace negotiations, but also concerning to their credible and effective participation in peace processes. Women's under-representation in this field takes place in spite of the growing participation of women in politics and the security sector, the higher awareness about the differentiated and greater impact of armed conflicts on women and girls, the important role they can play in peacemaking and peacebuilding and evidence that peace processes characterized by a high civil society involvement are more likely to be successful (UN Women, 2012, 1). The credible implementation of UNSCR 1325 and the subsequent ones[4] is crucial to strengthen the meaningful position of women in conflict resolution efforts and further engagement with civil society in order to meet this goal (UN Women, 2012, 1). It is also essential to focus both on men and women in gender equality awareness-raising and to reconstruct positive masculinities through long-term approaches and transformative changes (Kaya and Luchtenberg, 2018, 33). Educating girls is another powerful tool for women's empowerment. With this regard, education provides women with the knowledge, skills and self-confidence they need to empower themselves (OECD, 2012, 9–10).

WOMEN'S PARTICIPATION IN PEACE PROCESSES

Facts and figures evidence the severe gender inequality that women suffer also regarding their political empowerment around the world. Based on the Global Gender Gap Report 2020 (World Economic Forum, 2019), it will take 95 years to close the gender gap in political representation, with women in 2019 holding 25.2% of parliamentary (lower-house) seats and 21.2% of ministerial positions. Women's political empowerment is not only their right, but also a "role model effect" in terms of leadership that empower other women and benefits all the population. Moreover, their hidden talent is indispensable to advancing toward gender equality and sustainable peace.

STATE OF THE ART OF WOMEN'S PARTICIPATION IN PEACE PROCESSES

Firstly, with regard to the patterns of women's participation in peace processes, it is necessary to differentiate between individual women engaged in an official role in the peace talks and the ones who participate on behalf of women as a social group (speaking on behalf of a coalition of representatives of women's civil society groups). In this respect, women participate in peace processes through several modalities (UN Women, 2012, 7–11):

- As mediators or as members of mediation teams. It should be pointed out that most official peace processes are initiated or complemented by informal initiatives which can be facilitated by people from the conflict regions, although external mediation used to be more visible while the peace agreement is negotiated.

- As delegated of the negotiating parties discussing and agreeing on the provisions of the peace accord, setting the agenda and structure of the process (which includes setting conditions on who participates and how). It is worth noting that women do not always employ a gender perspective or advocate for provisions that would improve women's rights in the peace agreements texts.
- As all-female negotiating parties representing an agenda for women.
- As signatories.
- As witnesses, attending officially the talks and the signing ceremony and in most cases, also signing the agreement on behalf of the country or countries which sponsor the agreement.
- As representatives of women's civil society with an observer role.
- Participating in parallel forums or movements, which is the most frequent method employed by women, many times as a reaction to their exclusion from the official peace talks.
- As gender advisers to mediators, facilitators, or delegates, which supposes one of the most effective strategies to ensure the inclusion of appropriate gender-related provisions in the text of the agreements.
- As members of technical committees or working groups dedicated to gender issues to work on the technical details of the implementation of the agreement.

It should be highlighted that there is no best approach among the methods explained above. Accordingly, every of the peace processes is unique and the best way forward the inclusion of women's rights, needs and priorities is shaped by some key issues such as political culture, the particular circumstances of the conflicts, women's situations or the kind of international support and available resources. (UN Women, 2012, 7–11). Moreover, the particular characteristics of individuals participating in the peace processes are other key points to consider. Women are more and more struggling to become empowered actors in conflict and post-conflict settings as advocates, activists and fighters across the globe. But, as stated before, women's role in peace processes is frequently unrecognized, marginalized and under-valued around the world. Women have been historically absent in formal negotiations and peace processes, although they are active in advocacy, informal and grassroots processes that hide behind formal negotiations (United Nations Department of Peace Operations. Gender Unit, 2020). They are often excluded from peace talks, formal conflict resolution processes, political dialogue and post-conflict peacebuilding systems, which are the mechanisms and institutions responsible for the implementation of peace accords and post-conflict planning processes. And when they are indeed involved in such processes, they are often not taken seriously. It is noteworthy that regarding women's roles in major peace processes between 1992 and 2018, global data trends[5] show little progress due to women making up only 3% of mediators, 4% of signatories and 13% of negotiators in peace processes. Moreover, the majority of peace agreements signed from 1990 to the first months of 2020 did not include any female signatory (Council on Foreign Relations).

The involvement of women in peace processes is both their own right because of the disproportionate impact of conflicts on their lives but also a driver in increasing the chances of conflict resolution and a catalyst for the sustainability of peace. In this sense, robust data shows that women's participation in peace negotiations makes the resulting agreements 64% less likely to fall (Nilsson, 2012, 258) and 35% more likely to last at least fifteen years (O'Reilly, Súilleabháin, and Paffenholz, 2015, 16).

Moreover, there is a strong correlation between peace agreements signed by female delegates and sustainable peace. Evidence-based research has shown that agreements signed by women reveal a larger number of peace agreement provisions aimed at political reform, and higher implementation rates for these provisions than those not signed by women (Krause, Krause, and Bränfors, 2018, 1005–1007). Specially mediation is a powerful tool to change the dynamics of peace negotiations. Mediators can convey the concerns and ideas of women peacemakers who are excluded from the formal peace processes to the warring parties, empowering women's voices and supporting them for their better representation in final agreements (Dayal, 2018).

THE ROLE OF CIVIL SOCIETY AND INTERNATIONAL ORGANIZATIONS

Although women are full actors of the peace processes, they are frequently considered only as victims (United Nations Department of Peace Operations. Gender Unit, 2020). The lack of women from civil society groups in formal roles has major implications for the achievement of women's rights and gender equality due to they often represent and give voice to women's priorities and concerns (sometimes silenced voices), being more likely to do so than women within negotiating delegations, who are bound to their particular party's interests (UN Women, 2012, 3).

Research shows that the inclusion of civil society actors, such as the related to women's organizations, in the peace settlement increases the durability of peace (Nilsson, 2012, 262–263). Further evidence proves that peace processes which include the involvement of civil society actors and political parties in combination are more likely to be successful and sustainable. The outcomes also indicate that inclusion of civil society from wide spectra of society in the peace accord is the way of strengthening the peace and building legitimacy for the peace process, having also a significant impact on the prospects for global peace in nondemocratic societies. Their participation has been successfully institutionalized across all national, regional, and global peace and security fora. But access for women's organizations to vital deliberations spanning national security, conflict prevention, cessation of hostilities, countering violent extremism, protection of civilians and even humanitarian responses, remain in many places contested, politicized and even dangerous (Allen, 2019, 8–11). Krause, Krause and Bränfors (2018) state that linkages between female signatories and women civil society groups explain the positive impact of women's participation with respect to the sustainability of peace. These linkages between diverse women groups are essential for reporting the negotiation process and the inclusion of provisions that address social inequalities, particularly gender inequality. Women networks that emerge from such kind of collaboration during negotiations and the expertise that women gain from participating in these processes are very important for improving the quality of the implementation of peace agreement provisions. Consequently, collaboration and knowledge building among diverse women groups contribute to a better content of peace agreements and higher implementation rates of agreement provisions.

It should be noted that there are a large number of women's peacebuilders and mediators networks working for the advancement of gender equality in the field of women's participation in peace processes. In this regard, some of the outstanding women's civil society organizations are the African Network of Women in Conflict Prevention and Peace Mediation, FemWise-Africa; the Mediterranean Women Mediators Network; the Commonwealth Women Mediators Network; Afghan Women's Network or, the Global Alliance of Regional Women Mediator Networks. In sum, women's civil society organizations play a critical role in realizing positive change for women, in trying to make decision-making inclusive and in advocating for the achievement of gender equality in conflict and post-conflict contexts (PeaceWomen).

Because of that, the strengthening of women's leadership and women's civil society organizations is critical to support the implementation of the Women, Peace and Security Agenda. For that purpose, the United Nations Department of Peace Operations points out some good practices and lessons learned on enhancing women's participation (United Nations Department of Peace Operations. Gender Unit, 2020):

- High-level advocacy is an effective tool to foster women's leaderships and women's networks to engage in peace and political process meaningfully.
- Strong partnerships among women leaders correlate with their greater participation in national peace processes.

- Communities' ownership of peace processes increases with major awareness-raising, communication and engagement with local women's organizations.
- Monitoring mechanisms for women's participation in peace processes remain low.
- Strategic gains from informal processes and local processes are not being systematically translated to formal, national political processes.
- Women's leadership should be enhanced in a holistic way, including women's meaningful participation in peace, electoral and other political processes at the local and national levels.

GLOBAL CHALLENGES

Gender inequality in power structures reduces women to victims or passive spectators of decision-making. Because of that, this perception of women needs be challenged and replaced with the recognition of women as active agents of change and leaders of positive peace. In this regard, it should be noted that the narrative of the global agenda on Women, Peace and Security has generally focused on a vision of women as victims, overlooking the widespread nature of women's direct participation in contemporary armed conflicts and the reality that women are frequently agents of political violence, acting as supporters or combatants in a large number of contemporary armed groups (Henshaw, 2017, 1–2). The slightest attention to women as agents of violence in the Women, Peace and Security Agenda may be due to the lack of visibility among women in armed insurgent groups. This results from the fact that while women are active members of insurgencies as a general rule, they use to be concentrated in roles away from combat and, as a consequence, less visible in the organization of the armed groups. The inclusion of their voices in peace processes and post-conflict transitions may produce potentially important consequences for the success of long-term efforts to conflict prevention. In relation to the above, disarmament, demobilization and reintegration programs should respond to the particular needs of women who are demobilized from armed groups (Henshaw, 2017, 7).

Moreover, in spite of the significance of gender-sensitive language in peace agreements to establish a basis for gender inclusion during the peacebuilding process, it should be highlighted that most of the agreements do not explicitly address gender equality or women's rights. Between 1990 and 2018, only 353 of 1,789 agreements (19.7%) referred to more than 150 peace processes that included provisions addressing women, girls or gender. In 2018, out of ffity-two agreements across a variety of questions, only four (7.7%) included gender-related provisions, down from 39% in 2015 (UN Women, 2019).

Research shows that the unspoken message is still that women should be grateful to be allowed to sit in the negotiation tables because participation is not always allowed (Azarbaijani-Moghaddam, 2019, 51). Because of that, women need to see themselves as a key part of the peace processes, not as bystanders who are only given access at moments that are chosen by men.

To generate change, women need to receive information, skills, access to resources and have their voices heard to negotiate their positions and to develop changes that would benefit their societies. But women are frequently brought as silent witnesses into male-dominated structures and networks without opportunities to engage and initiate real change. As if that was not enough, they are blamed for not achieving results (Azarbaijani-Moghaddam, 2019, 50). Furthermore, it is necessary that all members of mediation teams or peace process support actions develop gender-sensitive conflict analysis and advance women's meaningful participation, avoiding the limited approach of allocating just one individual (frequently a gender advisor or focal a point) to work in such a significant task (UN Women, 2018, 41). For that purpose, they all should be trained on gender analysis and women's human rights and be able to know how to apply evidence, normative and legal obligations for the inclusive participation of women in peace processes. Following in this line, the UN, regional organizations, donors, NGOs and other entities should ensure that all the panels at meetings, conferences, seminars, training and another kind of activities they organize, co-organize or support regarding peace processes include gender equality and women's meaningful participation in these contexts. Based on practical hurdles that may prevent women from participating at the various stages of the peace processes, it is of particular interest the need of developing rapid response funds and mechanisms such as the securing of visas to represent themselves at international meetings in order to meet women's requirements concerning travel, caring, security or translation needs. The policy discourse on women's inclusion in peace processes should also consider the diversity of women groups and potential female delegates into account. In this sense, more attention needs to be paid to the potential roles of female combatants, women within the political wing of an armed group and female government representatives during peace negotiations (Krause, Krause, Bränfors, 2018, 1005–1007).

CASE STUDY: AFGHANISTAN

Women have been systematically marginalized by successive regimes in Afghanistan over the last four decades (Larson, 2015, 30), they were also excluded from the country's peace talks. Since the Taliban government fall in

2001, Afghan women achieved some rights, hope and opportunities. In this regard, as of 2019 these achievements included: a) Million of women voted in local and national elections and of parliament's 320 members, sixty-three were women (furthermore, eighteen women hold seats as ministers or deputy ministers and four serve as ambassadors); b) More than 68,000 women worked as instructors in schools and universities; c) More than 6,000 women served as judges, prosecutors, defense attorneys, police or as personnel of the Armed Forces; d) Approximately 10,000 women among Afghanistan were working as doctors, nurses and health professionals; e) Around 1,070 female journalists were working throughout the country and f) 1,150 women entrepreneurs invested $77 million in their businesses, having provided job opportunities for 77,000 Afghan women and men (Ahmadi, 2019). But notwithstanding the advancement in terms of women's rights in the first two decades of the 2000s in the country, gender inequality was severe before the Taliban return to power. Based on official data sources from the Gender Inequality Index 2020[6] (GII) (United Nations Development Program. Human Development Reports), Afghanistan ranked 169th out of 189 countries in this Index. Unfortunately, Afghan women's situation has deeply worsened.

The status of women in Afghan society has remained extremely fragile (Naderi, 2018) due to political, social and religion-related elements which attempt to reverse some of women's rights advances and to prevent the further promotion of gender equality. With this respect, Afghan women have remained victims of grave human rights abuses, gender-based violence, harmful cultural practices and systematic discrimination, but this perspective of women as victims has overlooked their participation in conflict and conflict resolution (Oxfam, 2014, 6). Based on their persistent exclusion from peace negotiations, many Afghan women were concerned that their rights were being traded away as part of the negotiations of the peace deal which was being addressed to end the conflict, despite the Afghan government and international community had continuously ensured to be devoted to prioritizing women's rights (Oxfam, 2014, 8). Women civil society leaders in Afghanistan (including the ones of the High Peace Council) warned about their deliberate exclusion from negotiations and in strategy discussions

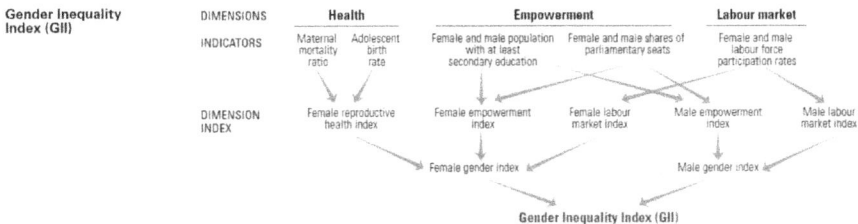

Figure 3.1. Gender Inequality Index

to address insurgencies and violent extremism. In this regard, research data based on Afghan women's inclusion in the former peace efforts showed that only 5% of them were taking part in negotiation roles (Council on Foreign Relations). The fear that the closed-door negotiations ignored and undermined women's rights, empowerment and freedom of speech was real, with huge implications for the future. In this sense, women in public roles were being increasingly targeted across Afghanistan, whether they were teachers, politicians, members of civil society organizations, human rights defenders or employed in sectors such as the related to the police and security (Allen, 2019, 8–11). Accordingly, Afghan women leaders suffered from insecurity and risk (International Civil Society Action Network, 2019).

The Afghan Women's Network[7] reported on its continuous exclusion in official and informal national and international meetings on Afghanistan's peace process and the use of the symbolic presence of women in the High Peace Council (Afghan Women's Network). This included their lack of support from the US and the international community in the Afghan women's way toward inclusive peace. With the aim of achieving their meaningful participation in the peace process, the Afghan Women's Network asked the government of national unity to ensure their active participation in all the peace talks and to fully implement the Afghanistan National Action Plan for Women, Peace and Security; to guarantee transparency and accountability regarding women's rights throughout the whole peace process and to prevent that any national or foreign groups represented the views, needs or recommendations of 15 million of Afghan women.

In addition, the Afghan Women's Network called the international community, particularly the countries involved in the Afghan peace process, for ensuring their meaningful participation in peace talks and their active role in decision-making processes, transparency and accountability. Moreover, the Afghan women demanded not to be the victims of the deals of the international community and other parties involved in the conflict. Sustainable peace could not be achieved when over half of the population was being excluded from the peace table. A leading activist for women's rights who served on the government's High Peace Council and as executive director of the Afghan Women's Education Center, stated that Afghan women needed to know their own rights and how to articulate them in a framework of Islamic values (Kakar, 2019).

CONCLUSIONS

The achievement of gender equality, the strengthening of women's leadership and ensuring women's civil society organizations meaningful participation in peace processes are the most effective ways to advance toward sustainable and long-lasting peace. Women's credible inclusion in peace processes is an imperative, not a gift, being their rights not negotiable between parties involved in peace negotiations. With this aim, international organizations, donors, states and other stakeholders must ensure that women especially from civil society organizations are included as part of the design and implementation of the peace processes and guarantee that their priorities are fully incorporated. They must also include compulsory gender requirements in the call for grants in peacebuilding processes, promote the building of inclusive security, gender-sensitive institutions and legislation at the national, regional, provincial and local levels. For that purpose, National Action Plans with substantial and sustained funding and monitoring mechanisms, transparency and accountability for implementing Security Council Resolution 1325 on Women, Peace and Security must be a priority of the international community. Women's peacebuilders and mediators networks are key actors for advancing toward gender equality and sustainable peace. Consequently, they should be supported at all levels (including key issues such as economic resources, security or training) to identify and empower more women mediators; to share best practices, lessons learned and contacts and, to participate in regional and international networks and meetings to maximize positive results. Regarding women's meaningful inclusion in peace processes, special efforts must be done not only in the number of women included but also in the quality of their participation. In addition, reliable data gathering is necessary to implement policies or actions when required to ensure that women's needs and priorities are being observed.

BIBLIOGRAPHY

Afghan Women's Network. Afghan Women Call for Fair and Lasting Peace, and Lasting Peace Requires the Full, Equal and Meaningful Participation of Women. news.un.org/en/story/2021/09/1100252

Ahmadi, B. (2019). Afghanistan Talks: No Women, No Peace, Analysis and Commentary, United States Institute of Peace. Retrieved April 5, 2020, from www.usip.org/publications/2019/03/afghanistan-talks-no-women-no-peace

Allen, L. (2019). Women Civil Society—the Bedrock of the Women, Peace and Security Agenda, Resilience and Resolution. A Compendium of Essays on Women, Peace and Security, The North Atlantic Treaty Organization. Retrieved March 20, 2020, from www.nato.int/nato_static_fl2014/assets/pdf/pdf_2019_03/20190307_190308-wps-essays-en.pdf

Azarbaijani-Moghaddam, S. (2019). From "Invisible" to "Invited" to "Invincible"-Women Build Peace, Resilience and Resolution. A Compendium of Essays on Women, Peace and Security, The North Atlantic Treaty Organization.

Retrieved March 20, 2020, from www.nato.int/nato_static_fl2014/assets/pdf/pdf
_2019_03/20190307_190308-wps-essays-en.pdf

Council on Foreign Relations. Women's Participation in Peace Processes. Retrieved
March 20, 2020, from www.cfr.org/interactive/womens-participation-in-peace
-processes/

Countryeconomy. (2018). Global Gender Gap Ranking 2018. Retrieved March 25,
2020, from countryeconomy.com/demography/global-gender-gap-index

Dayal, A. (2018). Connecting Informal and Formal Peace Talks: From Movements
To Mediators, The Georgetown Institute for Women, Peace and Security.
Retrieved February 10, 2020, from: giwps.georgetown.edu/resource/connect
ing-informal-and-formal-peace-talks/

Henshaw, A.L. (2017). Making violent women visible in the WPS
Agenda. Centre for Women, Peace and Security. LSE. Retrieved
April 2, 2020, from blogs.lse.ac.uk/wps/2017/07/07/mak
ing-violent-women-visible-in-the-wps-agenda-alexis-leanna-henshaw-72017/

International Civil Society Action Network. (2019). Why Are
Women Peacebuilders at Risk? Retrieved March 15, 2020, from
icanpeacework.org/2019/08/22/why-are-women-peacebuilders-at-risk/

Kaya, Z.N.; and Luchtenberg, K.N. (2018). Displacement and Women's Economic
Empowerment: Voices of Displaced Women in the Kurdistan Region of Iraq.
Gender Action for Peace and Security, The LSE Centre for Women, Peace and
Security, Women for Women International. Retrieved November 25, 2019,
from www.lse.ac.uk/women-peace-security/assets/documents/2018/LSE-WPS
-DisplacementEcoEmpowerment-Report.pdf

Krause, J.; Krause, W.; and Bränfors, P. (2018). "Women's Participation in Peace
Negotiations and the Durability of Peace," *International Interactions*, 44(6),
985–1016.

Larson, A. (2015). Afghanistan, Women in Conflict and Peace, Institute for
Democracy and Electoral Assistance. Retrieved March 10, 2020, from www.idea
.int/sites/default/files/publications/women-in-conflict-and-peace.pdf

Library of Congress (2017). S.1141 - Women, Peace, and Security Act of 2017,
Congress of the United States of America, Retrieved March 15, 2020, https://www.
congress.gov/115/plaws/publ68/PLAW-115publ68.pdf

Lieberman, A. (2020). Where are the women in the peace Afghan talks?,
Devex. Retrieved March 20, 2020, from https://www.devex.com/news/
where-are-the-women-in-the-afghan-peace-talks-96740

Naderi, M. (2018). Women and Peacebuilding: The Key to Achieving SDG
5 in Afghanistan, Impakter. Retrieved March 15, 2020, from impakter.com/
women-peacebuilding-key-achieving-sdg-5-afghanistan/

Nilson, D. (2012). Anchoring the Peace: The Civil Society Actors in Peace Accords
and Durable Peace, *International Interactions*, 38: 2012, Routledge, Taylor &
Francis Group.

O'Reilly, M.; O'Súilleabháin, A.; Paffenholtz, T. (2015). *Reimagining Peacemaking:
Women's Roles in Peace Processes*, International Peace Institute.

Oxfam. (2014). Behind closed doors: The risk of denying women a voice in determining Afghanistan's future, Briefing Paper. Retrieved 1 April, 2020, from www.oxfamamerica.org/explore/research-publications/behind-closed-doors-the-risk-of-denying-women-a-voice-in-determining-afghanistans-future/

PeaceWomen. Civil Society. Retrieved March 20, 2020, from www.peacewomen.org/civil-society

Sustainable Development Goals Development Platform. Retrieved December 18, 2019, from sustainabledevelopment.un.org/sdgs

Ulrich, R. (2019). The known knowns and known unknowns in data on women, peace and security, Centre for Women, Peace and Security. Research at LSE. Retrieved April 2, 2020, from www.lse.ac.uk/women-peace-security/assets/documents/2019/WPS19Nagel.pdf

United Nations Department of Peace Operations. Gender Unit. (2020). Leaders and changemakers. Women shaping peace. Women, peace and security highlights of UN Peacekeeping in 2019, Retrieved March 15, 2020, from peacekeeping.un.org/sites/default/files/dpo_wps_2019_digital_1.pdf

United Nations Development Program. (2010). Price of Peace. Financing for gender equality in post-conflict reconstruction, Synthesis Report. Retrieved November 15, 2019, from content-ext.undp.org/aplaws_publications/3190612/price-of-peace-financing-for-gender-equality-in-post-conflict-reconstruction.pdf

United Nations Development Program. Human Development Reports. Gender Inequality Index (GII). Retrieved March 20, 2020, from hdr.undp.org/en/indicators/68606

United Nations Security Council. (2000). Resolution 1325 on Women, Peace and Security. Retrieved November 28, 2019, from documents-dds-ny.un.org/doc/UNDOC/GEN/N00/720/18/PDF/N0072018.pdf?OpenElement

UN Women. Virtual Knowledge Centre to End Violence Against Women and Girls. Causes and Contributing Factors. Retrieved April 1, 2020, from www.endvawnow.org/en/articles/1475-causes-and-contributing-factors-.html?next=1476

UN Women. (2018). Women's Meaningful Participation in Negotiating Peace and the Implementation of Peace Agreements, Report of the Expert Group Meeting, Retrieved April 5, 2020, from www.unwomen.org/en/digital-library/publications/2018/10/egm-report-womens-meaningful-participation-in-negotiating-peace

UN Women. (2019). Facts and Figures: Peace and Security. Retrieved March 25, 2020, from www.unwomen.org/en/what-we-do/peace-and-security/facts-and-figures

World Economic Forum. (2019). Global Gender Gap Report 2020. Retrieved April 2, 2020, from www3.weforum.org/docs/WEF_GGGR_2020.pdf

NOTES

1. The UN Security Council declared as of 1992 that the organized, massive and systematic detention and rape of women in the former Yugoslavia was a international crime.

2. UNSCR 1325 (2000) can be consulted at: www.un.org/ruleoflaw/blog/document /security-council-resolution-1325-2000-on-women-and-peace-and-security/.

3. The 2030 Agenda for Sustainable Development can be consulted at: sustain-abledevelopment.un.org/post2015/transformingourworld.

4. The other nine key resolutions on Women, Peace and Security adopted by the United Nations Security Council after Resolution 1325 in 2000 can be consulted at: www.peacewomen.org/why-WPS/solutions/resolutions.

5. Further data can be consulted at www.cfr.org/interactive/womens-participation -in-peace-processes/explore-the-data.

6. Defined by a composite measure which reflects inequality in achievement between women and men in three dimensions: reproductive health, empowerment and the labor market.

7. The Afghan Women's Network reunited over 3,500 individual members and 125 women's organizations devoted to Afghan women's empowerment.

Chapter 4

Alice Shalvi as a Feminist Leader

Moria Ran Ben Hai

In an interview on December 5, 2010, answering the question—"How would you define yourself?—Professor Alice Shalvi stated:

> A wife. I am also a grandmother and great-grandmother. When I am asked to say what I am for a presentation or conference, I first say that I am socially recruited.[1]

The words of Professor Alice Shalvi, the Israel Prize laureate for her activities in education and the promotion of women, one of the leaders in the social-gender change in Israeli society, reflect her leadership self-perception. Shalvi, who sees herself first and foremost as a family woman, chooses to present herself outwardly as a mobilized leader for social purposes. Indeed, this is how the public perceived Shalvi:

> Prof. Alice Shalvi has always been revolutionary and groundbreaking with courage, intellectual integrity, and a long-term vision. In two main areas, intertwined, her special personal stamp is imprinted: in the field of education and the field of women's status and well-being.[2]

Alice Hildegard Shalvi (née Margulies) was born in 1926 in Essen, western Germany. In 1933, following the rise of the Nazis to power, her family immigrated to England and settled in London. They were Modern Orthodox observant Jews with an egalitarian gender view, according to Shalvi. Her parents were Zionists and community activists who encouraged her and her older brother to be educated and engage in society's needs. Shalvi completed a bachelor's and master's degree in English literature at Cambridge. As a student Shalvi took part in her college's Zionist delegation to the First Zionist Congress that was held after World War Two. After getting aware of the condition of the European Jews, she decided to switch her major from English literature to social work at the London School of Economics (LSE), in order to help the Holocaust survivors. In 1949, after graduating, Shalvi immigrated to Israel by herself and settled in Jerusalem.[3] After not finding work in assisting immigrants and Holocaust survivors, she began teaching in the English department at the Hebrew University and met Moshe Shalvi, who would quickly become her husband and an enthusiastic supporter of her work. Over the next two decades, Shalvi gave birth to their six children, finished her doctoral studies, and made progress in her academic path. In 1969, Shalvi was asked by the Hebrew University to establish and head the department of English Studies at the University of the Negev (later Ben-Gurion University). She held this position until 1972 when she first encountered gender discrimination. When Shalvi asked to be appointed dean, she was rejected because of her gender. She was told clearly and without fear of recrimination: "Because you are a woman!"[4]

Additional cracks began to appear in the gender-equality illusion that Shalvi held then, especially when she joined the government-appointed Namir Commission in 1975, which comprehensively examined the status of women in Israel following the United Nations' International Women's Year. Before that, in 1971, Shalvi met with Betty Friedan on her visit to Israel. Friedan tried to provoke a discourse with Shalvi about feminism, but Shalvi claimed that Israeli women "do not need liberation, they are already liberated."[5] Shalvi then, as an observant woman, a wife, and a mother, who headed an academic department, firmly believed that the State of Israel was advanced in its social attitude.[6] However, as Shalvi was exposed to discrimination and injustice against her and other women, and became acquainted with feminist work globally and in Israel during that decade, she became more and more feminist herself.

In addition to the Namir Commission, 1975 was also the year Shalvi took upon herself the management of the religious high school for girls, Pelech, in Jerusalem, where her eldest daughter studied. The former principals of the ultra-Orthodox institution could not handle the economic and administrative burden, so she volunteered to fill their place until a permanent principal will be found while working at the Hebrew University. The uniqueness of this high school, which was then indeed ultra-Orthodox, but operated under the supervision of the religious public education system, was its approach which combined excellence in both academic and Jewish religious studies as well as, surprisingly, cultural openness. Shalvi, who at that time belonged to the Religious Zionist society, sent her daughter to Pelech because she was disappointed with the Religious Zionistic educational institutions in Jerusalem. Like her, other Religious Zionist parents sent their daughters to the ultra-Orthodox high school and, in fact, the institution became more and more Religious Zionist in the mid-1970s. Upon taking office, Shalvi turned Pelech into an experimental educational institution and implemented an educational model she created based on the principles of democracy, pluralism, equality, and social leadership. Her model uses innovative teaching methods and project-based learning and served as a model for other educational institutions in Israel. To this day, when Pelech High School has become an educational network in Israel that implements Shalvi's educational model, Pelech is considered an institution that promotes girls and encourages them for leadership, academic excellence, and social, civic, and political involvement.[7] After fifteen years as Pelech's principal, Shalvi resigned, mostly because she acted independently on political issues that the Religious Zionistic educational institutions and many teachers and parents opposed. Her retirement was abrupt, and it was unclear who would run the high school in her place.[8]

In 1984 accord a formative event in Shalvi's life—an American-Israeli dialogue sponsored and initiated by the American Jewish Congress (AJC), on the topic "A Woman as a Jew, A Jew as a Woman: An Urgent Inquiry" that took place in the summer of 1984 at the Van Leer Institute in Jerusalem. In the dialogue, Jewish American women encouraged their Israeli cohorts to work to improve their religious and civil status.[9] This event was a turning point for Shalvi. She took an active role in the conference and, a few months later, led the establishment of the Israeli Women's Network (IWN). The goal was to create a comprehensive change in the status of women in Israel, whatever their identity may be. The IWN worked to raise public awareness of gender discrimination, develop international and local ties with other feminist organizations, promote women in politics and the military, improve the status of women in the media, dialogue, and when needed, even fight with the religious establishment regarding the issue of Agunot (women whose husbands refuse or are unable to grant them a divorce), and also act on violence against women issues. During Shalvi's tenure in the organization, the IWN's greatest achievements were: The Equal Retirement Age for Men and Women Initiative, 1987; amendment to the State-Owned Enterprises Law, 1975, that requires equal representation for both genders;[10] and Miller v. The Minister of Defense & others petition that paved the way for women in combat roles in the Israeli Defense Forces (IDF). Shalvi was chairperson of the IWN for fifteen years, until her final retirement in 2000.[11]

Her first retirement was against the backdrop of a change in the human fabric of the network's workers and volunteers. At first, they were mostly academic women and slowly the politicians multiplied and changed the spirit of the organization. Shalvi could not bear it, and several months before the 1997 election for the IWN's management, she announced that she would not run. Shalvi never trained a successor but supported one of the candidates and indeed this one was selected. After a year she resigned and Shalvi was asked to fill her place.

The tension between Shalvi and the other members of the IWN remained and even intensified. It led Shalvi to make significant decisions on his own, without consulting the rest of the activities, which is wrong in a democratic organization. Following the growing internal organizational pressures, Shalvi suspended herself from the chairperson position about two months before the 2000 election, and thus resigned from the organization for good.[12]

In addition to her two most notable accomplishments, the IWN and Pelech High School, Shalvi also headed the Schechter Institute, promoted Jewish-Arab coexistence in Israel, and promoted arts and sciences in Jerusalem. Even now, at the age of ninety-five, she is actively involved with the New Israel Fund and other initiatives.

BETWEEN THE PERSONAL AND
PUBLIC IN SHALVI'S LIFE

Shalvi's personal life and public persona had a complicated relationship. Although Shalvi played the "traditional woman" model and fulfilled its main purpose when she and Moshe established a large family, at the same time she also developed a demanding career while the children were still young, to which she added active roles in educational and social areas. Dew to her work she was away from home for long periods and, despite support from Moshe and others, her children and, later, she herself, felt the negative effects of her absence. Occasionally, her absence wasn't physical but emotional: she held an office at home but disconnected herself from the daily household life and parenting while working there. Additionally, Shalvi's house became a meeting place for her work, even during times that should have been for family, like the holidays or Saturdays. Often, there was little separation between her private home life and the public roles Shalvi occupied, roles that many times overshadowed the needs of other family members.[13] Furthermore, Shalvi often said and acted in the political, religious, and feminist fields that put her family at the center of public attention. In one case, a threat to Shalvi's life was recorded on her home answering machine because of her work for Jewish and Arab coexistence.[14] The family's public exposure to the mother's activities made it difficult to maintain an intimate family lifestyle for her children.

Romantic partnership often has a key role in the identity development of public activists and carrier persons.[15] Moshe, who was Shalvi's passionate partner in her work in the IWN and Pelech High School, also shared with her a new vision of marriage life. As the kids grew up, he often took on more "feminine" roles like cooking and cleaning, served as his wife's secretary, and was her occasional driver (Shalvi did not hold a driving license). Shalvi's dedication to her work was made possible by Moshe's support and financial aid from her older brother, Ze'ev Margulies, who stayed in England to run the family business and frequently sent Shalvi and her family money over the years.[16] Combining family life and public enterprise action is not the domain of many and therefore feminist leadership is often done by affluent women, as has occurred in the various waves of feminism. Shalvi certainly fits this assumption.

Shalvi's uniqueness is that she had a large family during her public career and was able to shine in many areas: the academic world, education, feminism, political and social activism. However, it is important to note that when Shalvi volunteered to become principal of Pelech, her youngest daughter was nine; she only established the IWN a decade later, when her children were adults and she could commit to activities for the public. Shalvi encouraged other women not to give up on family life or on having a career or becoming activists. She worked hard to promote laws that would allow both men and women to combine parentage and career.[17]

In both her enterprises, the gap between Shalvi's abilities and resources and those of her followers was evident. The teaching staff of Pelech, the school graduates, and the members of the IWN—all felt that Shalvi set a very high bar that was unattainable for them. They struggled to meet her demands of devoting time and efforts, but most of them did not have the financial resources and support Shalvi received from her family. This gap often created resentment toward her but did not damage her inspirational qualities since she remained close to the women she led and behaved modestly in her interactions with them. It helped that Shalvi dedicated all her abilities and resources to her public initiatives, often at the expense of her family. Her followers appreciated this since they could not and did not want to do the same. They saw Shalvi as the reason the enterprises succeeded.

SHALVI'S CONTRIBUTION TO THE DEVELOPMENT OF FEMINISM IN ISRAEL

Shalvi's two enterprises spearheaded her public work both by creating a vision and by putting it into practice. Shalvi created an innovative but realistic vision, both in her eyes and the eyes of the associates. As the principal of Pelech and chairperson of the IWN, she initiated systemic and comprehensive processes in order to realize and fulfill her vision. Her influence was felt in many areas: The Pelech model dealt with education methodology and content and tried to establish an active female religious model. The model included many innovations regarding the management of the high school, teaching

methodology, content, openness, and pluralism in religious education. Her
ideas about education were groundbreaking compared to what was existed at
that time and many of them would later be implemented in the public education system. Additionally, other "Pelech" schools opened in Israel: three
for girls and one for boys.[18] Shalvi was a pioneer when it came to women's
education in the sense that she gave her female students the tools to study
Torah and Talmud and encouraged them to focus on religious studies, in the
mid-1970s, when only two women's *midrashot* (institutions of high level
religious Jewish studies for women) existed in Israel. She fought for her
female students to receive high level Torah studies and to be allowed to sit
the Talmud matriculation exams, that were previously almost solely taken by
male students. The graduates of her school and teachers nurtured by her had a
meaningful role in expanding her revolution and establishing it as a religious
norm for girls. Many of them work in teaching Jewish religious studies in
schools and the academic world.[19]

Shalvi also encouraged her students to participate in leadership roles and
be actively involved in society. She was one of the first school principals
to run a personal volunteer program for her students in the 1970s that later
become a mandatory project for all high school students in Israel in the 1980s.
Shalvi continuously encouraged her female students to serve in the IDF: this
was, at the time, considered unacceptable for girls graduating from religious
schools in Israel, while it was a compulsory service for secular girls. Her
influence is evident in the rise of religious girls serving in the IDF and the
establishment of *midrashot* and programs aimed at preparing religious girls
for their military service along with high level religious studies, starting in
the 1980s in Israel.

Shalvi served as a female religious pioneering role model for students
and teachers, and she encouraged them to use her model in their life. Being
a religious woman at the head of a feminist organization encouraged other
religious women to take more of a part in feminist activism and raised public
awareness of the status of women in religious society. Over a decade after the
IWN began its work, in 1998, Kolech Forum was founded as an organization
that represents Orthodox feminist women.[20] Among its founders were members of the IWN. The effects of Shalvi's activism were felt in the Religious
Zionist and Modern Orthodox community in Israel: during her active years
and mostly afterward, there has been significant development in the status of
women in the Orthodox world.[21]

During the 1980s, both Shalvi and the IWN had a clear feminist message,
unlike earlier feminist organizations. It was a politically unaffiliated feminist
organization and therefore unique. The IWN's brand of feminism was liberal,
not radical, unlike most second wave feminist organizations at the time. This
unique aspect meant that women from all walks of life could identify with

the IWN and it granted the IWN legitimacy in the eyes of the Israeli public. Furthermore, the fact that Shalvi, who headed the organization, combined both traditional and modern identities added to the legitimacy of the organization. The IWN under Shalvi played an important role in the development of feminism in Israel: the IWN operated using multiple different ways to achieve the gender equality its members aspired to. As part of this systemic and comprehensive vision, it worked to influence the government, legislation, judicial law, media, education, and religious authority, all at the same time. The IWN was the first organization to engage in all these fields without being involved in social work.

The IWN had various modes of operation, some unique to the organization: The majority of their work was lobbying to promote legislation and raising public awareness of issues. The IWN had a public relations unit whose purpose was to turn the IWN into a central factor in the development of women's rights in Israeli society. Shalvi created a network of collaboration with female members of the Knesset and existing feminist organizations to increase the influence of the IWN. These collaborations strongly contributed to the female members of the Knesset and the organizations adopting a clear feminist declaration, one that would become stronger and clearer with time. Under Shalvi's leadership, the IWN promoted female feminist leadership in all sectors of Israeli society. The IWN initiated and conducted studies about the status of women in Israel to present the decision-makers with up-to-date data. The IWN also turned itself into a source of knowledge and information regarding women and feminism thanks to its library and archive. The IWN operated a women's legal aid center to help them fight for legal rights in the supreme court. By all of these, Shalvi, during her fifteen years of heading the IWN, had a significant impact on the development of feminism in Israel and created a new gender dynamic in Israeli society.[22] In addition to heading her two enterprises, Shalvi, because of her actions and strong personality, became a female role model for many women and shaped the next generation of religious women and feminist activists, as will be shown.

THE DEVELOPMENT OF FEMINISM IN ISRAEL AND ITS ATTRIBUTES IN VIEW OF SHALVI'S PHILOSOPHY

Israeli feminism is divided into four main waves, similar to Western feminism. The first wave was liberal, the second radical, the third multicultural, and the fourth empowered women and made use of Internet tools.[23] The IWN operated during the second and third waves. With the establishment of the state of Israel, the myth of gender equality in the modern state was created until, in the late 1970s, the report of the Namir state Commission concerning the status of women refuted it. Even before the report, radical feminism began to grow in Israel, but its spread was limited because it was deemed too extreme for Israeli society. An additional reason for its limited influence was the movements' avoidance of collaborating with the establishment and furthermore, their focus on criticizing the establishment. Many of the women active in the feminist movement were new immigrants from Western societies who were wealthy and well educated.[24] During the 1980s and 1990s, due to the Namir Commission report, liberal feminism took hold in the state and helped establish sectorial and multicultural feminism from the 1990s onwards. In the sectoral feminist organizations, Israeli-born women from all walks of life were active. During that period, the feminist message of those organizations became clear.[25]

One can point to Shalvi and the IWN's contribution in the transition between the second and third waves, the establishment of liberal feminism from the 1980s onwards, the improvement of women's organizations, and raising public awareness of feminism, which led to sectoral feminist initiatives by Israeli women in the third wave. Similar to radical feminism, the IWN was first established by white bourgeois new immigrants. Their goal was to create a common base in order to form a supra-party organization with a diverse representation of sectors in Israel. For this reason, the IWN avoided the issues of personal freedom, such as sexual preference and political stances regarding Palestinian-Israeli conflict, issues that had made it difficult for the feminist movement in Israel to achieve wide-scale acceptance. Shalvi represented a female model with multiple identities, including traditional ones, and believed then in liberal feminism, which is a softer version of feminism compared to the radical one. This enabled the organization to achieve wider acceptance in Israeli society. Additionally, the IWN aimed its activity at the Israeli establishment out of collaboration and initiated many changes via legislation, judicial action, and education. However, the IWN did not hesitate to criticize the establishment and recruit organizations, both women and civil-oriented, that were part of the establishment to achieve its goals. This flexibility was a new way of operating, compared to other feminist organizations in Israel, and it encouraged women's organizations that were part of the establishment to adopt feminist views.[26]

Shalvi saw the IWN as a natural place for both religious and secular women, Jewish and non-Jewish Israeli women, and, as such, the IWN attempted to be an umbrella organization for all women and feminists in Israel. The change of generations in the IWN in the 1990s expressed the appearance of a new generation of Israeli feminists that, unlike their formers, wanted a clear and sharp feminist expression, in the cultural, religious, and political arenas. This new feminist wave was made possible by the previous waves and by making feminism a part of Israeli society as the IWN, headed by Shalvi, attempted to do, and by her actions in Pelech that helped establish religious feminism in Israel.

Shalvi's identity was influenced by Western and Israeli, Zionist, religious, and humanist culture and society. She was able to hold all of these identities together and therefore failed to see a conflict between the Jewish orthodoxy and feminism. In her eyes, their values complemented each other and Jewish Halacha could be reinterpreted to match modern egalitarian values. This view was unpopular in the traditional society in Israel, and so its buds came from new immigrants like Shalvi. As a change agent who served in key educational and social rules, the application of her concepts in her enterprises has made a significant contribution to the advancement of civil and religious feminism in Israel.

RELIGIOUS FEMINISM: SHALVI'S CONTRIBUTION TO THE AMALGAMATION OF FEMINISM AND ORTHODOXY

In light of Shalvi's story, the combination of feminism and Orthodoxy is possible but not straightforward and entails many struggles. Shalvi handled the gap between the Orthodox world in which she grew up and the feminism she sought later on by repeatedly examining Orthodox Halacha versus values of equality. She took it for granted that these two worlds could coexist. Shalvi was both open-minded and very pluralistic in her actions, which enabled her to handle such complexity. Shalvi's image provided a new archetype: one that combined the Orthodox lifestyle, democratic values, and a modern way of life. Deborah Weissman, a pioneer of religious feminism and one of the founders of both the IWN and Kolech Forum, talks about her trip with Shalvi for a dialogue of Jewish and Palestinian women in Brussels in 1989. The dialogue lasted several days, including Friday and Saturday (Jewish Shabbat). They both made Kiddush and had a Shabbat meal in Alice's room on Friday night. The next day, when they came to the dialogue on Shabbat, Alice, who was the first speaker, explained she would not use the microphone because of the religious prohibition on using electricity on Shabbat. The audience understood and she naturally continued her lecture. Weissman's testimony shows how Shalvi kept the religious rules and stayed true to her faith, her actions promoting her political and democratic views, and how she combined the two easily and naturally. Weissman stated that, in this manner, Shalvi paved the way for religious women in the conference.[27] Later, this trip would be a source of conflict between Shalvi and the head of the religious public education system together with the teaching staff at Pelech. They could not accept Shalvi's complexity of combining Orthodox beliefs and left-wing politics.[28]

By heading a girls' educational institution and being a religious-educational leader, Shalvi provided a space for women, led by women, that helped grow future female leaders.[29] Out of an egalitarian conception and out of an awareness of the importance of halakhic practice in responding to the changes she sought to bring about in the status of women in Orthodoxy, Shalvi paved the way for the attainment of the Torah literacy abilities for women. She tried to get Pelech to adopt feminist religious rituals that were accepted then in the United States, such as women's prayer groups and *zimmun* before meals. Her students, however, were often less than receptive to such changes. Chana Pinchasi, a Pelech graduate and today a Doctor for Gender Studies who specializes in Talmud education, said: "We always suspected that the act of doing a *zimmun* like the men was more important to her, for feminist reasons than the grace after meal itself."[30] As mentioned, Shalvi encouraged her students to be socially involved as citizens in a democratic state, to join the IDF or volunteer to full national service, both for two years at least, and to take a political stand in their adult life. As part of Shalvi's social involvement, she confronted the Rabbinical establishment concerning civil status, divorce refused wives, and Agunot. She called to improve the status of women in Halacha and when these calls were not answered, she protested against the Chief Rabbinate of Israel along with other women from the IWN and feminist organizations. Shalvi barning *ketubah*, a Jewish marriage contract, as part of a protest in front of the Chief Rabbinate offices in Jerusalem after many attempts of dialogue in order to find solutions for *Agunot*, 1994. In many ways, her actions unsettled the traditional status of women in the Orthodox world and helped incorporate gender equality values in the orthodox society in Israel in the decades of her operation. Orthodox feminism in Israel today is characterized by religious halachic education for women, that for the first time in Jewish history, allowed women to become *toenet rabbanit* (advocates in the rabbinical courts), and halachic advisors in the subject of Tahara (family purity) as well as make halachic rulings in other fields. This education has enabled the rise of religious female leadership, a leadership that is growing stronger in *midrashot* and various Orthodox communities, as well as in the wider public. Additionally, partnership and egalitarian prayer minyans (congregations) have popped up in various Orthodox communities around Israel and worldwide.[31] Shalvi's work in religious girls' education, in the 1970s, planted the roots for these features. They are a melding of modernity and traditionalism that came about from a desire both for religious observance and practice and for gender equality. As mentioned, Shalvi played a key role in women's halachic learning revolution, and women took an active role in religious rituals. Another key feature of this type of feminism is the presence of religious women in the public sphere: in politics, the media, and key educational roles. The Kolech Forum was established, partly by women from the IWN, and today it has taken the lead on subjects concerning religious Orthodox feminism as sexual harassment, or even rape, by religious authorities, struggles against the rabbinical institution for Agunot, and legal fight for Rabbinical exams for women.[32]

The development of feminism in the Orthodox society in Israel runs parallel to Shalvi's early growth and the development of her feminist consciousness. However, once her awakening was complete, Shalvi quickly created an innovative and revolutionary vision for religious girls and women that was unpopular with the public for most of her years in Pelech. Her move from the Orthodox movement to the Conservative one was a dramatic statement about the way she perceived the relationship between feminism and Orthodoxy and teaches us about how she chose to create change: in the beginning, together with the establishment and from within and, when that failed, abandoning the establishment and choosing the path of extreme protest. The way she ran the IWN was the same. In retrospect, her vision was a guidepost for the development of religious feminism to this day.

Leah Shakdiel, one of the Israeli pioneers of Orthodox feminism who was a member of the IWN, remembers her surprise when she met Shalvi and discovered the IWN. According to Shakdiel, Shalvi was her own kind of pioneer. One can hear, in Shakdiel's words, the way Shalvi's complex personality was perceived by orthodox women in Israel: "I discovered the work done by this woman, and that group and suddenly—hey, she was religious! She was a teacher! She was the principal of a religious girl's high school! She was a community activist in the Katamon neighborhood where new immigrants were crammed, across from my childhood home! And she had just started a national organization for women! She could have been my mother! . . . Thank you, Alice, for being there a few decades ahead of us all! Not just before us, Ahead of us!"[33]

To conclude this section, Shalvi's unique contribution to the development of Israeli feminism in general, and religious feminism in particular, can be seen in two main aspects: identifying social changes, leading them, and making their messages available to the public. Shalvi identified social changes from the very beginning and created her vision from them. Sometimes, she created the change herself but, for the most part, she noticed changes happening at the edges of the social and religious reality and drew them into the mainstream. The changes she sought to create concerning the status of women were a new revolutionary message for social change in Orthodox society and gender equality in Israel.

This dual mission, both in the religious world and Israeli society, expressed different aspects of Shalvi's personality and increased her influence. Her unique and complex identity created a varied image of burgeoning Israeli feminism. Because of her identity and her leadership abilities, Shalvi was able to make feminism accessible to the Israeli public. A public which, at the time, tended to be conservative and traditionalist but was also ready to reexamine its values in many areas including social, political, and religious ones.

SHALVI AS A LEADER

Shalvi turned to public activism at an older age, with life experience and flexible thinking. She constantly drove to improve reality. Two main drivers guided her leadership and social activism: her desire for wide-scale social justice between genders, races, and social classes; and her personal crises and experience. The combination of the two shaped her feminist perceptions from the 1970s onwards. Most of the Pelech graduates, Pelech teachers, and members of the IWN that I interviewed spoke enthusiastically about Shalvi's leadership. One of the Pelech graduates spoke of the whole range experience of learning in Pelech under Shalvi's leadership: "The experience of Pelech enabled me to become someone with a personality, to gain life experience, the ability to cope, education, and much much more."[34] Rachel Lipshitz, who was a teacher at Pelech, described Shalvi as a motivator and enabler of ideas: "every idea that I had, I was given the space to enact it, and I had a lot of ideas! . . . Shalvi was always there."[35] "Alice was like an engine, she motivated us all fantastically."[36] Galia Golan, one of the founders of the IWN says looking back. "Not to mention the work environment with Alice, the same environment that inspired me and which I always try to preserve," wrote one of the office employees in the IWN in 1998.[37] Her words, as well as others, repeatedly came up in different ways in interviews I held with women from the IWN. Most of them mention Shalvi's ability to motivate them, to help them identify difficulties in their life and environment, and work to find creative solutions to those problems.[38] Shalvi was most certainly a leader, but was she a feminist leader?

THREE DEFINITIONS FOR FEMINIST LEADERSHIP

Some say that feminist leadership is leadership that derives its worldview from the feminist perspective; that encourages the identification of injustice and oppression in reality. A feminist leader, by this definition, is driven by a feeling of fairness, justice, and equality and so acts to raise awareness of issues of gender, race, and social class. This type of leader seeks to change social reality, focuses on both society and the individual, and is willing to take personal risks.[39] Another opinion sees feminist leadership as leadership that acts for social change, but according to this opinion, to create change, one must first develop high self-esteem and gain tools and resources. This enables the leader to join the ranks of the decision-makers, and create change in her own and adjacent communities and society. This leadership can be compared to small waves that eventually lead to large change.[40]

In the past, there have been those who have objected to the idea of "feminist leadership." According to this opinion, there is no difference between female leadership and feminist leadership other than the socio-political perspective. Therefore, women, like men, need to be leaders, to begin with, to be able to lead society to their ideas.[41] Today, studies point to distinct feminist leadership styles. These include people-oriented, nurturing, participative, democratic, and transformative leadership styles. All seem to be more supportive of employee participation in the decision-making (PDM) process compared to traditional leadership styles or masculine leadership styles that include control-wise, autocratic, top-down approach, and coercive leadership.[42] In light of these definitions, it would seem that Shalvi is indeed a feminist leader: her actions stemmed from a deep internal view of justice, a desire for wide-scale equality, and a feminist purpose. During her years in the IWN, Shalvi sought to create an egalitarian social reality in Israel. Even before Shalvi created her group of decision-makers, through which she empowered women and helped them infiltrate key roles in Israeli leadership, Shalvi built up her self-esteem. It had begun during her childhood: she grew up with idealistic and supportive parents; it continued when she became an educated young adult; a member of the academic world; and a woman who took advantage of the opportunities she was presented with. Shalvi had plenty of resources. She had emotional support from her parents and Moshe, her spouse, and she had financial resources from her brother. Both enabled her to develop personally and dedicate time to being chairperson of the IWN despite the lack of salary. She used different types of collaborative leadership styles. This also was her weakness, as I will later show. I will now show other aspects of her leadership to demonstrate Shalvi's unique brand of feminist leadership.

BIOGRAPHICAL BACKGROUND AS A
LEADER PORTRAIT DESIGNER

In her life's story, one can see that, like her parents, Shalvi sought meaningful work. Her activity in her two main enterprises came from a deep sense of social justice, a desire for wide-scale equality, and a feminist purpose. The values she obtained as a child in an active Zionistic gracious family and as a child who grew up under the Nazi threat, shaped her personality and over the years become operating forces within her. The difficulties and distresses of others, motivated her to a widespread action, again and again. This is visible throughout her youth, when she was active as a college student in the Zionist Congress, and when she chose to study social work to aid Holocaust survivors; It could be seen also when she faced gender discrimination while advancing in her academic path; and it could be seen later in her life, in the dilemmas she faced in her encounters as a woman with the Orthodox world; her children's struggles in the schools; the distress of the Rosenblüths who established Pelech and had to retire due to economic and administrative difficulties they had running the school; the low status of women in Israel and the gender discrimination exposed in the Namir Commission; as the principle of Pelech and as the head of the IWN. Like her nuclear family, Shalvi was drawn to social activism and dedicated her personal and familial financial resources to it.

From a young age, Shalvi had high self-esteem. Her parents supported her desire to study, even though higher education for Jewish women was uncommon at the time, and encouraged her to realize her Zionistic aspirations, even though it meant being separated from her. This support was also financial and became a strong base that allowed Shalvi to become the strong pioneering woman she is. Self-confidence and esteem characterized her leadership as will be shown. Additionally, her parents' full support can also be attributed to her being an encouraging and empowering factor toward women in her leadership, as they were for her. In her marriage, Moshe's admiration toward Shalvi and her ideas, and his full cooperation with them, continued the support she got from home and enabled her long years of public activism.

A LEADER FROM THE OUTSET AND
A LEADER EX POST FACTO

As an educational leader, Shalvi took advantage of opportunities that came her way to accomplish goals in the management of the education system and the content the system should deliver. Her management of Pelech was a productive combination of her educational aspirations, social ideas, and intellectual skills. Her position allowed her to use her skills and ideas that had not been utilized in her previous roles. This illustrates the value Shalvi placed on education as a key instrument of influence in society, both for the individual and society at large. Unlike her role in Pelech, Shalvi became the head of the IWN because she was suited to the role and believed she should lead the work on behalf of women. After the AJC conference, Shalvi worked to turn this idea from a single encounter into a proper organization, under her leadership. She has fully harnessed her talents and resources for the benefit of this role.

Shalvi did not see feminist activism as a secondary goal, but a primary one, and so was completely dedicated.

Shalvi saw both her enterprises, the one that she filled by chance and the one that was planned, like missions to take on and means to change society. In both her fields of leadership, the relationship between the two areas of activism, the religious within the framework of an establishment (school) and the civic one that worked with various establishments and against them, within social activism, was evident. The gains of knowledge and power from each influenced the other. Shalvi began her educational and public activity at the same time: she became the principal of Pelech just as she joined the Namir Commission to examine the status of women in Israel. Her exposure to the gaps Israeli women and religious girls faced, made Shalvi create innovative methods to actualize her feminist viewpoint. With her success in education and establishing herself as an educational leader after a decade of running Pelech, Shalvi felt empowered and took on a greater social leadership role leading the IWN. In this position, Shalvi took a stronger feminist stance and radical methods of operation. The way she conducted herself in this field affected her educational work and this could be seen also in Pelech, where it sped up her resignation from the school. In the 90s, the IWN reached the peak of its activity and achievements: this could be because Shalvi stopped working in Pelech and dedicated all her energy to civil causes. In both of her leadership roles and her public works, one can see many of her leadership characteristics. I will now discuss the most prominent ones.

SHALVI'S LEADERSHIP CHARACTERISTICS

Charisma

In her leadership, Shalvi was self-confident and ambitious which, together with her oratory skills, created a charismatic personality. She has succeeded to motivate many people to achieve goals over time. In both her enterprises, Shalvi felt a deep connection to the community she worked within and to the goals she sought to reach. Together with her charm, these characteristics made her able to create a feeling of a "peer group" among women with different ideological, political, religious, and social associations and to enable them to work together. She began her work in the 1970s by uniting female university professors to discuss discrimination in the academic world, in the Hebrew University where she worked, and other institutions. This ability served her well in Pelech where she recruited teachers from different religious and ideological backgrounds to implement the unique educational model she created. More so, the charisma is more evident in her leadership of the IWN and her desire to create an apolitical umbrella organization for all the women of Israel, and in her work when various women, members of the IWN, members of the Knesset, and other public figures found themselves identifying with Shalvi and her views and joining her.

As a multi-faceted feminist leader, Shalvi excelled at making revolutionary messages accessible and legitimate in the eyes of the public. Frances Raday, one of the founders of the IWN, defined her as "moderate in expression, radical in mind."[43] True, in Pelech, in the religious environment where her ideas often clashed with the halachic authority and with common traditional practice, her ability to make her messages accessible was limited. As mentioned, the majority of her influence was on the women who would become religious leaders in years to come after her. However, in her work in the IWN, she managed to introduce liberal feminist ideology and vision, which were uncommon views in the Israeli public, into the mainstream.

Shalvi could convince people to follow her even when her vision was far from reality. Some of her ideas were ahead of their time, and society was not ready for them. Such as her attempts to institute women's Torah readings in the 70s and 80s at Pelech which the student rejected then, and is still considered a revolutionary act for Israeli Modern Orthodoxy. Others were not possible because of the conditions of the time, such as her plan to create an umbrella organization for women at a time when society had sectoral aspirations.

Like other charismatic leaders who rely on charisma for their authority, Shalvi's main weak point came when she tried to turn her enterprises into establishments and had to relinquish authority and collaborate with subordinates. Weber marks this stage as the reutilization of charisma.[44] If this stage is not completed, loss of leadership is one of the results. This happened to Shalvi both at Pelech and at the IWN where, as a revolutionary woman, she struggled to work according to established methods.

Reading Reality and Formulating a Vision

Shalvi's leadership is the type of leadership that creates and shapes a vision. As a leader, she presented an image of a better reality for the future, captivated her followers, and created the hope that this vision would be realized shortly. She established goals, analyzed reality, and expressed herself in a way that the public could relate to and that seemed realistic. Shalvi identified social changes, some of them very early on, and could read reality and create goals from a personal vision that would change reality at large. She was an ideological, educational, and social leader. She led by ideas that she occasionally developed through action as a reaction to reality. Shalvi worked to consolidate moral and principle issues and define ideological goals. She created her vision independently; thus, her enterprises reflected her personality.

Shalvi's leadership was characterized by long-term planning and recruiting the women she led to realize her vision. She created practical methods to accomplish it and motivated others to do the same. She expressed her philosophy in writing, orally, and in practice. She worked hard on the practical aspects of her goals and led the daily activities in both her enterprises. Her work was not always successful, according to her followers: the teachers of Pelech reported a feeling of chaos; the IWN required organizational counseling, but even then, Shalvi felt that she had practical capabilities in both cases.

Cohen, which researched Jewish religious women leaders in Israel in the turning the century, lists four fields of female religious leadership. One of them, which does not require religious halachic knowledge, is the organizing and planning of public religious actions.[45] Shalvi worked in this field in her educational leadership. By creating the Pelech educational model and putting it into practice, Shalvi set out a path and vision for religious women and the religious Orthodox society. From her place as the principal of an educational establishment, Shalvi attempted to influence the place of religious women and created the path to the realization of a new female-religious-civic model in Israel. Her influence on the changes in the status of women in the religious sphere is evident. Most of her ideas were realized, both in religious education and in the status of women in religious society. This is shown by the many women of the halakhic authority that exist today, the Pelech High School network that has been established in recent decades, as well as the entry of religious women into leadership positions in politics and society. All of these were a distant dream for the observant woman in the 1970s, but for her, it was a realistic vision.

Establishing Interpersonal Relationships

In her leadership, Shalvi's life experience, sensitivity, and tolerance for the other, her ability to contain complexity and express ideas, including the revolutionary ones, in a way that was palatable to the other side, all came into view. This ability for moderation allowed Shalvi to generate a bridge between different audiences and her feminist vision, both at Pelech and the IWN activities. As a transformational leader, Shalvi excelled at finding common ground between her followers, creating social and practical connections, and uniting groups with various ideologies but which acted toward common goals, both at Pelech and the IWN. This trait caused women from different social, political, and religious backgrounds to follow her. This quality of Shalvi was born out of deep elements of her complex personality: from childhood, she had been educated to hold many values such as Judaism, Zionism, humanism, justice, and, above all else, openness and independent thinking, and she was the one who created time after time a unique synergy between them all.

One can see this expressed in the foundation of the IWN in 1984. After she received support from the Jewish American Congress at the end of the conference, Shalvi bravely made her beliefs the goals of the new organization. Her private agenda was evident in all the actions of the IWN from the very beginning. This similarity, between Shalvi and the IWN, was accepted by many women mostly because of the multi-faceted identity Shalvi portrayed: an observant Jew, a feminist, an Israeli, a new western immigrant, an academic, an educator, a mother of six, and a wife. These identities brought many women from different sectors to identify with her and follow her ideas. Additionally, according to her cohort, her open and friendly personality, her pleasant appearance, and her charisma were all evident in her ability to make revolutionary social ideas seem legitimate and acceptable to the public at large, and were what made her popular.[46]

Another well-remarked upon ability was Shalvi's gift for finding quality, talented, and educated women that were dedicated to the goals of the organization. Shalvi adopted them, strengthened their feeling of having a mission and ideological work, and encouraged them to be daring and creative.[47] She gave them the feeling that they had both the responsibility and ability to make a difference, as a democratic transformational leader.[48] Additionally, Shalvi connected these women and created a social network between them despite being religiously, politically, and sectorally different. She located their common ground and used them to create a tight-knit female network.

Another aspect of her *transformational* leadership was her close relationship with her followers. Shalvi was a sympathetic ear, a cheerleader, and a motivator to her followers. She helped them believe in themselves and their ability to live up to their potential, in and outside of her enterprises. In her close leadership, she evaluated and measured their work often but still sent them the message that she believed in them. They felt this and attributed their success to her in various fields later in life.

Her strong ability to create warm social ties made her seem accessible and a "first among equals" type of leadership rather than a pretentious and aloof leader. When she failed to create these connections, as happened with the second generation of the IWN beginning in the mid-1990s, or when she harmed existing connections the way she did right before she resigned from Pelech by taking over too many authorities, her leadership was damaged and she was forced to resign.

Flexibility

Shalvi was characterized by flexibility, both in her worldview, her daily life, and her organizational conduct. She had trouble accepting reality when she saw it as negative and conforming to society, both in her personal life and her leadership. She faulted the existing gender dynamic and challenged it. In her vision, she saw a different reality: different education than what existed, a higher status for women, and a reality of peace rather than national conflict.

This flexibility characterized the way she worked to achieve her goals from the establishment. She saw Pelech and the IWN as agents of social and educational change; she utilized systemic leadership both in the wide fields she worked in and in her desire to influence complete systems: the educational system, status of women, religious society, and even Israeli society. Her utilization of different ways of operating teaches us much about her ability to match methods of operation and her goals.

Shalvi was flexible in creating change. Firstly, she worked with and within the established system; however, when she had no choice and her goals were not achieved, she abandoned the system and chose the path of radical protest. This happened in Pelech where for fifteen years she worked within the Religious Zionist sector; but when her ideas were rejected by the head of the religious school system, the teachers, and the students, and led to her early retirement, she pointedly transferred to the Conservative movement. This characteristic could also be seen in the way the IWN operated: they collaborated with agents of the government and the religious authority but when these methods were ineffective the women of the IWN did not hesitate to criticize the establishment and turn to radical protest methods.

Her style of leadership was not fixed. Shalvi combined cooperation and moderation on the one hand, and authoritarianism and daring on the other. Shalvi's leadership is a complex model that combines two types of leadership which, at the time, were usually associated with men and women separately. Shalvi, however, used them both according to the necessities of reality like in the androgynous leadership model.[49] Her style of leadership had the main characteristics of transformative leadership: charisma, a focus on emancipation, democracy, equity, and justice, and personal attention to her followers.[50] They felt Shalvi enriched them, challenged them with her creative worldview, and led them forward according to her vision which soon became their vision too. She could draw people to her cause and motivate many to action. She delegated authority and gave her followers a lot of power, whether they be colleagues or students. Thus, she stimulated them intellectually and practically and gave them confidence in their ability to create change. Her followers were won over by her strong personality and felt important and empowered.

This type of leadership is democratic, usually, and characterizes leaders who define themselves as feminists, like Shalvi.[51]

However, her leadership style was also authoritarian as in the autocratic leadership style.[52] Many times Shalvi created policy, set goals, made decisions independently without consulting her followers. Mostly, Shalvi felt she could achieve faster results by operating in an authoritarian and decisive manner rather than using the accepted democratic process. Throughout their time working together, her followers criticized the flaws in the democracy of her leadership; however, her unique talents, achievements, persistence, and total commitment to their goals made them willing to put up with her flaws. In the end, her authoritarian manner caused too much criticism and forced her to resign from her enterprises.

Education and Socioeconomic Status as Levers

Education is a central factor in determining social status and one's standard of living in the future.[53] Furthermore, education is a key to empowerment and creating the appearance of a leader for social activists. This effect is more powerful in women as can be seen on Shalvi herself. By gaining education, women's awareness grows and sharpens, they become agents of change for themselves and others, and they are filled with the desire and ability to influence their surroundings.[54]

Shalvi completed two university degrees and an academic certificate. Later in life, she completed a doctorate and became a professor at the Hebrew University of Jerusalem. Throughout her life, one can see the ambition that motivated her to intellectual stimulation and the discovery of leadership in her environment. The two, education and leadership, were tied together throughout her life, one motivating the other and vice versa. She thus directed her students to obtain a wide education and independent thinking and from there to take on a social stance and leadership role.

Female feminist leadership is characterized by women who are financially and emotionally stable since they can hold a longstanding leadership position without having to worry about daily life. This is true for public and educational leaders, and for women who lead long-term battles for women's rights.[55] In Shalvi's case, her education and her financial abilities were bolstered by her brother's financial support. This allowed her to fully commit to her public works: for twenty-five years her two most meaningful roles were done as a volunteer, with no financial compensation, and yet she put all her energies into them. It would seem that wealth and financial independence are powerful forces enabling female leaders to grow.

Self-Confidence and Faith in the Cause

One can point to the existence of feminist leadership characteristics in Shalvi's personal characteristics: self-confidence and high self-esteem, as well as motivation from personal connection to her causes. Shalvi's entry to the management of Pelech with no appropriate formal training and no experience in education teaches us about her high self-confidence, her assessment of her own abilities, and the faith the parents and teaching staff had in her. Her aforementioned flexibility helped her adjust to her new status, and give free rein to her hidden educational aspirations. The establishment of the IWN was a different case. She came to that position after having dealt with the status of women in Israel from multiple perspectives, personal and public. Despite her familiarity with feminism and feminist activism, Shalvi's appointment as chairperson received objections from female politicians. However, Shalvi stood her ground because she felt that this was the path ordained for her. With this faith in herself, she began to fulfill the destiny that she had started setting up a decade previously. These characteristics served Shalvi throughout her tenure in Pelech and the IWN and during her activism for peace. She was prominent thanks to her unconventional opinions and positions, which she stood by Even at the cost of personal harm, out of faith in her goals.

Shalvi's leadership style was characterized by taking safe steps and inspiring a sense of faith in her followers up until the point where she would give more weight to her own decisions. Shalvi's resignations from her public roles stemmed from events that were caused by Shalvi operating independently in a way that her followers saw as a no return point. Since her resignations happened because of personal issues, this brings into focus the fact that she was a multi-faceted leader. On the one hand, she was stalwart, motivated, and put into motion formidable innovative enterprises. On the other hand, that same active and self-confident personality increased antagonism against her.

RELIGIOUS FEMALE FEMINIST LEADERSHIP: SHALVI'S NEW MODEL OF LEADERSHIP

Now we will examine Shalvi's leadership versus existing leadership models: female leadership, feminist leadership, and religious leadership. This will enable us to see her unique leadership style Shalvi led women to influence society. She believed in the power of women to strove for gender equality. Being a leader of women in both her main enterprises, Shalvi placed herself as a feminist leader who endeavored, first and foremost, to improve the place of women in Israeli society. In the past, female leadership was considered transformational leadership.[56] As studies about female leaders show, religious

female leadership and feminist leadership are characterized by a transformative leadership style, openness and innovation, and a tendency toward
democratic leadership.[57] Shalvi's complex leadership style contained characteristics of these but presented a new model of female leadership: one that
is flexible, that creates change, and that transforms as in the existing female
model but also authoritarian and assertive.

Like in the feminist leadership model, Shalvi urged her followers to operate within the values of justice and equality. She focused on change for the
group and the individual and was willing to take active risks to create a new
reality. Shalvi stood out because of her strong connection to the groups where
she worked for women's rights, both in the religious Orthodox world and in
Israeli society. She was perceived by her varied followers as a female model
that realized their aspirations from a feminist point of view, hence the validity
of being a feminist leader.

Shalvi's flexible leadership style enabled the realization of her feminist
vision. She acted, for the most part, as a mother to her followers: she listened
and supported them, gave them confidence, and directed them toward her and
their vision; she also set the agenda and insignificant decisions demonstrated
assertiveness. This style is not usually associated with feminist organizations,
which usually lack hierarchy and are managed democratically, and therefore
is not considered a feminist leadership style. However, this study shows that
this flexible leadership was a powerful tool in introducing feminist values
to society and making feminist organizations successful. As long as Shalvi's
behavior achieved her followers' goals it was profitable for them and they
agreed to it.[58]

In addition to the resemblances between female religious leadership and
feminist leadership, such as democracy and *transformational* leadership,
religious leadership is characterized by combining family life and a public
role. This was manifest in Shalvi's leadership. In Jewish Orthodoxy, the
development of female religious leadership is based on the revolution of
religious halachic education for women. It is characterized by extensive
knowledge of the halachic world and literacy, and a desire for female leadership that stems from halachic authority or religious education, the existence
of a theological-feminist discussion, or the desire to guide followers.[59] Shalvi
played a central role in the expansion of women's religious education in Israel
and abroad, and for many, is a religious leader, but she had limited religious
knowledge herself.

The strong correlation between Shalvi's personality and way of life and
between her public activism raised Shalvi's public esteem and yet, revealed
her vulnerability. Despite her innovative path and vision, Shalvi was connected to religious society but at the same time was different, as was apparent
at Pelech. Shalvi's uniqueness compared to her environment was obvious in

several ways: educational, religious, feminist, and political. Her democratic educational vision, which was put into practice at Pelech, and her attempts to create an activist religious female model were new in the education system in Israel and the religious education system in particular. For the most part, Shalvi was highly esteemed for her innovative vision and work, but the combination of her unique traits, mostly her political tendencies and feminist activism as a religious woman, became her downfall both personally and professionally. In the late 1980s, there were repeated calls for her resignation from the religious education school system administration and, eventually, from the teachers and school board of Pelech. This was the personal, professional, and social price she had to pay. Shalvi, who never again found her place in the Religious Zionist and Modern Orthodox society to which she belonged, left for the Conservative movement.

The fact that she did not have wide halachic knowledge, along with her revolutionary concepts regarding women and her left-wing political views, made the Modern Orthodox public reluctant to accept her leadership. For this reason, Shalvi is usually perceived as *the leader of (female) religious leaders*, the one who had the vision and created the path, rather than a leader of the observant public. However, in her activity in the IWN, her political and religious views received wide acceptance, therefore, in civil society, Shalvi was perceived as a social and feminist leader, *a leader of the public.*

Shalvi's attempts to create religious female leadership and extensive female leadership in Israel are evident throughout the study. Her efforts were successful. However, with her leadership, Shalvi failed to train successors to continue her path after she retired. While she did gather talented and active women around her, women who were innovative in thought and action, she trained none to take her place. Both in her resignation from Pelech and the IWN, Shalvi approached potential successors shortly before she left, as a last attempt to find someone to follow in her shoes. In this, consciously or not, Shalvi maintained her uniqueness as a one-time female leadership phenomenon.

SHALVI AS A FEMALE ROLE MODEL

The second wave of feminism raised the cry: "the personal is political." Shalvi's personal life, too, was an active part of her leadership particularly because of her multi-faceted identity: an observant Jew, a feminist, an Israeli, a new Western immigrant, an academic, an educator, a mother, and wife. Many women from different sectors identified with Shalvi, felt connected to her, and saw her as a role model. The sources of her strength as a leader and female role model were her personal resources and the formal appointments she received.

Shalvi knew how to appeal to both logic and emotion together. As an educational and feminist leader, she was a source of emotional support for her students and the teaching staff at Pelech. For her friends at the IWN, she provided a rational model for how to realize their emotions in their life. Being an approachable role model for her followers made her a unique identity, someone to measure themselves again as they created their own identity. They held her model in high regard and, when it turned out not to be realistic for them, were very critical toward Shalvi as in the case of Chana Pinchasi, a graduate of Pelech. Pinchasi, a prominent religious feminist in Israel, principal of the teachers' school, deputy director of the program and researcher at the Hartman Institute, maintained a strong and honest relationship with Shalvi. In the interview, Pinchasi spoke highly of Shalvi as an inspiring figure for her, the one who gave her the power to lead.[60]

The validity of her being a role model for feminists in Israel emerges from the words of Naomi Chazan, an ex-member of the Knesset and one of the founders of the IWN: "Alice Shalvi the professor, the headmistress, the mother, and the human being has become the model for constructive activism for a generation of Israeli women. In her ability to combine wisdom and daring, experience and youthfulness, and insight with practicality, she serves as an ongoing inspiration for Israeli women and Jewish women worldwide."[61]

To summarize, it would seem that Shalvi presented a complex model of feminist leadership. We can define her as a feminist leader, according to the known studies, because of her social philosophy and her desire to create social change in her surroundings, all while being guided by justice and equality. In addition to feminist motivation, her leadership is constructed from different models of leadership: transformational, motivational, democratic, and authoritarian. Her tendency toward democratic leadership, her ability to find and recruit talented women to her mission through the delegation of authority and empowerment, are all the ones who underlie the leadership in feminist organizations. She also had qualities that are less prevalent in feminist leaders: a dominant ability to create the feeling of a "group of equals" among women who were separated by political, religious, and social ideology and thus to motivate them to work together from their commonalities. This trait also made her successful at gaining public acceptance and legitimacy for revolutionary messages, and in turning these ideas into the mainstream a few years later.

During her years of operation, Shalvi exhibited assertiveness which was not expected of her. Her inability to not be opinionated, even when her followers protested, made it difficult for her to operate. Her flexible thinking helped Shalvi to deal with the reality of discrimination in Israel. However,

Shalvi was mostly inflexible as a leader. She had trouble leading women who were different from her in a manner that suited them, and she did not manage to produce a successor for the benefit of the IWN. Shalvi, without acknowledging and intending, utilized different styles of leadership on a regular basis. One can see in her biography and her leadership of Pelech and the IWN another model of feminist leadership, a flexible model, one that is *transformational*, authoritarian, and charismatic all in one—the "mother" leadership style.

BIBLIOGRAPHY

Primary Sources

Interview with Alice Shalvi, December 5, 2010
Interview with Alice Shalvi, March 5, 2012
Interview with Alice Shalvi, May 10, 2012
Interview with Chana Pinchasi, December 7, 2014
Interview with Dorit Karlin, January 24, 2017 (Telephone)
Interview with Frances Raday, February 4, 2013
Interview with Galia Golan, October 18, 2012
Interview with Michal Cafrey, July 1, 2012
Interview with Naomi Hazan, July 30, 2012
Interview with Orit Sulitzeanu, September 11, 2012
Interview with Pnina Shalvi October 1, 2017
Interview with Rivka Meller-Olshitzky, October 10, 2012
Interview with Rachel Lipshitz, April 3, 2013
Email correspondence with Ayelet November 23, 2014
Alice Shalvi's private archive

Newspapers

No author, "The Sicarii (Dagger men) Threatened Shalvi," *Kol Ha'ir Newspaper*, December 22, 1989 (Hebrew).
Zonshine Idan, "Extremist Noam Party Demands to 'Amend' Gov't Protections for Women," *The Jerusalem Post*, April 1, 2021.

Film

Paula Weiman-Kelman (director), *Rites of Passage: The Spiritual Journey of Alice Shalvi Israel*, 1999.

Online

"About Kolech" on Kolech website https://www.kolech.org.il/en/about-us-en.html (retrieved on August 22, 2021).

Arguments of the judges of the Israel Prize Committee for the year 2007 on the *Israel Prize* website (Hebrew): cms.education.gov.il/EducationCMS/Units/PrasIsrael/Tashsaz/AliceShalvi/nmk.htm (retrieved on May 18, 2021)

Cohen Tova, Ran Ben Hai Moria "Leaders in Israel's Religious Communities," *Jewish Women Archive* June 23, 2021 jwa.org/encyclopedia/article/leaders-in-israels-religious-communities (retrieved on August 22, 2021).

Congress Monthly, February/March 1985, Vol. 52, No. 2, In: Berman Jewish Policy Archive (BJPA) www.bjpa.org/content/upload/bjpa/the_/THE%2020TH%20AMERICAN-ISRAEL%20DIALOGUE-WOMAN%20AS%20JEW%20MARCH%201985%20VOL%2052%20NO%202.pdf (retrieved on May 18, 2021).

Lawson Naomi, Atlas Rona, "Pelech Religious Experimental High School for Girls, Jerusalem" at *JWA*: https://jwa.org/encyclopedia/article/pelech-religious-experimental-high-school-for-girls-jerusalem (retrieved on November 22, 2021).

Lir Shlomit, "New Media and Fourth-Wave Feminism," *HBI Online Journal* April 25, 2018 https://blogs.brandeis.edu/freshideasfromhbi/on-new-media-and-the-fourth-wave-of-feminism/ (retrieved on November 28, 2021).

Lorberbaum-Pinhasi Hannah, "The Power of an Educator," *Haaretz* http://www.haaretz.co.il/opinions/1.1403658 (Hebrew) (retrieved on August 23, 2021).

Maryles Sztokman Elana, "Partnership Minyan," at *JWA*, last updated June 23, 2021 https://jwa.org/encyclopedia/article/partnership-minyan.

Shalvi Alice, "Israel Women's Network," *Jewish Women's Archive*, updated July 5, 2021 https://jwa.org/encyclopedia/article/israel-womens-network (retrieved on August 22, 2021).

Shilo Margalit, "Kolech: Religious Women's Forum," at JWA, last updated June 23, 2021 https://jwa.org/encyclopedia/article/kolech-religious-womens-forum.

Wishlah Charlotte, Sztokman Elana, "Alice Hildegard Shalvi" at *JWA* jwa.org/encyclopedia/article/shalvi-alice (retrieved on May 18, 2021)

Books

Adeniji-Neill Dolapo, *Empowered Women: Nigerian Society, Education, and Empowerment*, Bern: Peter Lang, 2020.

Arlene Agus (ed.), *New Israel Fund: Israel Women's Leadership award Dinner in Honor of Professor Alice Shalvi*, New York 1994. https://www.nif.org/people/alice-shalvi

Batliwala Srilatha, *Engaging with Empowerment: An Intellectual and Experiential Journey*, New Delhi, India: Women Unlimited, 2013.

Max Weber, *The Theory of Social and Economic Organization*, London: Free Press, 1947.

Ran Ben Hai Moria, *The Individual, the Feminine and the Public: The Portrait of Professor Alice Shalvi and Her Enterprises as a Reflection of the Development of Women's Status in Israeli Society*, Doctoral thesis, Ramat Gan: Bar Ilan University, 2018 (Hebrew).

Shalvi Alice, *Never a Native*, London, UK: Halban Publishers Ltd, 2018, pp. 191–199.

Articles

Ahmad Seher, "Family or Future in the Academy?" *Review of Educational Research* Vol. 87, No. 1, February 2017, pp. 204–239.

Barton Tracy R., "Feminist Leadership: Building Nurturing Academic Communities," *Advancing Women in Leadership*, Online Journal Vol. 22, Fall 2006.

Bunch Charlotte, "Women's Leadership: Why Should You Care?" in: *Power for What: National Dialogue on Educating Women for Leadership*, New Brunswick, NJ: Institute for Women's Leadership No. 2, May, 2002.

Cohen Tova, "Jewish Women's Leadership: Israeli Modern Orthodoxy as a Test Case," *Democratic Culture* Vol. 10, 2006, pp. 251–296 (Hebrew).

Dyczkowska Joanna, Dyczkowski Tomasz, "Democratic or Autocratic Leadership Style? Participative Management and its Links to rewarding Strategies and Job Satisfaction in SMEs," *Athens Journal of Business & Economics* Vol. 4, No. 2, 2018, pp. 193–218.

Feldman Yael S., "From 'The Madwoman in the Attic' to 'The Women's Room': The American Roots of Israeli Feminism," *Israel Studies* Vol. 5, No. 1, Spring, 2000, pp. 266–286.

Gray Mel, Schubert Leanne, "'Do Something, Change Something': Feminist Leadership in Social Work," in: Sarah Wendt, Nicole Moulding (eds.), *Contemporary Feminisms in Social Work Practice*, Routledge, London 2016, pp. 113–131.

Halperin-Kaddari Ruth, "Women, Religion and Multiculturalism in Israel," *UCLA Journal of International Law and Foreign Affairs* Vol. 5, No. 2, Fall/Winter 2000–2001, pp. 339–366.

Hartman Mary S., "Peggy Antrobus," in: Mary S. Hartman (ed.), *Talking Leadership: Conversations with Powerful Women*, New Brunswick, NJ: Rutgers University Press, 1999, pp. 29–44.

Houghton Jeffery D., "Does Max Weber's Notion of Authority Still Hold in the Twenty-First Century?," *Journal of Management History* Vol. 16, No. 4, 2010, pp. 449–453.

Kark Ronit, "The Transformational Leader: Who is (S)He? A Feminist Perspective," *Journal of Organizational Change Management* Vol. 17, No. 2, 2004, pp. 160–176.

Mohammed Shaed Maslina, "Participative Management Theory and Feminist Leadership Styles," *Malaysian Journal of Society and Space* Vol. 14, No. 4, 2018, pp. 332–345.

Morgan Stephan, *On the Edge of Commitment: Educational Attainment and Race in the United States*, Stanford, CA: Stanford University Press, 2005, pp. 35–56.

O'Brien Anne, "Feminine or Feminist? Women's Media Leadership," *Feminist Media Studies* Vol. 17, No. 5, 2017, pp. 836–850.

Park Daewoo, "Androgynous Leadership Style: An Integration Rather than a Polarization," *Leadership & Organization Development Journal* Vol. 18, No. 3, 1997, pp. 166–171.

Post Corrinne, "When Is Female Leadership an Advantage? Coordination Requirements, Team Cohesion, and Team Interaction Norms," *Journal of Organizational Behavior* 36, 2015, pp. 1153–1175.

Shalvi Alice, "Changing the Concepts "Work" and "Family," in: Anat Maor (ed.), *Women of the Rising Force*, Kibbutz Dalia, 1998, pp. 280–277 (Hebrew).

Shields Carolyn M., Dollarhide Colette T., Young Anita A., "Transformative Leadership in School Counseling: An Emerging Paradigm for Equity and Excellence," *Professional School Counseling* Vol. 21, No. 1b, Special Issue: School Counseling Leadership in Practice 2017–2018, pp. 1–11.

Sinclair Amanda, "A Feminist Case for Leadership," Joy Damousi, Kim Rubenstein and Mary Tomsic (eds.), *Diversity in Leadership Australian Women, Past and Present,* Canberra: The Australian National University, 2014, pp. 17–35.

Stephenson Lauren, "Developing a Leadership Education Framework: A Transformative Leadership Perspective" *Counterpoints* Vol. 409, 2011, pp. 321–341.

Wallace Jean E., Jovanovic Alyssa, "Occupational Similarity and Spousal Support: A Study of the Importance of Gender and Spouse's Occupation," *Relations Industrielles/Industrial Relations* Vol. 66, No. 2, Spring 2011, pp. 235–255.

Wallace Ruth A., "Women and Religion: The Transformation of Leadership Roles," *Journal for the Scientific Study of Religion* Vol. 39, No. 4, 50th Anniversary Issue, December 2000, pp. 497–508.

Way A. Danielle, Marques Joan, "Management of Gender Roles: Marketing the Androgynous Leadership Style in the Classroom and the General Workplace," *Organization Development Journal* Vol. 31, No. 2, 2013, pp. 82–94.

Weatherby Georgie Ann, "Overview: Women as Leaders in Religion and Religious Organizations," in: Karen O'Connor (ed.) *Gender and Women's Leadership: A Reference Handbook*. Thousand Oaks, CA: SAGE Publications, Inc., 2010, pp. 475–481.

Xiu Lin, Liang Xin, Chen Zhao, Xu Wei, "Strategic Flexibility, Innovative HR Practices, and Firm Performance: A Moderated Mediation Model," *Personnel Review* Vol. 46, No. 7, 2017, pp. 1335–1357.

NOTES

1. An interview with Alice Shalvi, December 5, 2010.

2. Quote from the arguments of the judges of the Israel Prize Committee for the year 2007 on the *Israel Prize* website (Hebrew): cms.education.gov.il/Education-CMS/Units/PrasIsrael/Tashsaz/AliceShalvi/nmk.htm (retrieved on May 18, 2021).

3. Charlotte Wishlah, updated by Elana Sztokman, "Alice Hildegard Shalvi" at *JWA*: jwa.org/encyclopedia/article/shalvi-alice (retrieved on May 18, 2021); This paper is based on my Ph.D. dissertation: Moria Ran Ben Hai, *The Individual, the*

Feminine and the Public: The Portrait of Professor Alice Shalvi and Her Enterprises as a Reflection of the Development of Women's Status in Israeli Society, Doctoral thesis, Ramat Gan: Bar Ilan University, 2018 (Hebrew).

4. Alice Shalvi, *Never a Native*, London, UK: Halban Publishers Ltd. 2018, pp. 191–199.

5. Interview with Alice Shalvi, May 10, 2012.

6. Laws of formal equality, such as the "Male and Female Workers (Equal Pay) Law, 5724–1964"; Interview with Shalvi March 5, 2012.

7. There are four branches to the network, apart from the first one in Jerusalem; Pelech at Zichron Yaacov, Pelech at Kiryat Ekron, Pelech Tel Aviv and even one for boys Jerusalem. Naomi Lawson, updated by Rona Atlas, "Pelech Religious Experimental High School for Girls, Jerusalem" at *JWA*: jwa.org/encyclopedia/article/pelech-religious-experimental-high-school-for-girls-jerusalem (retrieved on November 22, 2021).

8. Moria Ran Ben Hai, *The Individual, the Feminine and the Public,* pp. 113–143.

9. *Congress Monthly*, February/March 1985, Vol. 52, No. 2, In: Berman Jewish Policy Archive (BJPA) www.bjpa.org/content/upload/bjpa/the_/THE %2020TH%20AMERICAN-ISRAEL%20DIALOGUE-WOMAN%20AS%20JEW %20MARCH%201985%20VOL%2052%20NO%202.pdf (retrieved on May 18, 2021).

10. (Amendment No. 6) 1993. Today, the extremist, ultra-Orthodox-nationalist party, Noam, is trying to repeal this amendment, which they claim disrupts the Jewish tradition. Idan Zonshine, "Extremist Noam Party Demands to 'Amend' Gov't Protections for Women," *The Jerusalem Post*, April 1, 2021.

11. She was chairperson between 1984–1997, and again between 1998–2000: Ran Ben Hai, *The Individual, the Feminine and the Public*, pp. 207–247.

12. Ran Ben Hai, *The Individual, the Feminine and the Public*, p. 246.

13. For example, the parents' meeting at which Shalvi volunteered to head Pelech was held at their home. Interview with Pnina Shalvi, October 1, 2017; The film *Rites of Passage: The Spiritual Journey of Alice Shalvi Israel*, 1999, Directed by Paula Weiman-Kelman. Also in the words of Deborah Weissman, "Travels with Alice," in: Arlene Agus (ed.), *New Israel Fund: Israel Women's Leadership award Dinner in Honor of Professor Alice Shalvi*, New York 1994, are mentioned meetings of the IWN.

14. Author not mentioned, "The Sicarii (Dagger men) Threatened Shalvi," *Kol Ha'ir Newspaper* December 22, 1989 (Hebrew).

15. Seher Ahmad, "Family or Future in the Academy?" *Review of Educational Research* Vol. 87, No. 1 (February 2017), pp. 204–239; Jean E. Wallace and Alyssa Jovanovic, "Occupational Similarity and Spousal Support: A Study of the Importance of Gender and Spouse's Occupation," *Relations Industrielles / Industrial Relations* Vol. 66, No. 2 (2011 Spring), pp. 235–255.

16. Interview with Pnina Shalvi, January 10, 2017.

17. For example: Alice Shalvi, "Changing the Concepts 'Work' and 'Family,'" in: Anat Maor (ed.), *Women of the Rising Force*, Kibbutz Dalia 1998, pp. 280–297 (Hebrew).

18. Pelech Kiryat Ekron (est. 2000), Pelech Zikhron Yaacov (est. 2008), Pelech Tel Aviv (est. 2015) and Pelech for boys in Jerusalem (est. 2017). The fact that they were all founded about thirty years after the creation of the Pelech model shows that Shalvi is a pioneer and has a long-term vision, as well as the expansion of the public interested in such education.

19. Among the prominent figures are: Malka Puterkovsky, Hannah Pinhasi, Tamar Bitton, Miri Schlissl, Shira Breuer and others.

20. "About Kolech" on *Kolech* website (retrieved on August 22, 2021).

21. See for example the changes in Modern Orthodox women's religious leadership on Tova Cohen, "Leaders in Israel's Religious Communities," *Jewish Women Archive* updated by Moria Ran Ben Hai, June 23, 2021 (retrieved on August 22, 2021).

22. Alice Shalvi, "Israel Women's Network," *Jewish Women's Archive* updated July 5, 2021 (retrieved on August 22, 2021).

23. Shlomit Lir, "New Media and Fourth-Wave Feminism," *HBI Online Journal* April 25, 2018.

24. Yael S. Feldman, "From 'The Madwoman in the Attic' to 'The Women's Room': The American Roots of Israeli Feminism," *Israel Studies* Vol. 5, No. 1, Spring, 2000, pp. 266–286.

25. Ruth Halperin-Kaddari, "Women, Religion and Multiculturalism in Israel," *UCLA Journal of International Law and Foreign Affairs* Vol. 5, No. 2, Fall/Winter 2000–2001, pp. 339–366.

26. Moria Ran Ben Hai, *The Individual, the Feminine and the Public,* pp. 203–243.

27. "She spoke eloquently paving the way for the other two of us and showing the religious convictions need not stand in the way of a commitment to peace," Weissman, "Travels with Alice."

28. Moria Ran Ben Hai, *The Individual, the Feminine and the Public,* pp. 159–160.

29. Tova Cohen, "Jewish Women's Leadership: Israeli Modern Orthodoxy as a Test Case," *Democratic Culture* Vol. 10, 2006, pp. 251–296 (Hebrew)

30. Hannah Lorberbaum-Pinhasi, "The Power of an Educator," *Haaretz* www .haaretz.co.il/opinions/1.1403658 (Hebrew) (retrieved on August 23, 2021).

31. Elana Maryles Sztokman, "Partnership Minyan," JWA, last updated June 23, 2021 jwa.org/encyclopedia/article/partnership-minyan.

32. Margalit Shilo, "Kolech: Religious Women's Forum," JWA, last updated June 23, 2021 jwa.org/encyclopedia/article/kolech-religious-womens-forum.

33. Lea Shakdiel, "Religious Zionism Becomes Feminist," in: Arlene Agus (ed.), *New Israel Fund: Israel Women's Leadership award Dinner in Honor of Professor Alice Shalvi,* New York 1994.

34. Email correspondence with Ayelet, November 23, 2014. Ayelet asked to be mentioned without her last name.

35. Interview with Rachel Lipshitz, April 3, 2013.

36. Interview with Galia Golan, October 18, 2012.

37. The quote is taken from a letter from Bilha Dvori to Orit Sulitzeanu, March 31, 1998. Shalvi's private archive.

38. "It made us act against what bothered us and to bring about change." Interview with Rivka Meller-Olshitzky, October 10, 2012; "The lobby fulfilled a lot of

my expectations and even gave me a lot of new expectations . . . I was proud and satisfied with the organization, its skilled employees, the public management and your considered leadership." The words of Anat Hoffman, a longtime member of the network, in a letter to Alice Shalvi before her first retirement, June 2, 1997. Shalvi's private archive.

39. Tracy R. Barton, "Feminist Leadership: Building Nurturing Academic Communities," Advancing *Women in Leadership*, Online Journal Vol. 22, Fall 2006; Srilatha Batliwala, *Engaging with Empowerment: An Intellectual and Experiential Journey*, New Delhi, India: Women Unlimited, 2013, p. 179.

40. Mary S. Hartman, "Peggy Antrobus," in: Mary S. Hartman (ed.), *Talking Leadership: Conversations with Powerful Women*, New Brunswick, NJ: Rutgers University Press, 1999, pp. 29–44; Mel Gray, Leanne Schubert, "'Do Something, Change Something': Feminist Leadership in Social Work," in: Sarah Wendt, Nicole Moulding (eds.), *Contemporary Feminisms in Social Work Practice*, London, UK: Routledge, 2016, pp. 113–131.

41. Charlotte Bunch, "Women's Leadership: Why Should You Care?" in: *Power for What: National Dialogue on Educating Women for Leadership*, New Brunswick, NJ: Institute for Women's Leadership, No. 2, May, 2002; Anne O'Brien, "Feminine or Feminist? Women's Media Leadership," *Feminist Media Studies* Vol. 17, No. 5, 2017, pp. 836–850.

42. Maslina Mohammed Shaed, "Participative Management Theory and Feminist Leadership Styles," *Malaysian Journal of Society and Space* Vol. 14, No. 4, 2018, pp. 332–345.

43. Interview with Frances Raday, February 4, 2013.

44. Max Weber, *The Theory of Social and Economic Organization*, London, 1947, pp. 334–342; Jeffery D. Houghton, "Does Max Weber's Notion of Authority Still Hold in the Twenty-First Century?," *Journal of Management History* Vol. 16, No. 4, 2010, pp. 449–453.

45. Tova Cohen, "Jewish Women's Leadership: Israeli Modern Orthodoxy as a Test Case," *Democratic Culture* Vol. 10, Gender and Society in Israel 2006, pp. 251–296 (Hebrew).

46. Interviews with Frances Raday, February 4, 2013; Galia Golan, October 18, 2012; Naomi Hazan, July 30, 2012.

47. Interview with Orit Sulitzeanu, September 11, 2012; Interview with Naomi Hazan, July 30, 2012.

48. Interview with Orit Sulitzeanu, September 11, 2012; Telephone Interview with Dorit Karlin, January 24, 2017; Interview with Michal Cafrey, July 1, 2012.

49. Daewoo Park, "Androgynous Leadership Style: An Integration Rather Than a Polarization," *Leadership & Organization Development Journal* Vol. 18, No. 3, 1997, pp. 166–171; A. Danielle Way and Joan Marques, "Management of Gender Roles: Marketing the Androgynous Leadership Style in the Classroom and the General Workplace," *Organization Development Journal* Vol. 31, No. 2, 2013, pp. 82–94.

50. Lauren Stephenson, "Developing a Leadership Education Framework: A Transformative Leadership Perspective" *Counterpoints* Vol. 409, 2011, pp. 321–341; Carolyn M. Shields, Colette T. Dollarhide and Anita A. Young, "Transformative

Leadership in School Counseling: An Emerging Paradigm for Equity and Excellence," *Professional School Counseling* Vol. 21, No. 1b, Special Issue: School Counseling Leadership in Practice 2017–2018, pp. 1–11.

51. Amanda Sinclair, "A Feminist Case for Leadership," Joy Damousi, Kim Rubenstein and Mary Tomsic (eds.), *Diversity in Leadership Australian Women, Past and Present* The Australian National University 2014, pp. 17–35.

52. Joanna Dyczkowska and Tomasz Dyczkowski, "Democratic or Autocratic Leadership Style? Participative Management and its Links to rewarding Strategies and Job Satisfaction in SMEs," *Athens Journal of Business & Economics* Vol. 4, No. 2, 2018, pp. 193–218.

53. Stephan Morgan, *On the Edge of Commitment: Educational Attainment and Race in the United States*, Stanford, CA: Stanford University Press, 2005, pp. 35–56.

54. See for example latest study on Nigerian girls and women: Dolapo Adeniji-Neill, *Empowered Women: Nigerian Society, Education, and Empowerment*, Bern: Peter Lang, 2020.

55. Mary S. Hartman, "Peggy Antrobus," in: Mary S. Hartman (ed.), *Talking Leadership: Conversations with Powerful Women*, New Brunswick, NJ: Rutgers University Press, 1999, pp. 29–44.

56. Ronit Kark, "The Transformational Leader: Who Is (S)He? A Feminist Perspective," *Journal of Organizational Change Management* Vol. 17, No. 2, 2004, pp. 160–176; Ruth A. Wallace, "Women and Religion: The Transformation of Leadership Roles," *Journal for the Scientific Study of Religion* Vol. 39, No. 4, 50th Anniversary Issue (December 2000), pp. 497–508.

57. Georgie Ann Weatherby, "Overview: Women as Leaders in Religion and Religious Organizations," in: Karen O'Connor (ed.), *Gender and Women's Leadership: A Reference Handbook*. Thousand Oaks, CA: SAGE Publications, Inc., 2010, pp. 475–481; Corrinne Post, "When Is Female Leadership an Advantage? Coordination Requirements, Team Cohesion, and Team Interaction Norms," *Journal of Organizational Behavior* 36, 2015, pp. 1153–1175; Lin Xiu, Xin Liang, Zhao Chen and Wei Xu, "Strategic Flexibility, Innovative HR Practices, and Firm Performance: A Moderated Mediation Model," *Personnel Review* Vol. 46, No. 7, 2017, pp. 1335–1357.

58. Interview with Galia Golan, October 18, 2012.

59. Tova Cohen, "Jewish Women's Leadership: Israeli Modern Orthodoxy as a Test Case," *Democratic Culture* Vol. 10, 2006, pp. 251–296 (Hebrew).

60. Interview with Chana Pinchasi, December 7, 2014.

61. Naomi Chazan, "Alice Shalvi: A Tribute," in: Arlene Aggus (ed.), *New Israel Fund: Israel Women's Leadership Award Dinner in Honor of Professor Alice Shalvi*, New York, NY: Free Press, 1994.

Chapter 5

Who Is Zofia Rosenstrauch, née Naomi Judkowski?

Orit Miller Katav

It was at the Warsaw Polytechnic Institute after the war. Naomi had met one of her instructors there; it was then, after his short chat, that she decided not to continue her studies in Poland and go to Israel to study.

> Well, what about you? Are you still a Jew? Why should you be? Look what they did to your people. Forget it for your own sake and for the sake of your future children. Convert your religion into ours. Enough with your sufferings.[1]

Who is the young woman who was born as Zofia Rosenstrauch? Why did she decide to leave her life in Poland in her mid-twenties? Why did she decide to shed her previous identity and adopt a new one? The answer to these questions is clear: She wanted a fresh start, a new life. The upheavals of her life led her on paths saturated with blood, destruction, and death. In Poland, she lost her beloved family and friends, her familiar life, her innocence, and her identity. The decision to make Aliyah to Israel in 1948 with her husband by her side was clear to her. They joined the Ghetto Fighters' House Kibbutz.[2] As someone who took an active part in Jewish activities in the Warsaw ghetto, mainly smuggling, planning shelters, bunkers, and escape routes, she proved her heroism on a daily basis, as any such action could have ended in death for her. Even after the ghetto was liquidated and all the Jews were evacuated to Majdanek, her spirit was not broken. Her parents and sister died in this camp. In early August 1943, she was transferred to Auschwitz-Birkenau due to the Soviets' advance. Whatever horrors her eyes witnessed, her slender hands drew. She was the designer at the Jewish statehouse at the first exhibition in Majdanek in 1946. Her album of paintings[3] was a voiceless scream and description of what took place in the Auschwitz-Birkenau death camp. These paintings also became a dramatic and significant testimony in the Eichmann trial, which took place in Israel in 1961. Her album of twenty watercolor paintings described what happened in the death camp and helped the Israeli prosecution prove the veracity of the events.

Her life in Israel was productive and full of creativity. She studied architecture at the Technion in Haifa, designed dozens of buildings, and engaged in painting and art. She had two sons and several grandchildren. Until the day she died, she did not know what happened to her album of paintings since it was taken from her in Warsaw and she never knew what became of it after that. Naomi was a resilient woman and a talented artist. Her paintings captured the horrors of the Holocaust from the perspective of the artist but also from the perspective of the subject and the viewer. Just like the biblical name she chose for herself, Naomi, saved lives, devoted herself to others, and was a humble and courageous woman. Some would call her a heroine.

CHILDHOOD

Naomi was born Zofia Rosenstrauch on March 29, 1920, in Warsaw, Poland. Her father's name was Michael Wolf Rosenstrauch. His family was from Gdansk. Her mother's name was Justina. Her family was from a Polish village called Lomianki. Naomi had an older sister named Felicia and a brother named Ignacy. She was the youngest in her family. Naomi's story of survival could have been completely different had her parents decided to stay in the British Mandate for Palestine. In 1926, when she was six years old, her family took a risk and left their comfortable middle-class life on Nowolipki Street in Warsaw and became pioneers in Eretz Israel.[4] In Poland, the family engaged in the textile trade market and earned a very respectable living. Naomi grew up with a personal nanny in a nurturing environment. Her parents gave her a European education and enriched Naomi's curriculum in literature and poetry.

The family made their way to Israel by train from Warsaw to Constanta, Romania. From there they sailed on a Berge ship to Tel Aviv. The family bought a nice apartment at 13 Balfour Street. They hired women to help with the domestic chores. Naomi started her education at a local school and liked it very much. Coming from high standards of education and the arts, the adjustments to the new strange language, hot climate, and pioneer culture were difficult for the family. Tel Aviv was a cultural, economic, and social center in those years, in contrast to the other settlements during the pre-state period that focused mostly on agricultural work.

Her father started a local cream and butter production factory on Herzl Street, but the business suffered many losses and her father was forced to close it. The economic struggle was the crucial factor that drove the family back to Poland in 1929, after only three years.[5] The family's return to the poor part of Warsaw to Swietojanska Street was even worse,[6] yet the family continued to maintain a dignified existence. Her father went back to trade, her brother studied law, her sister did secretarial studies, and Naomi was accepted to study architecture at the Warsaw Polytechnic Institute. A few years later the family moved to a better apartment that used to be owned by one of the grandparents on Nalevky Street. She began receiving architectural jobs and was able to help the family financially.[7]

WORLD WAR II

"In this part of the world (Eastern and Central Europe), there are six million Jews . . . for whom the world is divided into places where they cannot live and places they cannot enter."[8]

Haim Weizmann

With Adolf Hitler's rise to power in Germany in 1933, anti-Semitism became the official policy and ideology of the German regime. In 1938 there was an organized campaign in Germany for the destruction of synagogues, mass arrests, the destruction and looting of Jewish-owned businesses, and the systematic registration of Jewish properties with the aim of expropriating them at a later date. Along with the Jews, members of other groups were also persecuted, such as Sinti and Roma (gypsies), homosexuals, and the mentally ill, all of whom were considered enemies of the Reich.[9]

With the outbreak of World War II on September 1, 1939, a new phase in German policy toward the Jews began. After Germany conquered Poland, the Jews were concentrated in ghettos in Eastern Europe, while in Western Europe the Jews began to be registered and dispossessed of their property. Antisemitic racist legislation was also enforced in North Africa, and in southeastern European countries Jews were recruited into forced labor by regimes that collaborated with Nazi Germany, and tens of thousands of Jews perished there. World War II changed the face of Europe and the whole world, resulting in the premeditated extermination of tens of millions of civilians of different nationalities and ethnicities.[10]

In November 1939 the first decrees were issued against the Jews and they were required to wear a white armband with a blue Star of David. A series of economic measures caused many Jews to lose their livelihood and ability to support their family.[11] By November 1940, 380,000 Jews were imprisoned in the Warsaw ghetto, making it the largest ghetto in Europe. Over 80,000

Jews died as a result of the appalling conditions, overcrowding, and famine. Despite this, artists and intellectuals continued their creative efforts. In July 1942, deportations from the ghetto to the death camps began.

A *Judenrat* (Jewish Council) headed by Adam Czerniakow was established in the ghetto.[12] The ghetto covered only 2.4 percent of the city, and the masses of refugees deported to Warsaw from the surrounding towns and villages increased the population of the ghetto to 450,000. After the mass deportations to Treblinka in the summer of 1942, the Jews of the Warsaw ghetto, led by Mordechai Anielewicz,[13] began to fortify themselves in bunkers.[14] In April 1943, during a German *aktion*, the Warsaw Ghetto Uprising broke out. After a month of heroic fighting, the uprising was suppressed, and the ghetto burned to the ground.[15] The ghetto Jews fought heroically. It was the first popular uprising in the urban territory in Nazi-occupied Europe.

Before the ghetto was burnt, when Naomi was twenty years old, she did everything in her power to work and help to provide for her family. Pestilence and disease began to spread through the ghetto, specifically lice, typhus, and dysentery. The Germans feared that their people would become infected, so they ordered the opening of pharmacies to sell disinfectants and cleaning products. Naomi found a job at a pharmacy. She started to work as a cleaner and then as a cashier. She made connections and was kept abreast of all the events happening in and around the ghetto. Her work was actually a cover for the other activities she was engaged in, such as smuggling food, notes, messages, and medications. After working hours, she planned structures of underground bunkers, smuggling her parents from one place to another to save their lives. At the end of the ghetto uprising, she was caught with her father, mother, and sister, and they were all transferred to Majdanek. Her brother escaped the ghetto but was caught by the Nazis and killed. They never saw him again.

PRISONER NO. 48035

Majdanek was a Nazi concentration camp built about four kilometers from the center of Lublin, Poland. The camp was established on October 1, 1941, by order of Heinrich Himmler. It served as a prisoner of war (POW) camp for the SS. In February 1942, the place was converted into a concentration and extermination camp. Between April 1942 and July 1944, approximately 200,000 prisoners in the camp, 80,000 of whom were Jews, were killed using Cyclone B in gas chambers and crematoria. The non-Jewish victims were Soviet POWs, Poles, and other national prisoners of war who were considered enemies of the Reich.[16]

Naomi wasn't killed on her arrival at the camp. She passed the selection with her mother and sister. Her father also went through the same routine and was sent to the men's section of the camp. They were sent to have a shower, were given used clothes with personal numbers on them, and sent to block number twenty-two. They were needed as laborers and kept alive. There, on the *koya*[17] in block twenty-two[18] she shared a bed with her mother and sister and four other women. Her sister became ill. An SS woman saw her in the camp and wrote down her prisoner number. The next day while Naomi was out working around the camp, her sister and mother were taken for selection. When Naomi returned to the camp, she noticed that they were standing in line for extermination along with other older and sick women. That was the last time she saw them. They were executed immediately afterward. A few days later, she found out from a friend that her father was slated for extermination in the same selection from the men's side. Her family was killed at the same time.[19]

As the Red Army advanced along with eastern Poland, the prisoners at Majdanek were transferred to other places or killed on the spot. Naomi was one of eight hundred and five Jews who were transferred to the Auschwitz-Birkenau concentration camp on July 1, 1943. This was the largest concentration and extermination camp on Polish soil, next to the Polish village Oswiecim, chosen to be the main camp for exterminating the Jewish people by means of several gas chambers and crematoria using Cyclone B gas, which was previously tested on Soviet POWs.[20]

In October 1941, another camp, Birkenau (Auschwitz II), was established three kilometers from Auschwitz, and in March 1942, extermination operations began in the new camp. It had four gas chambers and until November 1944 the camp was a "factory" for mass murder and received transports from all over Europe. Most of the transports were Jews, and they were immediately sent to the gas chambers. Only a small percentage passed the selection and were selected for forced labor in the camp and in armaments factories located in the satellite camps. Some were used in the "medical" experiments of Dr. Mengele[21] and his team. In the spring and summer of 1944, when the Jews of Hungary and the Jews of the Lodz ghetto were brought to the camp, the rate of extermination increased.

The selection and killing process was well planned and organized. When the train stopped next to the platform, the victims disembarked and their belongings were collected in a number of barracks in the area called "Canada." The prisoners were placed in two lines—one for men and boys and one for women and children—and SS doctors performed the selection. The prisoners were categorized by their appearance and their fate was decided randomly: forced labor or death. After their death, gold teeth were removed from their mouths and the women's hair was cut off by the *Sonderkommando*—a group of Jews who were forced to work in the crematoria.[22]

Every day was precarious because additional selections were held several times a day among the prisoners who were assigned to work. The weak and sick were taken out of line and sent to the gas chambers. There was a rigid regimen in the camp that was based on a system of punishment and torture and only a few managed to survive. In Auschwitz-Birkenau, more than 1,100,000 Jews, 70,000 Poles, 25,000 Roma and Sinti (gypsies), about 15,000 Soviet POWs, and other people from different countries were murdered.

When Naomi arrived at Auschwitz after passing the selection routine, the number 48035 was tattooed on her arm.[23] She worked at a sewing workshop in block twenty-seven with all the other women who weren't able to work in the fields.[24] In August 1944 she fell ill with typhus. She refused to move to the special block that was used as a hospital for sick women because no one was ever cured there.[25] Although her health was fragile, she worked, and it was good for her because eventually she recovered. Then, a worker with artistic abilities was needed and she was transferred to secretariat block no. 4. Once again, her drawing skills were to her advantage and she worked as a drafts-woman in a unit called *Baulietung* and moved into block number 2. With her were Vera Poltin, a Jewish architect of Czech origin, and Professor Blitsky, a Pole who was sent to the camp because he saved Jews. Working in this unit gave Naomi much better access to food and message delivery. She assisted a young girl named Simone with smuggling information and food. After the war, the girl returned to France and in time became Minister of Health and President of the European Parliament.[26] The two kept in touch after the war.

The three workers in the block decided that they had to hide the camp plans for the crematoria, buildings, and a general description of the camp in case the Germans burned everything and there was no evidence left. Naomi made drawings of everything, folded the drawings, and hid them inside socks. The socks were then placed in tin cans and buried under the dirt floor of the women's camp. After the war, her friend Christina Horshak passed the drawings on to Naomi, and today they are displayed in the Ghetto Fighters' Museum.[27]

On January 18, 1944, Naomi went on a death march with the other women prisoners in the camp.[28] The weather was freezing cold, and they weren't dressed warmly enough. The march was very difficult since their legs were stiff from the cold. It was snowing. Anyone who stopped or sat down was shot in the head and his body was left behind. To survive the march, one had to think and act like a robot, which is exactly what Naomi did. While marching she decided to escape the line with fifteen other women with the help of a Romanian soldier. His name was Fritz. They were saved. In the small village of Vilchavy, Poland, the Milek and Antonchick family saved Naomi and the other women who escaped the march. The Antonchick family brought her into their home and hid her in the attic, an act that might have cost the lives of the whole family or even the entire village. But the father of the family took Naomi in out of a firm belief in the need to save a living soul.[29]

AFTER THE WAR

By the time the war ended, in April 1945, at the age of twenty-five, Naomi returned to Warsaw. She wanted to see what was left of her life prior to the war. Desolation was everywhere. The ghetto was destroyed. There was no sign of a familiar face or place. At the Warsaw branch of the Central Committee of Polish Jews, she found a job as a painter,[30] and in exchange for her work she was given a place to sleep and vegetarian meals.

A new manager named Zvi Shner came to the art division of the Warsaw branch of the Central Committee of Polish Jews.[31] He had the idea of setting up an exhibition in the Jewish block in an international exhibition in Majdanek. The exhibition, called Week in Majdanek, took place September 15–22, 1946.[32] It was a Jewish exhibition because it was created by Jews and had Jewish characteristics, and also because the countries that were invited to take part in the exhibition sent only their country flag. The flags were each placed in a different block to show the ethnic origin of each nation. The exhibition took place in the Jewish block. All the items were curated and presented there. As David Rapp described it, "All the horrible contents, first testimony after the war, was screaming out of the walls of the Jewish block. On the tables was set an album with Judkowski's paintings that were a voiceless scream and description of what took place in that death camp."[33]

The album was actually a large notebook of paintings depicting moments she had witnessed in Auschwitz. With that portfolio, she applied to the art department and was accepted. The paintings show different moments and situations of life in the camp. They are her testimony of the war. The album contains twenty paintings, sized 26.5 x 36 cm, that were painted in watercolor and ink on paper. After the exhibition, committee member Emil Zomershtein, the Jewish senator of the Polish Senate took these paintings with him to the United States to present them there. Later, the paintings were sent back to Israel and used as testimony in the Eichmann Trial, which took place in Israel in 1961.

After the trial, the album was transferred to the State Archives, and then in 1996, it was transferred to the Yad Vashem Archives. Thirty years passed until it made its way to the Yad Vashem museum after it gathered dust in the state archives. The museum's senior curator, Yehudit Shender, chose to display the album in the archive's permanent display. Naomi never got the album back, although she kept copies of the drafts. When she passed away on December

5, 1996, at the age of 76, she never knew that it had been sent and exhibited at the Yad Vashem Museum of Art, where her paintings are displayed in an exhibition in her name.[34]

THE EICHMANN TRIAL

Two years after the establishment of the State of Israel, in 1950, the Knesset enacted the law to prosecute Nazis and their collaborators.[35] The law obliges the state to locate, capture, investigate, and prosecute in Israel anyone who took part in harming or exterminating the Jewish people during the Holocaust, or the citizens of Israel. There is a provision in the law that these acts do not have a statute of limitations. A decade later, valuable information reached the Mossad about the whereabouts of Adolf Eichmann, the man who orchestrated the extermination of European Jews during the Holocaust, under his false identity Ricardo Clement in Argentina. In 1960, the Mossad led a covert operation[36] where Eichmann was captured and brought to trial in Israel.

The trial in Israel of the war criminal captured the public's full attention. The desire for revenge and the pursuit of justice resonated in the national and international media. The courtroom was filled to capacity and the demand to attend the hearings greatly exceeded the available space, leaving many people who could not get a seat at the hearing immensely frustrated. In his opening speech, the Israeli Attorney General Gideon Hausner said: "When I stand before you here, Judges of Israel, to lead the Prosecution of Adolf Eichmann, I am not standing alone. With me are six million accusers. But they cannot rise to their feet and point an accusing finger towards him who sits in the dock and cry: 'I accuse.' For their ashes are piled up on the hills of Auschwitz and the fields of Treblinka and are strewn in the forests of Poland. Their graves are scattered throughout the length and breadth of Europe. Their blood cries out, but their voice is not heard. Therefore, I will be their spokesman and in their name I will unfold the terrible indictment."[37] Eichmann was found guilty and was executed by hanging. His body was cremated and scattered outside the territorial waters of the State of Israel.

A NEW LIFE IN ISRAEL

One afternoon Naomi met with Zvi Shner, her manager from the Central Committee of Polish Jews, at a cafe in Warsaw. He came with a friend of his, Boria (Boris) Judkowski, and it was love at first sight for the two. Boria walked Naomi home and they were together from that night on.

Boria was born in Yekaterinburg, Russia, and educated in Poland. Before the war, he was married and had a young child. During the war, he joined and fought with the partisans in Belarus. His wife and child hid with the other fugitives. One day the locals discovered their hideout and exposed everyone. They were executed on the spot. The next day, Boria arrived and discovered the tragedy. Near the end of the war, he joined the Red Army and was discharged with the rank of lieutenant. When the war ended, he came to Warsaw as part of his role as head of the Aliyah B organization in Eretz Israel. There, in Warsaw, he would hold meetings with the Central Committee of Polish Jews, which is how he met Naomi.

Naomi and Boria got married and planned to make Aliyah and raise a family in Israel. In 1948 they came to Haifa after spending some time together in Paris. From there they moved to Kibbutz Yagur, then they joined Kibbutz Alonei Habashan. They were part of the group that planned and established the Ghetto Fighters' House Kibbutz. At first, there were tents, then they set up barracks, and finally established permanent buildings. After settling into life on the kibbutz, she changed her name from Zofia to Naomi and took her husband's surname, Judkowski. The couple had two sons, Yigal and Michael, and numerous grandchildren. She completed her architecture engineering studies at the Technion in Haifa and worked in this profession for over forty years in Israel.

Naomi planned many buildings: a health center on Kibbutz Shefayim, libraries, and dining rooms for other kibbutzim in Israel. As a young member of the kibbutz, she also did her part in the children's house taking care of the children, like all the other female members. She continued to paint the entire time. In 1969, while Israel was fighting Egypt in the War of Attrition, their two sons served in the army. That same year, her beloved husband Boria, who had fought his entire life, died. She never remarried. Her art decorated the kibbutz's dining room walls as well as her own home. Her son Michael said: "I remember my mother's art, and I have some of her paintings in my house. But since her arrival in Israel my mother painted only landscape and nature paintings. I guess this was her way to express her new point of view, in her new life."[38]

CONCLUSIONS

The End of the Beginning / Wislawa Szymborska[39]
After every war
someone has to clean up.
Things won't
straighten themselves up, after all . . .

Naomi was one of many ghetto fighters who survived, but the only one whose art brought the Nazi war criminal Eichmann to trial and justice in Israel. Her art saved her life during the war and became her profession and passion after the war. The end of the war was the beginning of her new life, in a new country, profession, and with a new name of a woman who was known to save others: Naomi.

When a war ends and the clouds of dust and debris dissipate, the visible picture of destruction becomes clear: what was burned, what was destroyed, who was killed. The number of dead and injured can be counted and the scope of investment in the required rehabilitation can be assessed. However, it is impossible to describe the void left in the hearts of those who survived. The war also has dates: when it began, its main operations, and when it ended.

Everyone chooses whether and how to talk about their experiences. Some people find conversation a path to their healing while others keep silent. Each person chooses how to present their point of view: a poet writes a poem, a writer writes a story, a painter draws a picture. Each of these works of art will present things as reflected in the eyes of the observer. There are so many untold stories of Holocaust survivors in the world, including my own personal family history. But I chose to write about Naomi mostly because I wanted to understand who she was, and what her life was like prior to and during the war. In the opening of her book, Naomi wrote: "I would like this book to serve as a hand of remembrance for all those who did not leave an heir, to mourn all those dear to him who were murdered."[40]

These words describe the kind of woman Zofia Rosenstrauch was, and the kind of woman she became—Naomi. Her book provides information on so many research themes and I had to stay focused on her life rather than be drawn into other history fields. These are exactly the things that motivate me to research and write about. The truth behind the facts, the secrets waiting to be revealed to the reader and to the world. Naomi chose to tell the world about the atrocities she and others experienced firsthand. Her book and works present a broad picture of what happened, and here lie the additional secrets, hidden within a variety of colors, figures, and illustrations. The artist tells a story in his work and a viewer will see what he chooses to see in it.

I see the story of the biblical Naomi rise up and repeat itself in a modern version. A woman who lost her loved ones, leaves her home in a foreign land, and arrives in the Land of Israel where she builds a new life for herself. She was an independent woman who was not afraid to express herself, to promote ideological ideas while risking her life for the sake of others. She was a woman whose work saved her from death but also led to justice being served in Israel and to the construction and prosperity of communities in Israel. She was a woman whose deeds must be remembered.

The Sand Will Remember / Nathan Yonatan[41]
The sand will remember the waves
But the foam—will not be remembered,
Besides by those who passed
with the late night wind.

BIBLIOGRAPHY

Aharoni, Zvi, (1997). *Operation Eichmann: The Truth About the Pursuit, Capture and Trial*, Wiley Press.

Arad, Yitzhak, Guttman, Israel, Margaliot Abraham, (2016). *Documents on the Holocaust: Selected Sources on the Destruction of the Jews of Germany and Austria, Poland, and the Soviet Union*, Yad Vashem.

Arendt, Hanna, (2000). *Eichmann in Jerusalem: A Report on the Banality of Evil*, Bavel Publishing.

Bikont, Anna, (2002). "Things Like They Were Seen in Jedwabne," in: Silberklang David, *Yad Vashem Studies*, Jerusalem, pp. 7–18.

Blatman, Daniel, (2002). "Were They Ordinary Poles?," in: Silberklang, David, *Yad Vashem Studies*, Jerusalem, pp. 41 – 54.

Browning, Christopher, R., (1998). *Ordinary Men: Reserve Police Battalion 101 and the Final Solution in Poland*, Harper Perennial.

Browning, Christopher, R., (2004). *The Origins of the Final Solution: The Evolution of Nazi Jewish Policy, September 1939—March 1932*, Yad Vashem, Jerusalem.

Carmi, Shulamit, (1971). "About the Fourth Aliyah: Aliyah, Urbanization and the Crisis of the Process of Jewish Settlement in the Land of Israel in the 1920s," *Mebifnim*, 33, 1, pp. 22 – 49.

Chen, Shoshana, (April 9, 2021). "Mother Said She Won't Hold on the Witness Stand," *Yedioth Ahronoth.*

Drori, Yigal, (September 1982). "The Beginning of Economic Organizations in Eretz Israel During the 1920s," *Katedra*, 25, pp. 99–112.

Drori, Yigal, (June 1985). "Organization of the Middle Class in Eretz Israel—Attempts at Political Organization in the 1920's," *Katedra*, 44, pp. 116–125.

Erez, Yehuda, (1964). *The Third Aliya Book*, Am Oved, Tel Aviv.

Ferreira, Luis, Van Pelt, Jan, (2019). *Auschwitz: Not Long Ago, Not Far Away*, Abbeville Press, New York.

Geva, Sharon, (2010). *To the Unknown Sister: Holocaust Heroines in Israeli Society*, Migdarim (Genders) Series, Editors: Naveh, Hannah, (Chief Editor), Hertzon, Hannah, Kibbutz Poalim, Tel Aviv.

Guri, Haim, (2004). *Facing the Glass Booth: The Jerusalem Trial of Adolf Eichmann*, Wayne State University Press.

Grabowsky, Jan, (2012). *Rural Society and the Jews: Elders, Night Watcher, Firefighters, Hostages and Manhunts*, Yad Vashem, Jerusalem.

Grabowsky, Jan, (2013). *Hunt for the Jews: Betrayal and Murder in German—Occupied Poland*, Indiana University Press, Bloomington.

Gross, T. Jan, (2001). *Neighbors: The Destruction of the Jewish Community in Jeduabne,* Princeton University Press, Princeton, NJ.

Gvati, Haim, (1981). *A Century of Jewish Settlement in the Land of Israel,* United Kibbutz.

Hausner, Gideon. (1966). *Justice in Jerusalem,* Harper & Row Press.

Jacobson, Michael, (August 18, 2014). "An overview of the dining hall building on the Ghetto Fighters' House Kibbutz," *Back Window,* Israel.

Jacobson, Michael, (May 26, 2015). "An overview of the dining hall building on the Hagoshrim Kibbutz," *Back Window*, Israel.

Judkowski, Noemi, (1990). *Requiem for Two Families*, Ghetto Fighters' House, Israel.

Logan, W., Reeves, K., (2008). "Dealing with Difficult Heritage," *Places of Pain and Shame,* Routledge, London & New York.

Lewin, Eyal, Miller Katav, Orit, (2020). "A Moral Assessment of the Polish-Israeli Declaration Following the 2018 Polish Anti-Defamation," *Journal of Education, Culture and Society,* Vol. 11, No. 2.

Mendelsohn, Daniel, (2013). *A Search for Six Million,* Harper Collins, New York.

Morris, Heather, (2018). *The Tattooist of Auschwitz,* Harper, New York.

Pearlman, Moshe, (2015). *The Capture of Adolf Eichmann*, Normanby Press, New York.

Rapp, David, (August 21, 2005). "Zofia from Auschwitz Is Naomi from the Ghetto Fighters," *Haaretz.*

Rees, Laurence, (2006). *Auschwitz: A New History,* Public Affairs Press.

Roman, Zipura, (May 11, 2011). "Who Is a Heroine? The Israeli Society and Women in the Holocaust," *Laisha.*

Shalem, Motti, (July 10, 2018,). "When Poles Burned Hundreds of Jews in the Barn," *Ynet.*

Silberklang, David, (2006). *Yad Vashem Studies*, Jerusalem.

Szymborska, Wislawa, (2001). *Miracle Fair: Selected Poems of Wislawa Szymborska,* W.W. Norton and Company, Inc., New York.

Tsoffer, Ruth, (2007). "The Trauma of Otherness and Hunger: Ruth and Lot's Daughters," *Women in Judaism*, A Multidisciplinary e-journal, Vol. 5. No. 1.

Williams, P., (2007). "The Surviving Object Presence and Absence in Memorial Museums," *Memorial Museums: The Global Rush to Commemoration Atrocities*, Berg Publishers, New York.

Witz, Yehiam, (1997). "The Law for the Judgment of the Nazis and their Aides and the Attitude of Israeli Society in the 1950s to the Holocaust and its Survivors," *Chair*, 82.

Wright, L.D., (2002). "Curatorship and Content Development" in: Lord, B., Piacente, M. *Manual of Museum Exhibitions,* Second Edition, Rowman & Littlefield, New York.

Yablonka, Hannah, (1997). "The Law for the Judiciary of the Nazis and their Assistants: Another Aspect of the Question of Israelis, Survivors and the Holocaust," *Chair*, 82.

Yablonka, Hannah, (2001). *State of Israel v. Adolf Eichmann*, Yad Ben Zvi, Sefri Hemed, Tel Aviv, Jerusalem.

Yehuda, Amichai, (1998). *Patuach Sagur Patuach: Shirim (Open Closed Open: Poems),* Shoken, Tel Aviv.

Zakovitch, Yair, (1990). *Ruth: Mikra Leyisrael, Magness*, Jerusalem.

Internet sources

www.yadvashem.org/yv/he/exhibitions/eichmann/index.asp

www.massuah.org.il/תערוכות-מקוונות/grp_681/התקשורת-בראי-אייכמן-משפט

www.youtube.com/watch?v=DfQPDrVu9TU&feature=youtu.be

www.gfh.org.il/תערוכות/79/מול_תא_הזכוכית

www.knesset.gov.il/exhibits/EichmannCapture/intro.htm

GFH page for Naomi Judkowski's pictures from her album

IDEA - ALM - תוצאות חיפוש (infocenters.co.il)

NOTES

1. Naomi Judkowski, *Requiem for Two Families* (Israel: Ghetto Fighters' House, 1990), 92. The Hebrew version.

2. The kibbutz is named after the Warsaw Ghetto Uprising.

3. Judkowski called the album FKL Oswiecim (women's concentration camp, F—Frauen, K—Konzentration, L—Lager).

4. The fourth Aliyah, also called the Grabski Aliyah after the Polish Finance Minister, is the great wave of Aliyah between 1924 and 1931 to Eretz Israel. The number of immigrants during this period is estimated at about 70,000, while the number of those leaving the country during this period is estimated at about 20,000. Haim Gvati, *A Century of Jewish Settlement in the Land of Israel* (Israel, United Kibbutz, 1981). Shulamit Carmi, "About the Fourth Aliyah: Aliyah, Urbanization and the Crisis of the Process of Jewish Settlement in the Land of Israel in the 1920s," *Mebifnim*, (Israel, 33, 1, 1971). pp. 22–49.

5. Many pioneers returned to their home country due to the difficulties in adjusting to the harsh conditions prior to the establishment of the Jewish state. Yehuda Erez, *The Third Aliya Book (Am Oved, Tel Aviv, 1964).*

6. Naomi Judkowski, *Requiem for Two Families* (Israel: Ghetto Fighters' House, 1990), 52–60. The Hebrew version. GFH memorial page for Naomi Judkowski: www.loh.org.il/viewpage.asp?pagesCatID=576&MemorialPage=1 &Personkey=gf45g9g878878377832128321vx1&siteName=lohamei

7. Naomi Judkowski, *Requiem for Two Families* (Israel: Ghetto Fighters' House, 1990), 33–35.

8. The words of Haim Weizmann, the first president of Israel.

9. Yad Vashem, Nazi Germany and the Jews, 1933–1939. Arad, Yitzhak, Guttman, Israel, Margaliot, Abraham, "Change in the Legal Position of the Jews," *Documents on the Holocaust: Selected Sources on the Destruction of the Jews of Germany and Austria, Poland, and the Soviet Union,* (2016, Yad Vashem, Jerusalem), pp. 83.

Christopher R. Browning, *The Origins of the Final Solution: The Evolution of Nazi Jewish Policy, September 1939—March 1932* (2004, Yad Vashem, Jerusalem), pp. 123–150.

10. Yad Vashem, The Outbreak of WWII and the Policy Towards the Jews.

11. Arad, Yitzhak, Guttman, Israel, Margaliot, Abraham, "Marking in Jews in the General Government," *Documents on the Holocaust: Selected Sources on the Destruction of the Jews of Germany and Austria, Poland, and the Soviet Union* (2016, Yad Vashem, Jerusalem), p. 143. Ibid., "Smuggling Food to the Ghetto," pp. 182. Ibid., "The Jewish Fighters Organization," p. 233. Christopher R. Browning, *The Origins of the Final Solution: The Evolution of Nazi Jewish Policy, September 1939–March 1932* (2004, Yad Vashem, Jerusalem), pp. 123–150.

12. The *Judenrat* was the Jewish Police who tried to maintain order in the ghetto also by carrying out the Germans' orders. Adam Czerniakow committed suicide in the ghetto on July 23, 1943 because he was unwilling to continue cooperating with the Germans and handing over lists of Jewish names for extradition to the extermination camps.

13. Mordechai Anielewicz was the commander of a Jewish organization fighting in the Warsaw Ghetto Uprising. He was killed on May 8, 1943 in a battle with the Nazis in the ghetto. He was gifted with outstanding leadership skills, and after his death his personality was engraved as a symbol of courage and sacrifice. He was twenty-four at the time of his death.

14. Naomi was the one who planned the bunker path system and maps. Jewish Fighting Organizations in the Ghetto were: Hashomer Hatzair, Dror, Akiva, Poalei Zion Party, Jewish Military Union: ACI, ZZW.

15. Yad Vashem, The Outbreak of the Warsaw Ghetto.

The Israeli Holocaust Memorial Day is on the 27th of Nisan, a week after the end of Passover. The date was chosen because it is close to the date the Warsaw Ghetto Uprising broke out, which symbolizes Jewish heroism and fighting spirit.

16. Yad Vashem, Majdanek.

17. *Koya* was a bunk bed made of wood.

18. There were 227 blocks in total in the camp.

19. Naomi Judkowski, *Requiem for Two Families* (Israel: Ghetto Fighters' House, 1990), pp. 60–62.

20. Yad Vashem, Auschwitz-Birkenau. Christopher R. Browning, *The Origins of the Final Solution: The Evolution of Nazi Jewish Policy, September 1939—March 1932* (2004, Yad Vashem, Jerusalem), pp. 469–480.

21. A doctor and SS officer, known as the Angel of Death of Auschwitz. He conducted numerous pseudo-medical experiments, as well as performing selections among the Jews brought to the camp. During these selections, most of the Jews were immediately put to death in the gas chambers and a minority were selected for forced labor. Mengele concentrated his experiments mainly on children and young twins and dwarfs. His experiments involved all kinds of abuse. After the evacuation of Auschwitz, Mengele was transferred to the Mauthausen concentration camp. After that camp was liberated on May 5, 1945, he disappeared without a trace.

22. Yad Vashem, Auschwitz.

23. Heather Morris, *The Tattooist of Auschwitz* (2018, Harper, New York).

24. Those who were very thin and pale were called *Muselmann* and they were usually separated from the others to isolate them from people who were more physically robust.

25. The prisoners sarcastically called the hospital "Riviere."

26. Simone Veil.

27. Naomi Judkowski, *Requiem for Two Families* (Israel: Ghetto Fighters' House, 1990), The Hebrew version, pp. 72–78.

28. Yad Vashem, Death Marches: Toward the end of the war, when the German army retreated on all fronts, Nazi Germany began to evacuate the camps that were close to the Eastern Front and march the prisoners west toward Germany. Despite their inevitable defeat, the Nazis were determined to prevent the survivors in the camps from being liberated by the Allies. In the death marches, the prisoners were forced to walk vast distances in freezing cold weather, with a minimal amount of food, water, and rest, if any. Those who were unable to continue walking were shot along the way. Liberation was just beyond the horizon but for those victims, it was the beginning of another phase of terrible suffering. Many of them perished in the final months and days of the war.

29. Naomi Judkowski, *Requiem for Two Families* (Israel: Ghetto Fighters' House, 1990), The Hebrew version, pp. 82–87.

30. The Committee was established on November 12, 1944.

31. Shner was the first museum manager at the Ghetto Fighter's House Kibbutz.

32. I received this information by e-mail from Aleksandra Skrabek, head of exhibition and publication in Majdanek.

33. David Rapp, "Zofia from Auschwitz is Naomi from the Ghetto Fighters," *Haaretz*, August 21, 2005.

Naomi Judkowski, *Requiem for Two Families* (Israel: Ghetto Fighters' House, 1990*)*, 95. Yad Vashem Museum archive, the scanned album created by Naomi.

34. David Rapp, "Zofia from Auschwitz is Naomi from the Ghetto Fighters," *Haaretz*, August 21, 2005.

Shoshana Chen, "Mother Said She Won't Hold on the Witness Stand," *Yedioth Ahronoth,* April 9, 2021.

35. Knesset: "The Law for the Judiciary." See also: Weitz (1997). The Law of Justice. Jablonka (1997). The Law of Justice. Jablonka (2001). State of Israel v. Adolf Eichmann.

36. Operation Finale.

37. Yad Vashem: Eichmann Trial.

38. On December 31, 2019, I spoke with her son Michael on the phone. He doesn't remember his mother ever talking about her former name or the reason for choosing the name Naomi. He told me that his mother's art still decorated his house, but mostly her later work. After the war, she painted mostly landscapes in soft pastel colors. All the historic art she had was given to the Ghetto Fighters' House Museum. Only her notebook with the original war paintings was given to Yad Vashem Museum (as mentioned before, she never knew about that). Naomi Judkowski, *Requiem for Two Families* (Israel: Ghetto Fighters' House, 1990*)*, 10–14.

39. Wislawa Szymborska, *Miracle Fair: Selected Poems of Wislawa Szymborska,* W.W. Norton and Company, Inc., 2001. Wislawa Szymborska was awarded the 1996 Nobel Prize in Literature.

40. Naomi Judkowski, *Requiem for Two Families* (Israel: Ghetto Fighters' House, 1990), 7.

41. Nathan Yonatan is a renowned Israeli poet.

Chapter 6

The Gambia Gender Policy

Trajectory of Women's Collective Action

Fatou Janneh

The year 1970 marked a turning point for The Gambia because the country became a republic on April 24, 1970.[1] Gambians ceased to be subjects of Britain and became citizens of their own sovereign state, free to frame a constitution that attended to their wishes and aspirations.[2] Prime Minister Dawda Kairaba Jawara was sworn in as the country's first president soon after the announcement of results of the referendum in which seventy percent of the electorate voted for the republic.[3] Hence, Sir Farimang Sighateh's position as Governor General came to an end. To secure the referendum vote for the republic in place of the monarchy, women assured the People's Progressive Party (PPP) and its leader of their support. This victory arguably could not have resulted without the political involvement of a broad network of women's grassroots organizations.[4]

Scholars agree that grassroots activism created an avenue for political participation in national campaigns for the decolonization process and independence in Africa.[5] Many African women, however, were sidelined by colonial states, the fight for the independent state, and later, economic crises and political failure.[6] This marginality had strongly influenced Gambian women both individually and collectively. They developed strategies to defend their economic and political interests within the colonial and post-colonial environments. They became significant allies of politicians and political parties with the expectation that these individuals and parties would resolve their plight. Since authorities failed to serve their interests, Gambian women resorted to using collective action to overcome their challenges through *kafoolu* and *kompins* operating in the rural and urban areas.[7] They shifted their drive toward grassroots women's organizations that focused on social and political change. Their collective efforts were composed of women from various backgrounds. Between the late 1950s and early 1960s, these women's grassroots organizations became visible in national politics.

The Gambia's colonial past continued to have a significant effect on its socio-economic formation, geography, and constitutional and political orientations. The country is surrounded by neighboring Senegal on all sides except for the west, where its boundary is the Atlantic Ocean. This was not a historical coincidence. Britain and France, who controlled the colony of Senegal, demarcated the boundaries of The Gambia in the late 1880s and made subsequent modifications in the 1890s and 1970s.[8] The country is the smallest on Africa's mainland with a population of 1.8 million.[9] An American journalist, Berkley Rice, described the Gambia at independence as the "birth of an improbable nation" due to the country's weak economy, poor infrastructure, and massive illiteracy, among other factors.[10] These challenges likely informed Richard Burton's harsh description of Bathurst (former capital of The Gambia, now Banjul) as "nothing but mud, mangroves, malaria and miasma."[11] This impoverishment was profoundly apparent in the rural areas, which concentrated more than half of the population at the time. The country relied exclusively on the export of peanuts for the revenue to support the government in its provision of services such as health and education, which were mostly centralized. The condition became deplorable during the rainy season due to a shortage of food, as farmers depended on their crops which they had to harvest and could not do so under these conditions.[12] This period was locally called the *hunger season*. All these factors had influenced negative perceptions of the country's socio-economic and political prospects. Despite the uncertainty of the country's ability to survive as a nation, Gambians proceeded undeterred in their strive for self-rule.

This chapter argues that women acting through *kafoolu* and *kompins* were important political actors in the process of Gambian independence. These organizations grew in significance as they helped women negotiate economic survival and access to land. The women cultivated political patronage with male political leaders to achieve their economic goals; that patronage was cashed in by political leaders who needed popular support to buttress their political power under the new republican government. Thus, women helped build the new government, but from a position of political clientelism (exchange of services for political support), rather than a position of political authority.

BRITISH COLONIAL INFLUENCE AND HISTORICAL
PAST OF WOMEN'S ORGANIZATIONS

British colonial rule influenced the organization of the political life and culture of Bathurst. British colonialism, and settlement of liberated Africans or repatriated free slaves from the New World called Aku, brought European education, Christianity, and foreign languages, specifically English or Creole (Krio), among the Gambian people.[13] Although Western culture seemed to dominate, it coexisted with African culture among the indigenous settlers. This combination molded the ebb and flow of city life. Concurrently, Islam impacted people's lifestyles. It blended with some of the existing cultural practices and cemented male hegemony in the rural areas. A colonial report in the 1940s revealed that the colonial government, in recognition of the importance of Islam, desired to have a representative of the Muslim community in the Legislative Council. But it had to choose a man from Bathurst as there was no one in the Protectorate (inland territory) with sufficient knowledge of English to be able to follow the proceedings.[14] Thus, levels of Western education became one of the major differences between the urban and the rural areas.

British colonial education and Christianity introduced by the missionaries influenced women's organizations. As an illustration, members of social clubs were overwhelmingly educated Aku and Creole women and girls.[15] The present study has identified two categories of *kompins* that emerged during the colonial era in Bathurst. One was the group comprised of educated and working-class women; they were predominantly Christians. Women Contemporary Society, Gambia Women Federation, Women's Corona Society, Girl Guides, Girls friendly society, religious-based groups such as Methodist Women Association, Mother's Union, ex pupils' associations, namely Methodist Girls High School (MGHS), were examples.[16] The second category was less literate in the western education system, and overwhelmingly Muslim. They were married women, some of them were stay-at-home mothers, while most of their membership engaged in trade at the market or homemade canteens. Members served as a support system to one another with a common value system. They embarked on local banking schemes, *osusu*.[17] Occasionally, they organized entertainment programs, mostly *sabar,* as a way of strengthening the association.[18] Nonetheless, before the 1950s none of these groups were involved in mainstream politics.[19] They participated as electorate and office seekers between the 1930s and the 1950s. Christianity and education formed the basis of most of these associations, which had influenced their mode of operation.

Through *kompins,* women engaged in diverse activities such as educa-tion, health, entertainment, and humanitarian services. The educated or elite women's groups were dedicated to empowering women and girls across the country, although they began remotely in the city before expanding the advocacy into the interior. This is because educational opportunities were limited to Bathurst. For example, the Women Contemporary Society and Gambia Women Federation employed education as a tool for liberation. They organized reach outs and urged parents to send their daughters to school. As a founding member of the above-mentioned organizations, Busy Bees and Women's Corona Society, Rosamond Fowlis was known for her crusade in Kombo areas and provinces encouraging parents to enroll their daughters in school. These organizations rallied women of diverse backgrounds to deliber-ate matters of the common good. They organized a "baby award" annually and offered incentives to mothers of healthiest babies.[20] They sensitized the city residents on proper sanitation and hygiene, especially among poor families.

Members of these organizations were predominantly teachers and nurses, and virtually all were from the Aku ethnolinguistic population. Their inter-action with Europeans had a significant influence on their cultural lifestyle. Some of them were exposed to different educational environments that provided them with a broad awareness of social justice and the potential for social change experienced in other parts of the world, especially in British West African colonies between 1945 and 1960. For example, Fowlis was trained in England and was a science teacher for over three decades. Louise Njie studied at Achimota College in Gold Coast, Augusta Hannah Jawara proceeded to Edinburgh to study nursing after attending MGHS. Likewise, Lucretia S.C. Joof studied in London.[21] Studying abroad gave these women a sense of understanding the struggle for self-determination and internal self-rule. These women also resisted male hegemony that was blinded by gender stereotypes and discriminations. They paved the way for social change and the dismantling of gender barriers by advocating for mass education for girls.

The British colonial administration promoted the establishment of Gambian Women War Workers were prompted by the outbreak of World War II from 1939 to 1945; members attended to the conditions of wounded soldiers and their families. Such an act demonstrated not only owing allegiance to one's country but showing loyalty to the colonial power.[22] The leaders of this association were prominent women of Bathurst and were wives of important men of the city. Mrs. Njie was the wife of nationalist leader Pierre S. Njie, and Mrs. J.A. Mahoney was the wife of the first speaker of the Legislative Council, Sir John Andrew Mahoney. Despite the colonial government's inad-equate preparations to fund the humanitarian project, the association had an estimated account of nine hundred and ninety-four British pounds sterling in December 1941 from its members' fundraising.[23]

The rise in community service and the women's empowerment approach led these disparate categories of *kompins* to converge in the late 1950s and early 1960s. The Gambia Women Federation extended its membership to ex. Pupils' association, Old Girls of St. Joseph's association, and *Musu* kafoo society, with the aim of representing all women across the country.[24] By 1955 and 1956, many members of these organizations had identified with the emerged political parties through the women's wings. Whereas *kompins* followed a Western model of organizational structure, *kafoolu* have their roots in the precolonial era, originally as traditional associations. In essence, *kafoolu* and *kompins* became intertwined with the purpose of enhancing women's economic and social freedom.

The colonial system was discriminatory in its efforts to organize Gambian political life. Voting was restricted to the Colony, the area of jurisdiction under the direct administration of the British colonial government, and not every woman had the right to vote.[25] First, before a woman could exercise her franchise in Bathurst, such potential voters were required to possess property and have a steady income. Second, she had to be at least twenty-five years old at the time of the election, either to vote or to run for office. Unlike the Colony, the Protectorate was deprived of such legal rights or privileges enjoyed in Bathurst; women were disfranchised. Two years before the introduction of universal suffrage in 1960, chiefs refused female voting rights at the constitutional conference. In contrast, men were granted legal rights with or without property.[26]

There was disagreement between the Colony and the Protectorate's delegates over women's right to vote. Bathurst politicians were advocating for women's suffrage, but their counterparts were reluctant because they believed granting voting rights to rural women would cause insubordination to their husbands. Illustrating Gambian women's long struggle in politics, J.H. Price, quoted a renowned historian of West African History, Michael Crowder, stating:

> . . . one chief replied that he has seen the trouble caused in Bathurst by giving the women the vote and they didn't want any palaver with their women. I asked an Upper River Division chief later why he wouldn't accept the principle of women voting in the protectorate. He replied that personally he didn't mind the idea, but chiefs living near Bathurst had painted a grim picture of the troubles the men had with women because of politics. So he thought it best not to let it happen in the chiefdom.[27]

For these chiefs, female suffrage intrinsically could undermine male authority. These controversies left delegates failing to reach a consensus on the issue of equal voting rights. This conference held in Brikama on October 18 through

25, 1958, was nevertheless historic, giving rise to the 1960 Constitution that adopted Universal Adult Suffrage. This marked a significant development in Gambian politics because, for the first time, there was equal suffrage for adult men and women without discrimination.[28] The presence of women delegates, Cecilia Moore, and Rachel Palmer from Bathurst, gave women's issues momentum in the national discussion and the way forward. Two subsequent conferences continued in Georgetown and Bathurst in January and March of 1959, before the suffrage ultimately took effect in 1960 following the first House of Representatives election.[29] That said, this disenfranchisement of women shows an interconnectedness between the British colonial policy and indigenous patriarchal values that limited women's opportunity to participate in public life.

PATH TO INDEPENDENCE

Activism reinforced and heightened the decolonization process. Nationalist leaders such as Edward Francis Small struggled for independence for several decades and paved the way for different anti-colonial political actors.[30] He defied government policies and the unpopular reforms of governors such as Richmond Palmer and Arthur F. Richards to fight for the public interest using different platforms. Small engaged in massive civic awareness campaigns and he would sacrifice his sleep to enlighten villagers about current issues, which helped the farmers to understand the exploitative nature of the colonial system. Consequently, he helped them to organize themselves into cooperatives that would engage in mutual agreement on the prices of peanuts. He established Gambia Farmer's Cooperative Association in 1917, Bathurst Trade Union in 1929, and the first newspapers *Gambia Outlook* and *Senegambian Reporter*, among other initiatives.[31]

Small and other nationalist leaders linked the struggle for workers' rights to the struggle for self-determination.[32] The Workers' Unions, including dock workers, Rate Payers Association, Civil Service, and trade unions, were mobilized, and their energies were oriented toward the cause of national liberation.[33] Small's efforts culminated in the establishment of Urban Councils. He advocated for the expansion of Urban Councils to the rural areas, but the governor denied this request in 1934.[34] In his advocacy for equal representation, he fought for electoral reforms to the Legislative Council and was granted in 1946.[35] Due to paucity of material, little is known about the direct involvement of women in this struggle, and to what extent they participated before the 1940s. Could it be that the banner of gender equality was not prioritized by anti-colonial activists who were not paying particular attention to gender disparities? Based on Small famous slogan, "no taxation without representation," it would be fair to conclude that women were his concern as he vied against colonial rule not only in The Gambia, but also in the African continent, and elsewhere.

The mid-twentieth century witnessed the wooing of *kafoolu* and *kompins* by the emerging political parties. This quest to appeal to these women's organizations was pursued with the goal of benefiting from women's endorsement. The Gambia Democratic Party (GDP), Gambia Muslim Congress (GMC), and United Party (UP) all targeted the *kompins*. Political activities were outlawed in the rural Gambia (the area governed by traditional rulers called chiefs who were under the supervision of the colonial administration).[36] It was a strategic move by the British to prevent the rise of nationalism or independence movements among its subjects. But more importantly, to contain the use of violence as experienced in other British colonies. In Kenya nationalist groups led by the Mau Mau Movement clashed violently with British colonial authorities as they protested discriminatory and exploitative land policies that favored white settlers.[37] Fearful of a similar outcome in The Gambia, British authorities limited indigenous political parties' influence on local politics, to urban areas.

The four political parties that were formed in the 1950s were relatively inclusive. Specifically, Hannah Forster was instrumental in financing and establishing GDP on February 25, 1951, led by Rev. John Colley Faye. She was a wealthy entrepreneur and among the country's first women political activists.[38] In 1959, Forster also urged provincial chiefs to enfranchise rural women by participating in politics at the All-Party Conference held in Georgetown. In the same way, women supported Garba Jahumpa's GMC formed in January 1952.[39] Under the leadership of Yadicone Njie, Bathurst women endorsed Pierre Sarr Njie when he became the leader of UP in 1954.[40] Because women proved active mobilizers and volunteers, and effective in amplifying political messages, most parties recognized the necessity of involving them, increasing their visibility in the political space. This is evident in the case of Rachel Palmer who was the only woman out of the ten delegates of the London Constitutional Conference of 1961.[41]

The rapid development of women's grassroots organizations was driven by socio-economic conditions in Bathurst and Kombo St. Mary's.[42] Through their collective action, women opposed colonial policies. Female traders at the Albert market organized to protect themselves from colonial tax collectors and public health officials' harsh treatment. The 1920s exemplified a mass demonstration of women in Bathurst against prices increases.[43] Essentially, these forms of collective actions were means of empowerment for their members. Women's resistance against colonial taxation laws was also found in other parts of Africa such as in the Tamne-Mende crisis in Sierra Leone and the Akan protest in the Gold Coast in the last years of the nineteenth century.

Marc Matera et al. show extensive historical analyses of Aba women's resistance in 1929. The British colonial administrators in southeastern Nigeria imposed special taxes on the Igbo market women which culminated to protest between market women against colonial government and the warrant chiefs.[44] Similarly, Abeokuta Women's Union under the leadership of Funmilayo Ransome-Kuti led a series of protests between 1940s and 1950s against tax increment. Those protests were a major cause of the abdication of Alake Ademola II, the traditional ruler of Agba in January 1949. The Women's Union also advocated for enfranchisement of all women in Nigeria.[45] In Guinea, in 1948, the market women defiled colonial regulation and market tax. By 1955, these women succeeded in getting the colonial government to reduce taxes.[46] Consequently, these actions led to the growing interest in self-help groups.

The formation of women's grassroots organizations in The Gambia empowered women to challenge the status quo. This is certainly true in the case of Women's Contemporary Society and Women's Federation, two organizations that promoted political awareness and women's rights. One of the founding members of these organizations was Augusta H. M. Jawara, who became the first woman to run for a national election in 1960 under the PPP ticket. Through these organizations, Lady Jawara built a strong network and support for the PPP. She led a group that participated in a house-to-house campaign and spoke to women's groups. Yet, she lost Soldier Town to her male opponent, Alieu Badara Njie, the candidate for Democratic Congress Alliance (DCA).[47] Lady Jawara's candidacy was a litmus test for women's ability to win national elections.

In 1965, The Gambia attained independence and held its first referendum the same year. The citizens were to decide whether to change the political system from a parliamentary monarchy to a republic.[48] Women were visible in celebrations of independence as they chanted and danced on that momentous day of February 18, 1965. Almost every woman had sewn a new dress bearing the face of Jawara with inscriptions such as the Gambia independence 1965 or progress peace and prosperity. Since the eve of independence, women dressed in a variety of colors. Several people arrived from upriver districts to join the rest at the McCarthy square.[49] Around midnight, the union jack was brought down and replaced by the Gambian flag; its red, white, blue, white, green colors were displayed on the flagpole while fireworks lit the sky and people sang the national anthem and liberation songs in unison.[50] It was an emotional moment as Gambians looked forward to a better future; there were tears in the eyes of the people. They were tears of joy, hope, freedom, and uncertainty. The weeklong celebration started three days earlier. There was jubilation everywhere, in every village and every corner of the country.[51]

To honor this day, the most women stayed at home instead. As the city was aroused with a festive mood so were other parts of the country.

Nine months after The Gambia's independence, the first referendum was held on November 26, 1965. However, it was lost due to the government's inability to achieve a two-thirds majority.[52] Most of the electorate seemed to be unaware of the relevance of the referendum or what sovereignty entailed at the time. The referendum would give people the mandate to make informed choices that would facilitate constitutional change, stipulate the type of government, and shape various institutions to run the affairs of the state of the Gambian people. It gauged whether the electorate preferred to govern themselves or to be governed by a foreign power, and if citizens were willing to cut the umbilical cord between the country and its colonial master. Some politicians, however, opposed the proclamation of a republican state stating that the country was unprepared for a transition because of its limited resources. The UP and its leader, Pierre S. Njie, strongly disapproved of the republican state because they felt it was unwise for the people to take total control to run the affairs of the state. Many were of the view that the country's future statehood was uncertain, and its high poverty rate would cause its failure.[53] This referendum, therefore, failed to attain the two-thirds majority by less than eight hundred votes.

ORIGINS AND WORKINGS OF *KAFOOLU*

Gambian women's ability to cultivate solidarity strengthened their collectivity. Despite the hostility of the colonial environment, women contested and negotiated with the system that gagged them. Women adopted different strategies to defend their economic and political interests within the colonial environment, which led to collective action efforts by groups from various regional and ethnolinguistic origins. Bala Saho's work portrays women's sense of solidarity in the Cadi court during the colonial era; "women-built networks along kinship lines at a social gathering, and through the market."[54] One woman's success in court was a success for other women. One of such instances was the landmark case of Horrijah Jobe.[55]

There is a long-standing history of women networks in rural Gambia. But to date, little evidence has been found stating exactly when *kafoolu* were created. By way of illustration, community development practitioner Njaga Jawo concedes that:

We did not form kafoos; we found them there. People will claim that they form kafoos, normally that is what people will say, but kafoos were here from days immemorial, even before we were born. What we did know is that we

strengthened the kafoos and empowered them, but we found them there. So even
before you and I were born, we found kafoos in our villages.[56]

For Suwaibou Touray, women *kafoolu* emerged after independence. He
claimed that the culture (farm work for well-to-do families in the farming
communities in return for reward) was that "it was the male and female youth
who were in this culture before independence. Women *kafoos* only came into
being later after independence to engage in the farm work of this type or
simply work for pay. It was these women *kafoos* that were infiltrated by politicians who then patronized them to gain their support. This culture was borrowed from the Bathurst area to the provinces deforming the word *kafoo* to
that of *kompin* and for Mandinka *kompinoo.*[57] According to Sulayman Touray,
kompins were made up of different women and men but the members were
usually within the same age bracket or generation.[58] Binta Jammeh-Sidibe
and Omar B. Jallow, asserted that the idea of *kafoo* was brought to the city
by rural-urban migrants, consequently, metamorphosing into the concept of
kompin in Bathurst and its surroundings.[59] As Saho states that the Colony
could not provide "ethnic and kinship security," the formation of social network became inevitable as a survival technique to the changing conditions
in the urban areas.[60] These alliances were motivated by ethnolinguistic and
economic aspirations and interests as in the case of Mankinkas from Badibu
of the North Bank Region and Serahuli from Garawuli of the Upper River
Region.[61] These Bathurst *kafoolu* and *kompins* were based on strong ethnolinguistic community ties and grouped men who were mostly clothes and textile
traders who usually operated in Albert market. Most of them had lived in
different areas in Bathurst called *Half-Die* and *Tobacco* road.[62]

Jammeh-Sidibe and Touray highlighted that both women and men formed
kafoolu to attain specific objectives and to address the community's needs.
These necessities varied from one community or village to another. With
time and a rise in population, individual *kafoolu* represented distinct groups
and their respective identities. For example, secret societies for blacksmiths,
leather workers, farmers, women groups, age grade, and weavers represented
the interests of members of these occupations.[63] For the most part, in these
groups, women were under the guidance of men in craftworks. In urban areas,
however, women became more independent in handicrafts. They created their
market where they predominantly sold to tourists. These women seemed to be
more prosperous than their rural counterparts even when they crafted similar
products, such as dyed cloth and other fabrics.[64]

In the rural Gambia, *kafoolu* became a means for women to join forces to
promote their economic interests. They were created for socio-economic reasons aimed at improving members' income-generating potential by offering a
support system for women's businesses and trades to become relevant actors

in the informal sector of the country's economy.[65] Nonetheless, individual women faced challenges when attempting to secure a living or profits from commercial activities.[66] By forming these groups, they exerted more pressure on local and regional leaders to protect their interests.

Members of *kafoolu* have been mostly farmers and food providers. For example, the Banjulinding, Bakau, Sukuta Women and the Ndemban Garden Associations. The Gambia Women Farmers' Association (NAWFA) was later created as an umbrella body.[67] Involvement in food production made many of these women breadwinners within their households.[68] They engaged in horticultural ventures and the breeding of livestock for the provincial market, *lumo*, and the Islamic feast *tobaski*. These women's labor contributed to the country's economy. Still, these women's ability to shape economic policy or gain political influence remained limited and subject to male authority.

Kafoolu were formed by women and their membership includes mostly women. Nonetheless, men have a limited presence in *kafoolu* to help women with certain labor in some cases including fencing gardens and digging wells. These coopted male members constituted between three and five men and they participated as associate members.[69] These men served as advisers and helped women with their records in some cases. The members sometimes had their organizations' aims and objectives recorded in written documents. Even when that was not the case, they agreed about their goals and know them by heart.[70]

Kafoolu were instrumental in the collaborative work of their communities. Their act of voluntary service in their communities predated colonial rule. They participated in social and religious activities such as funerals and naming ceremonies. Members of *kafoolu* played a complementary role to men in terms of clearing farms, weeding, and harvesting. They worked on individual farms as a way of mutual aid to their fellow members or sometimes for cash in exchange for their labor. They partook in other duties such as fetching water and firewood and community cleaning. In addition to cash, they received grains such as rice, corn, and millet in return for their services. Members would visit somebody's farm such as a relatively wealthy person, very respectable individual, or successful merchants. They would also help the needy who were incapable to work on their farm. Members were also involved in other economic ventures such as soapmaking and cloth dyeing to support themselves.[71]

EMERGING POST-COLONIAL LAND TENURE POLICIES

Kafoolu worked on changing land tenure policies to protect women's access to land. Although a few women had access to land ownership, most depended

on lands owned by their male relatives, such as husbands and fathers, to conduct their business. Some women were able to use the communal property.
Government policies and customs have complicated women's rights to land
in the rural Gambia. Their reliance on collective action as a solution was
increasingly being recognized. Women employed different strategies to cultivate connections with people in the position of power and influence regarding
land policy decisions. The essence of this strategy was to cultivate patronage
relationships. During the colonial era, Mandinka women had relied on custom
to access and control land (*kamanyango*) which could also be transferred to
their daughters.[72] It was a common practice in swamps areas particularly, in
the Central River Region cleared by women for food production, rice cultivation in particular.

The dynamic of colonial legacies which manifested in the post-colonial
Gambia created layers of complexities in land ownership. For instance, the
land was grouped into freehold land, customary tenure, and leasehold.[73] The
freehold land tenure, introduced during the British colonial rule allowed for
gifts of land to individuals and companies outrightly for different motives.
The beneficiaries had free access and use of the gifted land. In comparison,
customary land tenure had its root in the provincial areas and was highly
influenced by Islamic law and cultural practices.[74] Usually, the person who
claimed a piece of land would become the founder and regulator of the property locally called *Alkaloo*. Such land could pass to later generations through
inheritance. This family or clan often followed customary land tenure for sub-
sistence farming. The leasehold land tenure system in The Gambia involved
a mutual agreement between the landowner and someone for temporary land
use in exchange for rent.[75]

Kafoolu utilized their power of collective action to have access to land for
agricultural purposes. Due to its increase in value, land has become politicized. The politics of land ownership led to a major source of conflict.[76] As
a result, *kafoolu* had to collaborate with local authorities (namely *alkalolu* or
individual landowners), to borrow land usually on a seasonal basis. In Kiang,
for instance, women *kafoo* borrowed land from individual owners instead.[77]
Similarly, in Kenya, women's groups accessed land for their food production
through similar means. Their approach, however, appeared to be more radical. This practice was exemplified in the research of Leslie Gray and Michael
Kevane. According to them, organized women's groups acted politically
to challenge the existing conditions.[78] These groups marched and protested
against local state authorities. Their collective action helped to enhance their
voice and allowed them to influence outcomes in land tenure cases.[79]

In the post-colonial Gambia, *kafoolu* approached donor agencies to obtain
funds. For example, Action Aid, European Union, and locally-based NGOs
provided *kafoolu* farming tools, seeds, fertilizers, and technical advice.[80]

These organizations assisted women through *kafoolu* to fence their garden plots. Additionally, the drought experienced in The Gambia from the 1970s led to the introduction of development initiatives to address access and control to land issues in the North Bank Region. It took collaborative efforts of different actors to diversify the rural economy response to the drought crisis.[81] These interventions were sponsored by small grants from agencies interested in Women in Development (WID), NGOs, voluntary agencies, and the state. This initiative was meant to help promote small-scale businesses operated by women, such as the cultivation of fruit tree orchards. Businesses and the orchards, however, were mainly controlled by men. Another initiative was a joint land for rice cultivation for family consumption purposes dominated by women. Specifically, in Badibu Kerewan, *kafoolu* were funded by NGOs. The project lasted for more than twenty years, starting in 1977 and over one hundred communities of women gardeners benefited from donor support across the country during this period.[82]

The increased land reforms witnessed in the 1980s were influenced by the customary system's failure to promote security and agricultural investment of land. The absence of clearly defined and enforceable property rights, as well as an appropriate policy that would take the right direction, were the causes of these challenges.[83] Pauline Peters argued that land reforms became priority areas of development for African governments since independence.[84] But such progress created a contradiction between "statutory and customary law, formal and informal land tenure."[85] Some of these reforms and titling programs from the 1970s to 1980s failed to achieve their goals of promoting agricultural investment and productivity. Nor did they enforce the use of land as collateral in loans for small farmers. Consequently, it deprived the very people who should have been protected of support through titling. It, therefore, widened unequal access to land mostly based on gender and other categories, including ethnicity and class.[86] In the case of women, their lack of collateral limited their financial opportunities especially when seeking loans either from foreign or Gambian banks.[87]

As has been noted, an increase in land value caused a tremendous decline in women's access to land due to discriminatory laws and customs.[88] Women's access to agricultural land that provided income was generally the only right they exercised. For instance, some men took advantage of their authority to dominate women. Those women whose rights to farm plots were endorsed through the help of their husbands because of their marital status often lost their land rights once they faced a marital crisis, and it has led to much more economic and social uncertainty for women.[89] Although granting farmlands to women was progressive, it had created inconsistency in land access and control caused by socio-cultural factors.

Scholarship has demonstrated the relevance of women farmers in Gambian agriculture.[90] In the Gambian context, the land is an asset; it was a source of income, power, and influence. But family dynamics and gender shaped the possession of the land. Rural women had engaged in rice cultivation in "traditional swamplands." Nonetheless, agricultural transformation led to the rise of the "garden boom" in the 1980s and 1990s, causing a dramatic change in irrigation schemes. This transformation led to more demand for farmlands. While rice production declined due to low rainfall, the garden boom allowed women to cultivate all year round without interruption.[91] This demand for communal labor was evidence of a rise in *kafoolu* as a powerful platform for rural women as they continued to strive to become relevant actors in the country's informal sector.

In recent time, *kafoolu* has adopted a radical approach through a collaborative effort with local agencies and local authorities to register farmlands that would give permanent ownership to these women. An interviewee who was instrumental in this process explained that:

> . . . We go to the villages, talk to the villagers, to the local authorities, talk to the landowners through our own approach, we don't use legal approach, we are using our own approach because in every district we have our committee, a land advocacy committee and that constitutes the chief, the *alkalos* of the villages, an extension worker, community development worker and the women leader in that community.[92]

NAWFA embarked on Land Advocacy for Rural Farmers, mainly women. Through such collaboration with the Female Lawyers Association of The Gambia (FLAG), *kafoolu* were able to register over three thousand hectares.[93] The process of land ownership passed through a hierarchy of authorities.

First, the land process began with a commissioner—now changed to a governor—of a region who would summon all the chiefs for a meeting. This step was followed by a report from a *kafoo*, and once the governor accepted, chiefs would have to give their consent in favor of it. Some interviewees observed that they were surprised to discover that sometimes *alkaloolu* possessed no land.[94] This is because people assumed an *alkalo* to be sole owners of land in rural Gambia; however, some of them were involved in unscrupulous activities by selling land to multiple individuals, all of whom believed they were the sole proprietors. Through collective efforts of an *alkalo* and *kafoolu*, the legal owners of land were invited for discussion and encouraged to give their consent to women's access to the land.[95] Once the owner, usually a man, responded in positive all the parties, landowners, members of a *kafoo* and the governor had to sign the legal documents FLAG prepared. This would establish a legal authorization to use the land and to transfer ownership. Some of these arrangements were not free of charge. Most of the local authorities were provided tokens to participate in the process. It was claimed that without incentives, these authorities were not expected to consent to address the conditions of women. To justify this action, Jawo pointed out that " . . . this is development politics, once you get the consent of the governor, the governor will summon all the chiefs, and nobody dares to be absent. This one is the top-bottom approach."[96]

Other times, the approach began from the bottom with the *alkaloo*. But the problem associated with this approach was that some of them sometimes refused to meet these women's groups. As a result, different means were used to conduct such courtesy call. By way of demonstration, one of such means was to:

> . . . convince the governor with nice workshops, nice lunch, nice allowance . . . they will be motivated to do something. Then once you get the governor, the governor will summon all the chiefs on a Saturday, they will come and when they come the governor will say yes it makes sense, what you say yes makes sense. And he summons the chiefs in various chieftaincies to summon all the *alkalos* to make sure that they support these people because these people are here to support our women. Then we meet the *alkalos* and the incentives were a continuous process, we give it to different levels may be different amounts [laughs]. This is development politics, so now the chief will call the *alkalos* and the *alkalos* will come . . .[97]

Substantially, *kafoolu* made concerted efforts to access village land by embarking on different approaches. This way they were able to explore political collaborations with local authorities and politicians to attain a socio-political and economic advantage.

POLITICAL PARTNERSHIP OF WOMEN AND POLITICAL LEADERSHIP

Gambian politicians have used political patronage to gain support. This practice was evident in the 1960s with the emergence of new political parties competing for a strong political base. Women mobilized to secure political patronage. Ethnicity and regionalism were cultivated and promoted for political ends. This resulted in fostering division between the urban and rural areas. In other words, British officials purposefully created political fragmentation by encouraging regional political identities. For example, the formation of the PPP was a major political shift because, until 1959, the rural population was unrepresented. Thus, it came to symbolize the marginalized Protectorate. The extension of enfranchisement to the rural areas exacerbated the struggle for recognition among parties. Knowing the political rivalry between the UP and the PPP, Governor Sir Edward Henry Windley in 1961 appointed Pierre S. N'Jie as the first chief minister despite UP having a smaller number of seats (five versus nine seats of the PPP). As a protest to this appointment, Jawara and Sheriff Sisay resigned from the Executive Council. Therefore, the 1962 election cemented partisanship, ethnicity, and political patronage in the country's history.[98] During this election, the major parties were UP and the PPP. The leader of UP, Pierre S. N'Jie who was also the Chief Minister, gained the support of the chiefs.[99] The PPP, however, embarked on a face-to-face campaign and concentrated on the farmers' support.[100] From this date onwards, the PPP came to symbolize with rural population who were legally excluded from the national political scene by the colonial government.

Kafoolu and *kompins* provided resources and support for political parties. As indicated previously, women's collective action led political parties to recognize their potential local influence and seek the support of women's organizations during elections. *Kompins* became political allies with GMC, UP and PPP who sought to work with these women groups. They directly linked with the women's wing of political parties led by *yai kompins*. A *yai kompin* literary means "mother of association" but technically referring to a female leader or representative. They have played mentorship roles to community members and have made sure that members recognize the need to participate in development work. Through these activities, they have become a strong mobilization force, instrumental to politics. Most interviewees agreed women in advanced age assume the position of *yai kompins*. These women are eloquent, relatively "wealthy," and from "important" families and traits that propelled them to a position of leadership. Many were the wives or daughters of important local men, such as an imam, *alkalo* or successful trader themselves.[101] They are opinionated, skillful individuals who worked to expand their organization's political engagement with a diverse national population. Women's grassroots organizations endorsed and canvassed votes for their candidates during elections because voters listened to them. They sometimes supported the political goals of men close to them. Also, they hired vehicles to transport voters to polling stations.[102]

Kafoolu and *kompins* embarked on fundraising and persuasion thereby facilitating political conversations as well as local diplomacy. They collaborated with the Women's Bureau; an institution put in place by the Gambia government to investigate policies concerning women issues. It aimed to promote women in national development.[103] Through them, politicians were able to collaborate with urban and rural women for political gains. Much of that influence was also the product of the effective advocacy of these women. Using contributions of their members, women's organizations supplemented the organization and entertainment efforts of political parties and candidates, providing, among other things, *asobee*, food, water, and drinks for their political gatherings.[104]

African women's collective action was instrumental to liberation struggles across the continent. Scholars such as Filomina Chioma Steady, Susan Geiger, Deborah Pellow, Elizabeth Schmidt and Ampofo Akosua Adomako have examined the way women's political participation transformed societies and the roles movements played either in societal success or failure.[105] Geiger describes women as being "neglected" despite their efforts and linked this constraint to patriarchy. These scholars hold the view that African women's political participation diminished after independence largely due to illiteracy.[106] The findings of the present study, however, suggest that women's grassroots organizations were significant political actors in spite of their illiteracy.

Kafoolu and *kompins* have increased women's political engagement through the organization of political activities.[107] Their pivotal role in the 1970 referendum emblematizes their achievement of political influence at a decisive moment in Gambian history. During the change to a republican government, Prime Minister Jawara faced massive opposition after his administration decided to hold the referendum. But in October 1969, women in Saba assured Jawara that they would campaign for its success. Similarly, in Fass Chaho, women affirmed their support during Jawara's visit.[108] Women were therefore at the forefront of the PPP campaign for the republic. Gambian women were loyal followers of the PPP leader. Their position was not grounded so much on political ideology but on the notion that "God chooses a leader," more of a cheerleader role. He was charismatic and had the firm support of women. Consequently, UP, which opposed the call for a republican status, failed to secure the majority vote. The success of the PPP during this referendum made numerous personalities from various parties shift allegiance to the PPP. This erratic changing of loyalty speaks volume of the country's political leadership and its direction.

From all indications, the political relationship and collaboration that existed between women and the country's political leaders remained asymmetrical. These women used their resources, energy, and time, but their compensation has been inconsequential compared to their political input. They calculated that politicians would work to create solutions to their problems by providing them social amenities such as markets, schools, boreholes, health centers, and good roads. By focusing their efforts on securing votes for their candidates, instead of promoting critical political debate on policy issues, women in these organizations ended up doing the bidding of political parties. As a Prime Minister, Jawara had the authority to appoint the cabinet members of his government. All eight appointed ministers were men except

Lucretia St. Claire Joof who was nominated to the House of Representatives two years earlier.[109]

The ability of these women to contribute to this referendum was connected to their extensive networks across the country, specifically the *kafoolu*'s well-established history in the rural Gambia and *kompins*' political trajectory in Bathurst. These women's organizations grew their members' socio-economic and political advancement. Yet it failed to lead to women's increased political representation. Their collectivity was a useful mechanism in partnership with politicians. It, therefore, enhanced a significant transformation, especially where *kafoolu* have made concerted efforts to gain increased access to village land. Political partnership of women's organizations contributed to the success of the referendum. Yet this relationship culminated into political patronage between the *kafoolu/kompins* and the male-dominated parties and government.

BIBLIOGRAPHY

Action Guide for Advocacy and Citizen Participation. Warwickshire: Practical Action Publishing, 2007. https://justassociates.org/en/resources/new-weave-power-people -politics-action-guide-advocacy-and-citizen-participation

Almeida, Ralphina P. *A Panoramic Portrait of the Contribution of Gambian Women to National Social, Political and Economic Development: 1880–2014.* Banjul: Ralphina A. Phillot-Almeida, 2014.

Berger, Iris. *Women in Twentieth Century Africa: New Approaches to African History.* Cambridge: Cambridge University Press, 2016.

Carney, Judith. "Converting the Wetlands, Engendering the Environment: The Intersection of Gender with Agrarian Change in the Gambia." *Economic Geography* 69, no. 4 (Oct. 1993).

Carney, Judith and Michael Watts. "Manufacturing Dissent: Work, Gender and the Politics of Meaning in a Peasant Society." *Africa* 60, no. 2 (1990).

Ceesay, Ebrima J. *The Military and Democratization in The Gambia: 1994–2003.* Victoria, BC: Trafford, 2006.

Ceesay, Hassoum. *Gambian Women: An Introductory History.* Kanifing: Fulladu Publisher, 2007.

———. "Women's Association and Social Development in Bathurst, 1925–1965." In *Africa History and Culture*, edited by Mariama Khan and Mkodzongi, 32–42. Dubuque: Kendall Hunt publishing, 2020.

Chant, Sylvia. "Dangerous Equations? How Female-Headed Households Became the Poorest of the Poor: Causes, Consequences, and Cautions." In *Feminisms in Development: Contradictions, Contestations, and Challenges.* Eds. Andrea Cornwall, Elizabeth Harrison, and Ann Whitehead, 35–47. New York: Zed Books, 2007.

Chant, Sylvia and Isatou Touray. "Women and Gender in *The Gambia: Problems, Progress and Prospects.*" In *State and Society in The Gambia since Independence, 1965–2012*, edited by Abdoulaye Saine, Ebrima Ceesay, and Ebrima Sall. New Jersey: African World Press, 2013.

Chuku, Gloria. "Igbo Women and Political Participation in Nigeria, 1800s-2005." *International Journal of African Historical Studies* 42, no. 1 (2009).

Fallon, Kathleen M. *Democracy and the Rise of Women's Movements in Sub-Saharan Africa.* Baltimore, MD: The Johns Hopkins University Press, 2008.

Finkel, Steven E. "Civic Education and Mobilization of Political Participation in Developing Democracies." *The Journal of Politics* 64, no. 4 (Nov. 2002): 994–1020.

Fourshey, Cymone. "Women in the Gambia." Faculty Contributions to Books, 2019.

Gailey, Harry A. *A History of The Gambia.* London: Routledge and Kegan Paul, 1964.

Geiger, Susan. "Women in Nationalist Struggle: TANU Activists in Dar es Salaam." *International Journal of African Historical Studies* 20, no. 1 (1987): 1–26.

Geisler, Gisela. "Troubled Sisterhood: Women and Politics in Southern Africa: Case Studies from Zambia, Zimbabwe and Botswana." *African Affairs* 94, no. 377 (Oct. 1995): 545–578.

———. *Women and Remaking of History in South Africa: Negotiating Autonomy, Incorporation and Representation.* Uppsala, Sweden: Nordiska Afrikainstitutet, 2004.

Gray, John M. *A History of The Gambia.* London: Frank Cass, 1966.

Hughes, Arnold and David Perfect. "From Green Uprising to National Reconciliation: The People's Progressive Party in the Gambia 1959–1973." *Canadian Journal of African Studies* 9, no. 1 (1975).

"Gambian Electoral Politics: 1960–2912." In *State and Society in The Gambia since Independence, 1965–2012.* Edited by Abdoulaye Saine, Ebrima Ceesay, and Ebrima Sall. Trenton, NJ: African World Press, 2013.

———. *A Political History of The Gambia: 1816–1994.* Rochester, NY: University of Rochester Press, 2006.

Jawara, Dawda K. *Kairaba.* West Sussex: Domtom, 2009.

Jonson-Odim, Cheryl and Nina Emma Mba. *For Women and the Nation: Funmilayo Ransome-Kuti of Nigeria.* Chicago: University of Illinois Press.

Kea, Pamela. *Land, Labour and Entrustment: West African Female Farmers and the Politics of Difference.* Boston: Brill Publishing, 2010.

Le Vine, Victor T. "The Fall and Rise of Constitutionalism in West Africa." *The Journal of Modern African Studies* 35, no. 2 (1997).

Longwe, Sara Hlupekile. "Towards Realistic Strategies for Women's Political Empowerment in Africa." *Gender and Development* 8, no. 3 (Nov. 2000).

Matera, Marc Misty L. Bastian and Susan Kingsley Kent. *The Womens War of 1929: Gender and Violence in Colonial Nigeria.* New York: Palgrave Macmillan, 2012.

Olagbaju, Oladotun Opeoluwa. "Research Article Adult Literacy and Skill Acquisition Programmes as Correlates of Women Empowerment and Self-Reliance in The Gambia." *Hindawi Education Research International* (Feb. 2020)

Pearson, Ruth. "Reassessing Paid Work and Women's Empowerment: Lessons from the Global Economy." In *Feminisms in Development: Contradictions, Contestations, and Challenges,* edited by Andrea Cornwall, Elizabeth Harrison, and Ann Whitehead. New York: Zed Books, 2007.

Pellow, Deborah. "Solidarity among Muslim Women in Accra, Ghana." *Anthropos* 82, no. 4/6 (1987): 489–506.

Perfect, David. *Historical Dictionary of The Gambia,* 5th ed. New York: Rowman and Littlefield, 2016.

Saho, Bala. Contours *of Change: Muslim Courts, Women, and Islamic Society in Colonial Bathurst, the Gambia, 1905–1965.* Michigan: Michigan State University Press, 2018.

Saine, Abdoulaye. *Culture and Customs of Gambia.* California: Greenwood, 2012.

———. "The Coup d'états in The Gambia, 1994: The End of the First Republic." Armed Forces & Society 23, no. 1, (1996): 97–111.

———. "The Gambia's Elected Autocrat Poverty, Peripherality, and Political Instability." 1994–2006 Political Economy Assessment (Feb. 2008).

———.*The Paradox of Third-Wave Democratization in Africa: The Gambia under AFPRC-APRC, 1994–2008.* Lanham, MD: Lexington Books, 2009.

———. "The Soldier-Turned—Presidential Candidate: A Comparison of Flawed 'Democratic' Transition in Ghana and Gambia.*" Journal of Political and Military Sociology* 28, no. 2 (2000).

Sallah, Halifa. *The Road to Self Determination and Independence.* Serekunda: People's Centre for Social Sciences, Research, Civic Awareness and Community Initiatives, 2010.

Sarr, Assan. "Women, Land and Power in the Lower Gambia River Region." In *African Women in the Atlantic World: Property, Vulnerability and Mobility, 1660–1880,* edited by Mariana P. Candido and Adam Jones, 38–54. Woodbridge, UK: Boydell and Brewer Limited, 2019.

Schmidt, Elizabeth. *Mobilizing the Masses*: *Gender, Ethnicity, and Lass in Guinea, 1939–1958.* Portsmouth: Heinemann, 2005.

Schroeder, Richard. "Gone to Their Second Husbands: Marital Metaphors and Conjugal Contracts in the Gambia's Female." *Canadian Journal of African Studies* 30 (1996): 69–87.

Shipton, Parker. "The Control of Land on the Upper Gambia River: A Description with Policy Implications APAP." Collaborative Research Report, no. 352 (Sept. 1993): 12–14.

Sonko-Godwin, Patience. *Ethnic Groups of the Gambia.* Banjul: BPMRU, 1986.

———. *Leaders of the Senegambia Region: Reactions to European Infiltration 19th-20th Century.* Banjul: Sunrise Publisher, 1995

———. *Trade in the Senegambia Region: From the 12th to the Early 21st Century.* Banjul: Sunrise Publisher, 2014.

Steady, Filomina Chioma. *Women and Collective Action in Africa Development, Democratization, and Empowerment, with Special Focus on Sierra Leone.* New York: Palgrave Macmillan, 2006.

Sudarkasa, Niara. "The 'Status of Women' in Indigenous African Societies." *Readings in Gender in Africa* (2005).

Tamale, Sylvia. "Gender Trauma in Africa: Enhancing Women's Links to Resources." *Journal of African Law* 48, no. 1 (2004).

Thornton, John K. "Women in the Kingdom of Kongo: Historical Perspectives on Women's Political Power." *Journal of African History* 47, no. 3 (2006).

Tripp, Aili Mari, Isabel Joy Kwesiga and Alice Mungwa. *African Women's Movements: Transforming Political Landscapes.* Cambridge University Press, 2009.

Newspapers and Magazines

AWA Magazine, June to December 1991.

Foroyaa Newspaper, September 1988 to November 1991.

The Gambia Echo, October 1966.

Gambia Magazine, October 1989 to December 1995.

The Gambia News Bulletin, June 1975.

New Gambia, Bathurst, February to November 1966.

Weekend Observer, February to July 1995.

Archives

CSO 2/2466 The women war and Bust Bees

CSO 2/1695 Report on Methodist Girls High School

CSO 2/907 Land and Survey Ordinance

CSO 2/938 Domestic Training of Girls

CSO 2/938 Taxation Imposition on the People

CSO 2/850 Fish Control of Price

CSO 2/978 Domestic Training Scholarship

LGO 1/24 Women's Education

NGP 1 Gambia Echo, 1936–1971

Reports

The Gambia Government Development Program, 1964–67, Sessional Paper No 10. of 1964. Bathurst, Government Printer, 1964.

The Gambia Government Development Program, 1967–68 to 1970/71, Sessional Paper No 4 of 1967. Bathurst, Government Printer, 1967.

Report on the Progress of Gambianisation of the Civil Service, March 1962 to May 1964, Sessional Paper No. 20 of 1964. Bathurst, Government Printer, 1964.

NOTES

1. Dawda K. Jawara, *Kairaba* (West Sussex: Domtom, 2009), 274.

2. Alieu Jabang, "Halifa: April 24 Important in Gambian Calendar," *The Point Newspaper*, April 27, 2009.

3. Six months prior to the referendum, the Republic Bill was published and approved by the House of Representatives.

4. All interviewees unanimously asserted that women played a crucial role in Gambian politics. Binta Jammeh-Sidibe affirmed that her mother was a very active kafoo leader since the 1960s whose efforts and other women shaped her political orientation in serving people. Her future husband, Bakary Sidibe was also very active in politics and he was among the founding members of PPP. Sidibe was also a kafoo leader for men. Some interviewees claimed that women even sold their valuable such as jewelries to invest in politics in the 1960s and the 1970s.

5. Cheryl Jonson-Odim and Nina Emma Mba and Nina Emma Mba, *For Women and the Nation: Funmilayo Ransome-Kuti of Nigeria* (Chicago: University of Illinois Press, 1997), 99–152; Schmidt, "Women Take the Lead"; Hassoum Ceesay, *Gambian Women: An Introductory History* (Kanifing: Fulladu Publisher, 2007); Almeida, *A Panoramic Portrait of the Contribution of Gambian Women*, 4–25.

6. Gisela Geisler, *Women and Remaking of Politics in Southern Africa: Negotiating Autonomy, Incorporation, and Representation* (Nordiska Afrikainstitutet, 2004), 208.

7. *Kafoo* (pl. *kafoolu* meaning traditional associations in Mandinka) operates in rural and peri-urban areas. While *kompins* (meaning associations/ organizations in Wolof) operate in urban settings. The name, however, does not affect the membership. Both *kafoolu* and *kompins* constitute different ethnolinguistic references of The Gambia. Binta Jammeh-Sidibe, telephone interview, July 31, 2020; Dusuba Touray, interview, Wuli Sutukonding, August 17, 2020.

8. Arnold Hughes and David Perfect, *A Political History of The Gambia: 1816–1994* (New York: University of Rochester Press, 2006), 1–2.

9. "Gambia 2013 Population Census," n.d., https://www.gbosdata.org/downloads/census-2013

10. Berkeley Rice, *Enter Gambia: The Birth of an Improbable Nation* (Boston, MA: Houghton Mifflin, 1967).

11. Lamin Sanneh, "Foreword," in *State and Society: The Gambia Since Independence, 1965–2012,* eds. Abdoulaye Saine, Ebrima Ceesay, and Ebrima Sall (Trenton, NJ: African World Press, 2013), xxviii.

12. Ibid.

13. Some of Aku's descendants came from different parts of West Africa particularly, Sierra Leone and Nigeria. For an insightful reading, see Patience Sonko-Godwin, *Trade in the Senegambia Region: from the 12th to the Early 21st Century* (Banjul: Sunrise publisher, 2004), 177–240.

14. National Archive file C.58S; CSO 3/205 appointment of unofficial representation of Legislative Council.

15. Sonko-Godwin, "Impact of the Abolition of the Slave Trade and Slavery in the Senegambia Region," in *Trade in the Senegambia Region: From the 12th to the Early 21st Century* (Banjul: Sunrise Publisher, 2014), 148.

16. Some of these organizations had engaged in philanthropic work such as the women's corona society that supplied food and clothing to the poor and needy in the Gambian society.

17. *Osusu* is monetary contributions (but not limited to monetary value) that has been accumulated by members of a group. Such a contribution is collected by individual members on rotational basis either weekly, biweekly, monthly, or even daily; it depends on the goal of the association. It is a form of micro finance or cooperative society strategy for commonwealth. This kind of scheme cements the group to remain together and stay loyal to their political patrons.

18. Wolof dance of which sounds are created from the beating drum(s).

19. A few individuals such as Cecilia Moore and Hannah Forster, however, were prominent in the city council politics.

20. See Ceesay, *Gambian Women: An Introductory History,* 43 and 70.

21. See Sonko-Godwin, "The Settler Colonies of Sierra Leone and Liberia-Achievements and Contributions of Blacks to the Development of West Africa," in *Trade in the Senegambia Region*, 225–230.

22. See Ceesay, *Gambian Women: An Introductory History,* 41.

23. Ibid.

24. *New Gambia*, Friday, March 11, 1966.

25. The governor (with the assistance of the Legislative and Executive Councils) was responsible for administering the colony. He was accountable to the Secretary of State for the colonies. It is important to note that the British colonial rule led to dividing the country into Colony and Protectorate. While the former was directly governed by the British, they used the indirect rule system to administer the latter.

26. Ceesay, *Gambian Women: An Introductory History,* 94.

27. Quoted in J.H. Price's article on "Some notes on the influence of women in Gambian politics," published in Institute of Social and Economic Research, Conference proceedings, December 1958, 151–158.

28. See David Perfect, *Historical Dictionary of The Gambia,* 5th ed. (New York: Rowman and Littlefield, 2016), 99.

29. Governor Edward Windley was crucial in this process based on his efforts in convening these conferences. David Perfect noted that Windley was receptive to Gambians' proposal for constitutional reforms, unlike his predecessor.

30. Small was a nationalist journalist, and trade unionist. He became the first African to be elected to the Legislative Council in November of 1947.

31. See Nana Grey-Johnson, *Edward Francis Small: Watchdog of The Gambia,* 3rd ed (Banjul: Media & Development Specialists Publishing Co. Ltd., 2013), 1–122.

32. Swaibou Touray, telephone interview by author, October 17, 2020.

33. Ibid.

34. Small was a nationalist journalist, and a trade unionist. He won the first Legislative election in February 1947.

35. See *Foroyaa Newspaper,* February 21, 2016; Perfect, *Historical Dictionary of The Gambia,* 401–404.

36. See Sonko-Godwin, *Leaders of the Senegambia Region: Reactions to European Infiltration 19th to 20th Century* (Banjul: Sunrise Publisher, 1995), 85;

Sonko-Godwin, *Social and Political Structures in the Pre-Colonial Period: Ethnic Groups of the Gambia* (Banjul: Sunrise Publisher, 1986), 70. In *Leaders of the Senegambia Region,* Sonko-Godwin noted that the Protectorate was areas locally controlled by indigenous people. They appeared to be autonomous, but they were under the supervision of the British colonial government's representatives known as Travelling Commissioners who enforced the implementation of colonial laws. The Protectorate was divided into five divisions, each of which was sub-divided into districts.

37. The Protectorate was excluded from national politics. See Hughes and Perfect, *A Political History of The Gambia: 1816–1994,* 134–139; Arnold Hughes, "From Green Uprising to National Reconciliation: The People's Progressive Party in the Gambia 1959–1973," *Canadian Journal of African Studies* 9, no. 1 (1975): 62–65.

38. Almeida, *A Panoramic Portrait of the Contribution of Gambian Women,* 5–6.

39. Hassoum Ceesay, "I.M. Garba Jahumpa: Educationist, Nationalist and Pan-Africanist," *Weekend Observer*, February 7–9, 1995.

40. Most of the developments that occurred in women's struggle happened in the city. Little evidence was about women's political strife in the rural areas. From the evidence, one for this was the influence of Islamic religion and the practice of patriarchal culture. To many, the joy of womanhood was to have a successful marriage, and one's children become thriving in their endeavor as breadwinners of their families and good wives and mothers in their matrimony. Active politics was not a place for ordinary women in Gambian society. However, such perceptions became gradually replaced by an ambition to involve in politics, not to aspire as candidates in most cases but to vote for their male counterparts, usually along with religion or ethnic lines.

41. The delegates composed of Rachel Palmer, M.E. Jallow, Henry Madi who represented the independent voices, Omar Mbacke represented the chiefs, David Jawara, and Sheriff Saikouba Sisay for the PPP, I.M. Jahumpa and Rev. J.C. Fay for Democratic Congress Alliance, while United Party was represented by P.S. N'Jie and Michael Baldeh. Palmer's father was a secretary to the Legislative Council through she developed an interest and helped her father in writing minutes and clerical works where politicians knew. Her nomination was unanimously accepted said in her 1995 interview with the Foroyaa Newspaper. She was also instrumental in the National Consultative Committee (NCC) that set up a transitional timetable to a democratic constitutional order for the second republic in 1997. Palmer also served as the Director of the Gambia Red Cross Society for over 20 years and became the Principal of the School of Nursing. She is the mother of the late Poet L. Dr. Lenrie Peters, who served as the chair of the NCC to seek Gambia's opinion about the transition period of the AFPR. See "Women's Affairs," *Foroyaa Newspaper,* May 10, 1995.

42. Ceesay, "Women's Association and Social Development in Bathurst," 32–36.

43. Ibid.

44. Marc Matera, Misty L. Bastian and Susan Kingsley Kent, *The Women's War of 1929: Gender and Violence in Colonial Nigeria* (New York: Palgrave Macmillan, 2012), 1–11.

45. See Cheryl Jonson-Odim and Nina Emma Mba and Nina Emma Mba, *For Women and the Nation: Funmilayo Ransome-Kuti of Nigeria* (Chicago: University of Illinois Press, 1997), 63, 94–95.

46. Schmidt, *Mobilizing the Masses*, 122.

47. DCA was a merger of the Gambia Muslim Congress (GMC) and the Gambia Democratic Party (GDP) in March 1960. Soon after that, the party became inactive due to a slip-up of GMC to form Gambia Congress Party in October 1962. DCA later merged with PPP in 1965. Meanwhile, Augusta was a nurse, women's rights activist, and playwright. She came from a very prominent family in Bathurst. Because of her social status, some of her critics alleged that she would be favored. Augusta Jawara was the wife of the leader of PPP, D. K. Jawara and Sir John Mahoney's daughter, the country's first Speaker of the Legislative Council. The Gambia Echo's June 1960 publication dedicated an editorial paying tribute to the pioneering spirit of both the party and the candidate. The editorial allegedly stated that, despite a barrage of abuses aimed at opponents by some political parties, she stood firm. Through her literacy works and campaign, Augusta Jawara engaged in a variety of activities including sports and culture especially, at the Female Athletics Meeting organized by the Gambia Athletics Association. She attended seminars and based on her wide recognition; she represented the country in Dakar on November 19, 1962 on the theme Advancement of Women in Africa. The program was a concerted effort between the Senegalese government in collaboration with UNESCO. Lady Jawara was known for her exemplary leadership and intellect. She continued to advocate for women's political rights until her demise in 1981. For the detailed information, see Dawda K. Jawara, *Kairaba* (West Sussex: Domtom, 2009), 204–205; Almeida, *A Panoramic Portrait of the Contribution of Gambian Women,* 8–9; *Gambia Echo,* June 1960.

48. There were controversies around Independence because political leaders had different views on how to run the affairs of the state. Garba Jahumpa and P.S N'Jie's viewpoints failed to project complete freedom. Instead, they supported delaying independence. D.K. Jawara and some PPP members, on the other hand, demanded immediate internal self-rule in 1961.

49. See Berkeley Rice, *Enter Gambia; the Birth of an Improbable Nation*, 21–27; Dawda K. Jawara, *Kairaba*, 245–246.

50. Mrs. Julia Howe wrote the country's national anthem constituting three stanzas:
For the Gambia, our homeland
We strive, work, and pray
That all may live in unity
Freedom and peace each
Let justice guide our actions
Towards the common good
And join our diverse peoples
To prove man's brotherhood
We pledge our firm allegiance
Our promise we renew
Keep us, great God of nations
To The Gambia ever true.

51. See Dawda K. Jawara, *Kairaba*, 245–246.

52. Hughes and Perfect, *A Political History of The Gambia*, 2.

53. Lamin Sanneh, "Foreword," in *State and Society: The Gambia Since Independence*, xxviii.

54. Bala Saho, *Contours of Change: Muslim Courts, Women, and Islamic Society in Colonial Bathurst, the Gambia, 1905–1965* (Michigan: Michigan State University Press, 2018), 1–121.

55. The plaintiff who filed against Rex in 1887, was a coos seller locally called *chereh* at Albert market and was alleged of stealing a bag worth two pounds along with a few other items after involving in a barter trade with a destitute who wanted a plate of *chereh* but had no money instead gave her the bag. This act of fair exchange led to her arrest and detention at the Bathurst police station up to the time market women contributed to pay for the said amount. Due to this humiliation, she hired two outstanding men: lawyer Renner Maxwell and John C. Gray to defend her case. Eventually, she won the case. Despite the harsh policies of colonial rule, these women used the legal and economic opportunities to their advantage in the urban area. This detail is found in Saho, *Contours of Change*, 61.

56. Njaga Jawo, interview, Wellingara, October 9, 2020.

57. Swaibou Touray, telephone conversation with author, October 17, 2020.

58. Sulayman Touray, interview, Brikama, October 11, 2020.

59. Binta Jammeh-Sidibe, telephone interview, July 31, 2020; Omar B. Jallow, interview, Serekunda, July 28, 2020.

60. Saho, *Contours of Change*, 120–21.

61. The five Administrative Regions of The Gambia were referred to as Divisions before they were changed in 2007. These divisions were Western Division, North Bank Division, Lower River Division, Central River Division and Upper River Division and Banjul City. See the introductory chapter of the present study for administrative areas.

62. Although early settlers came to Bathurst in large numbers, they were fragmented. They constituted of Europeans who arrived from Senegal with their servants and technicians who were contributory to the construction of the colonial city. There was a group who arrived in search of greener pasture as in the case of Serahuli and Badibunkas. A few came for educational purposes and other opportunities that were available in the city. Among them was a group of settlers who came for safety reasons due to Muslim wars in the region for over five decades. For more detail, read Saho's work on Contours of Change.

63. Ibid.; Kaddy Dibba, interview, Sukuta Nema, October 11, 2020; Hon. Touray is a sitting National Assembly member for Wuli West since 2017.

64. Aja Sima, telephone interview, Bakau, October 11, 2020.

65. Telephone conversations with interviewees: Na Fanta Fatty, Tamba Sansan, Basse, September 10, 2020; Lisa Kanteh, Bundung Borehole, October 12, 2020; Aja Faya Camara, interview, Touba Kotou, Wuli, August 15, 2020; and Kaddy Dibba, interview, Sukuta Nema, October 11, 2010.

66. Na Fanta Fatty, telephone interview, Tamba Sansan, Basse, September 10, 2020.

67. Ya Sainabou Panneh was a leader of both kafoo and kompin in the North Bank Region. She has been instrumental in politics from Presidents Jawara, Jammeh to Barrow as a *yai kompin;* Fatoumata Jahumpa-Ceesay (former speaker at the National Assembly), in discussion with the author, August 28, 2020.

68. Judith Carney and Michael Watts, "Manufacturing Dissent: Work, Gender and the Politics of Meaning in a Peasant Society," *Africa* 60, no. 2 (1990): 207–241; Cymone Fourshey, "Women in the Gambia," Faculty Contributions to Books (2019), https://digitalcommons.bucknell.edu/fac books/179; Londa Vanderwal et al., "Participatory Approach to Identify Interventions to Improve the Health, Safety, and Work Productivity of Smallholder Women Vegetable Farmers in the Gambia," *International Journal of Occupational Medicine and Environmental Health* 24, no. 1 (2011): 36–47; William G. Moseley, Judith Carney, Laurence Becker and Susan Hanson, "Neoliberal Policy, Rural Livelihoods, and Urban Food Security in West Africa: A Comparative Study of The Gambia, Côte d'Ivoire, and Mali," *Proceedings of the National Academy of Sciences of the United States of America* 104, no. 13 (March 2010): 5774–5779.

69. Jaga Jawo was an agriculture extension and development worker. His work exposed him to every part of the country and he has been working with *kafoolu* across The Gambia.

70. Na Fanta Fatty, telephone interview, Tamba Sansan, Basse, September 10, 2020; Aja Faya Camara, interview, Touba Kotou, Wuli, August 15, 2020.

71. See Mawdo Jatta, interview, Wuli, October 18, 2020; Na Fanta Fatty, Tamba Sansan, Basse, September 10, 2020.

72. *Kamanyango,* a traditional practice of land acquisition meant purposely for women and not for family use (one meant for the entire family is called *maruwoo*). *Kamanyango* is an uncultivated arable land which she may clear for herself purposely for her personal use and it can be transferred to the woman's daughters, daughter in law or mother-in-law. Sanna Jaina, telephone conversation, December 14, 2020.

73. Abdoulie Dibba, telephone interview, November 21, 2020.

74. During colonial rule, the protectorates were "British protected persons" instead of subjects until 1960 when they had equal constitutional and legal rights as experienced in the colony. The term Protectorate was removed and renamed Provinces soon after independence in the mid-1960s. Till today, most people refer to the rural Gambia as provinces.

75. Dibba former columnist—"Farmer's eyes" at *Foroyaa Newspaper*, which monitors and reports on issues that hinder development in the rural Gambia. The 1990 Lands Act of The Gambia provides for 99-year leaseholds.

76. Such conflict caused intensified competition of land use, control, and ownership.

77. Rural women have no total or permanent control over land use and allocation in most cases. In most Mandinka communities, Kaur and Kuntaur specifically, women could receive land as a gift from their parents. These gifts could in return be inherited by their children including daughters. A similar practice is common among the Jola. Under such circumstances, the right to land is permanently owned. Some of the interviewees also emphasized that this applies to communal land, but the system is

changing. Women can secure land by themselves if they can purchase it either from individual owners or real estate. Most importantly, inheritance in Islam, daughters get half of what the sons have from their fathers' inheritance whereas they have an equal share of the property from their mother's inheritance.

78. Leslie Gray and Michael Kevane, "Diverted Exclusion: Women and Land Tenure in Sub-Saharan African," *African Studies Review* 42, no. 2 (Sept. 1999): 28–29.

79. Ibid.

80. Na Fanta Fatty, Tamba Sansan, Basse, September 10, 2020. Some women observed that sometimes assistance from donors through consultation with the government was selective on most occasions as to which *kafoo* was sympathetic to the government.

81. Richard A. Schroeder, "'Re-claiming' Land in the Gambia: Gendered Property Rights and Environmental Intervention," *Annals of the Association of American Geographers* 87, no. 3 (Sep. 1997): 487–508.

82. Ibid., 490.

83. Pauline E. Peters, "Challenges in Land Reform in Africa: Anthropological Contributions," *World Development* 37, no. 8, (2009): 1317–18.

84. Ibid., 1317.

85. Ibid., 1318.

86. Ibid.

87. Binta Jammeh-Sidibe, telephone interview, July 31, 2020. Jammeh-Sidibe has been a strong advocate for women's empowerment in the country. She was the Executive Director of the Women's Bureau and currently serves as the head of the local organizing committee for the 16th heads of state and government summit of the Organization of Islamic Cooperation. She is highly recognized by people both nationally and internationally through the service of working with women and girls as proprietress of SOBEYA (skill training schools in Churchills and Bakoteh).

88. Gray and Kevane, "Diverted Exclusion: Women and Land Tenure in Sub-Saharan African," 15.

89. Ibid., 32–33.

90. Richard Schroeder, "Gone to Their Second Husbands": Marital Metaphors and Conjugal Contracts in the Gambia's Female," *Canadian Journal of African Studies* 30, no. 1 (1996): 69–87; Pamela Kea, *Land, Labour and Entrustment: West African Female Farmers and the Politics of Difference* (Boston: Brill Publishing, 2010), 1–218; Assan Sarr, "Women, Land and Power in the Lower Gambia River Region," in *African Women in the Atlantic World: Property, Vulnerability and Mobility, 1660–1880,* eds. Mariana P. Candido and Adam Jones (Woodbridge, UK: Boydell and Brewer Limited, 2019), 38–54.

91. Schroeder, "Gone to Their Second Husbands," 69–72.

92. Njaga Jawo, interview, Wellingara, October 9, 2020.

93. Ibid.

94. *Alkaloolu* (sing. *alkaloo* meaning a village-head). This reason might as well explain why Kiang Kamben kafoo in the Lower River Region would borrow land from individual landowners rather than the *alkaloo.*

95. Ibid.; Ya Sainabou Panneh, interview, Fass Chaho, Niumi, August 30, 2020.

96. Njaga Jawo, interview, Wellingara, October 9, 2020.

97. Jawo was the coordinator of this process of land advocacy for rural women.

98. Arnold Hughes, "From Green Uprising to National Reconciliation: The People's Progressive Party in the Gambia 1959–1973," *Canadian Journal of African Studies* 9, no. 1 (1975): 61–62.

99. Despite N'Jie's appointment by the Governor General to head the Executive, full self-government was not attained until 1963.

100. Ibid.; Suwaibou Touray, telephone interview, October 17, 2020; Alagie Jambo Camara, interview, Sutukonding, August 15, 2020. Among the interviewees, Camara and Jatta gave an insightful discussion of the contestation for power between the UP and the PPP.

101. Ya Haddy Panneh's late husband was an alkaloo of Njawara in the North Bank Region. She succeeded him to chieftaincy during the Second Republic after facing opposition before she was unanimously approved. Aja Fanta Basse's husband was a Governor General representing Queen Elizabeth II before the republic. Fatounding Jatta was a successful merchant. Aja Fatou Sallah was also a strong woman of Muslim Congress and Democratic Alliance parties in the 1950s and 1960s.

102. Alagie Demba Sisawo, interview, Sutukoba, August 13, 2020; Fatoumata Jahumpa-Ceesay, telephone conversation with the author, August 28, 2020; Neneh Isatou Jallow, telephone interview by author, October 8, 2020; Sulayman Touray, interview, Brikama, October 11, 2020.

103. Jawara, *Kairaba*, 361; Alagie Jambo Camara, interview, Sutukonding, August 15, 2020.

104. Asobee is a party-uniform (resemblance of a garment worn by members of an association during occasions). It is not restricted to women, but they popularize the idea as an illustration of membership, cooperation, and unity. The word *asobee* may have originated from a Yoruba word, "aso ebi" meaning cloth or dress worn by family (but not limited to) for self-identification or to show solidarity and friendship during ceremonies.

105. Steady, *Women and Collective Action*; Schmidt, "Women Take the Lead"; Susan Geiger, "Women in Nationalist Struggle: TANU Activists in Dar es Salaam"; Deborah Pellow, "Solidarity among Muslim Women in Accra, Ghana," *Anthropos* 82, no. 4/6 (1987): 489–506, https://www.jstor.org/stable/40463476; Ampofo Akosua Adomako, Josephine Beoku-Betts and Mary J. Osirim, "Researching African Women and Gender Studies: New Social Science Perspectives," *African and Asian Studies* 7 (2008): 327–341.

106. Ibid.

107. Ceesay, "Women's Association and Social Development in Bathurst," 31; Almeida, *A Panoramic Portrait of the Contribution of Gambian Women* (2014): 2–3.

108. Ironically, the republican state witnessed the decline of a major opposition party, UP, who orchestrated the failure of the first referendum. Omar Jallow, telephone interview by author, July 18, 2020; Ya Sainabou Panneh, interview, Fass Chaho, August 30, 2020; Jawara, *Kairaba*, 271.

109. Earlier in August that year, a bill was passed to increase number of nominated members from two to four geared toward promoting women.

Chapter 7

Inclusive Education and Impact on Girls

Maria Santiago-Valentín

Access to equitable and inclusive education (IE) for girls was a challenge prior to the COVID-19 pandemic, and it is still a challenge in some countries with higher poverty rates (Acosta and Evans, 2020). Acosta and Evans (2020) analyzed the impact on education when global crises happened in the past. They found that learning loss, increment of household chores for girls, reduction of the countries' financial sources for education due to budget constraints that impact and increase the gender gap that already exists in education. Acosta and Evans (2020) shared that girls in some African countries experienced distress during the Ebola epidemic. For example, in Sierra Leone, girls sold stones, and in Liberia, girls became heads of households. In Zimbabwe, "school location, absent parents, religious beliefs, inadequate resources, irrelevant curriculum, hunger, poverty, early marriage, and teenage pregnancy" were high-risk factors that kept girls out of school prior to COVID-19 (Bucker et al., 2021). These challenges became even greater for some girls with a disability when 190 countries temporarily closed their schools (Carrey et al., 2020; Jones et al., 2021; Ord, 2020; UNICEF, 2020). The inequities and accessibility barriers that before COVID-19 were subtly hidden became visible and evident.

This chapter attempts to define IE, the principles of IE, the challenges families and girls faced to access IE (e.g., broadband access, accommodations modifications due to disabilities), the financial difficulties of the family and the girl after losing a parent or caregiver during the pandemic. The role of the teacher, the methods of instruction, the social-emotional wellbeing of the learners and the educators, and the digital or virtual experience will be reviewed to understand the barriers the educators faced to provide equitable and IE/instruction to girls during the pandemic. Online education aggravated existing inequalities with "an estimated 826 million students do not have a computer at home and an estimated 706 million lack internet access" (UNICEF, 2020, p. 7). Corlatean (2020) shared some alarming statistics from the United Nations Development Program of global learning loss as a result of the pandemic, like the estimated 60% of primary education students who did not have access to the Internet and the estimated 86% of primary education students who missed school in low-income countries. Corlatean (2020) shared that international organizations and agencies' reports showed increased domestic Violence Against Women (VAW) in different countries from Africa and South America, Asia, or Europe.

Among the dangers girls faced during the pandemic, forced marriages and violence were reported (Corlatean, 2020). Prior to the pandemic:

> Persons with disabilities are most at risk of exclusion and marginalization within society and education. In 2020, the situation deteriorated even further, resulting in more than an estimated 32 million children with disabilities being out of school. (GPS, 2021)

After the pandemic, the situation for girls with and without disabilities was exacerbated. Pfunye and Ademola-Popoola (2021) mentioned that the pandemic hit girls living in rural areas with the most challenging economic strains. Many girls were forced to marry for money that their family needed during the pandemic, like Cecilia, a 17-year-old girl in first grade from Zimbabwe, who during the pandemic was married off to an older adult for economic reasons to a man who had two wives and children at that time (Pfunye & Ademola-Popoola, 2021). The effects of the interruption in girls' education in emerging countries will be seen in the rollback of gains in areas related "to poverty reduction, health and wellbeing, inclusive quality education and gender equality" (UNICEF, 2020, p. 2). The closure of schools and jobs to mitigate the impact of the pandemic exposed millions of girls and women to severe risks in less economically distressed countries (Corlatean, 2020).

The UNESCO's COVID-19 Global Education Coalition reported and predicted an increase of 65% of adolescents' pregnancy across sub-Saharan Africa due to the school closings because of the pandemic (Acosta & Evans, 2020; Ord, 2020). Zimbabwe and Sierra Leone have lifted bans that impede access to education for pregnant students (Corlatean, 2020; Ord, 2020). The impact of the pandemic is crystal clear. In Zimbabwe, half of the adolescents reporting to classes are either pregnant, married, or not returning because they are working (Ord, 2020). During the pandemic, forced marriage and VAW, women will result in early pregnancies and girls dropping from school (Burzynska & Contreras, 2020; Corlatean, 2020). The situation in East Asia is alarming. The Malala Foundation reported that more than 20 million girls from k-12 systems are at high risk of leaving school and never returning (Ord, 2020). Mental health challenges were experienced by female medical students in the Philippines (Acosta and Evans, 2020) who might have some knowledge about coping mechanisms and where to seek help. The mental health challenges (trauma for loss, depression, anxiety, etc.) for girls and youth in lower-income countries within a k-12 education system during the pandemic should be investigated since their mental wellbeing determines their ability to learn and bounce back.

Another consequence of the school closures is the increase in dropouts from school for economic reasons. Burzynska and Contreras (2020) shared that parents kept daughters at home even after the schools opened again to have them help at home. If one of the parents in the household died because of COVID-19, the other parent took the financial toll, and as are a result of this, the girls became the caregivers and housemakers while that parent was and is working to support the family. To reimagine and build better education systems to address gender and disabilities, it is imperative to remove the accessibility barriers for children and girls whose socioeconomic conditions aggravated during COVID-19.

BACKGROUND AND SIGNIFICANCE

During the pandemic, access to equitable and IE became an unprecedented global emergency. The topic of IE and its impact on girls will be grounded on Bruner's constructivism and Gardner's multiple intelligences (MI) theories. Aligned with the theory of MI, the Universal Design of Learning (UDL), differentiated instruction, and the creation of a curriculum with a gender perspective will be discussed as best practices for the implementation of an inclusive curriculum. Bruner's classroom offers the learner the ability to put into practice the concepts learned, while Gardner's MI offers the learners the ability to learn through different platforms (online, face to face), modalities, and structures. Assuming all learners have access to digital tools and platforms sets a learning loss scenario for schools in rural areas (De Klerk & Palmer, 2021). By applying and putting together the theoretical frameworks of Bruner and Gardner, I proposed the benefits of hands-on and blended learning with the combination of brick and mortar and remote learning to foster inclusive and gender equity education (Wahyudin et al., 2018). UDL, which is an instructional approach based on the theory of MI, provides the space for differentiated instruction. Meanwhile, before the pandemic in some countries, girls with disabilities were seen as a burden. Their parents encourage marriage and early pregnancies rather than furthering these young girls' education (Hui et al., 2018). This chapter provides factual evidence of the benefits, successes, and challenges (needed to be addressed) after reviewing current articles and studies within seven years about IE and its transformational tenets for girls:

1. Investing in girls is the way to transform our countries and communities— "The correlation between investment in girls' education and economic growth was proliferated by 1980s World Bank research that illustrated how improved access and enrollment of girls in formal schooling led to increased GDP per capita; decreased infant mortality rates and increased life expectancies" (Desai, 2016).
2. Strengths of the countries' economy—only 46% of women participate in the global economy. The world needs educated women for safer, healthier, wealthier communities. It reduces unemployment and poverty.
3. Promotes the Inclusion of women in the job market and, more importantly, in Higher Education spaces as students, researchers, and educators. Creating global indicators for implementing a gender/women curriculum can help address gender equity and equality issues across nations (Canetto, 2019). A curriculum that also intersects with the disabilities and socioeconomic realities of learners in their countries.
4. Impacts their longevity and overall health for productivity—Canetto (2019) mentioned that girls' education may resolve national problems like the spread of STD and HIV, and overpopulation, among other problems. Educating a girl helps the growth of the global economy.

LITERATURE REVIEW

The access to inclusive and quality education for girls and women during the pandemic was problematic and disruptive in many countries (Green, 2021). It is important to remember that gender inequality prior to COVID-19 intersected with other areas such as race, migration status, refugees, gender stereotypes, discrimination, poverty, language barriers, sexism, sexual orientation, and disabilities. At the Global Education Summit, the United Kingdom partnered with Kenya to offer examples of IE (Green, 2021). The summit is an initiative of the organization Global Partnership for Education (GPE) that planned to meet to discuss global funding for education for children and youth with disabilities in countries that struggle with poverty. One of the themes of the summit was Gender Equality. It is essential to acknowledge that funding is needed to provide IE to girls. Gender inequality in education can be addressed if the following behaviors and strategies are put in place: the strength of partnerships, being able to create an educational system that acknowledges gender fluidity that moves away from stereotypes, adults' internal work to operate from a space liberated from bias and stigma, prejudice against students in disadvantage that harm such students. According to Minister of Education in Sierra Leone David Sengeh (GPS, 2021), the inequality goes even further when he acknowledges that the perpetuation of gender stereotypes leads to school bullying and VAW in Sierra Leone. Dr. Gilmore from Harvard University (GPS, 2021) mentioned that many global education systems perpetuate stereotypes by rewarding "gender compliant roles and behaviors." It is time to create a curriculum with inclusive and gender perspectives (GPS, 2021; UNICEF, 2020). Gender disparity in primary schools widens its gap in secondary school and higher education.

Funding and investing in a country's education are strategic for the country's economic growth. That funding includes Investment in better facilities, teacher training/professional development, resources for the teachers and the students. Challenging political systems and faith systems are also strategies to defy the bigotry against women and bring equality in education for poor girls and youth. These are challenging parameters for the leaders in countries who operate within an educational system that reproduces stigma and violence. It is also essential to consider what value education has for girls in low-income communities before creating programs that do not match their needs. Bucker et al. (2020), in their study, shared stories of girls who dropped and who dropped and returned to school, and for some of them, school is the way to mobilize socially, while for others, school or education becomes inconvenient when they are the caregivers and do not know if their younger siblings are being abused or not while they (the girls) are attending school. It became evident that these families need to solve economic and parenting needs before these girls can rejoin school.

Another example of education funding is the World Bank's Inclusive Education & Disability Inclusive Education in Africa Program attempts to solve the implementation of IE in poor countries in relation to funding (GSP, 2021) with small grants that support research and products for students with disabilities. Charlotte McClain-Nhlapo, World Bank Global Disability Advisor (GPS, 2021), explained that the funding for the World Bank's Inclusive Education & Disability Inclusive Education in Africa Program comes from the US and the World Bank manages it. This program, established in 2017 prior to COVID-19, wants to help the poorest countries in Africa and Asia develop and implement IE for students with disabilities and increase access to quality education. This program has three main components: diagnostic criteria to determine a disability and interventions for students with disabilities. It is now to strengthen such criteria in the educational systems of the selected countries, teacher training, and professional development.

BRUNER'S THEORY OF CONSTRUCTIVISM
AND INCLUSIVE EDUCATION

For reopening the schools after COVID, Bruner's classroom offers a project-based learning and hands-on environment for learners of all abilities. The learning environment is a student or learner-centric place for putting into practice the skills learned. Most of the girls might not return to school because they are the caregivers in a home where one of the parents passed away, or because they are the caregivers of younger siblings or had a child of their own due to a forced marriage or VAW need a differentiated curriculum to become sustainable for themselves and those, they are taking care of. Pagán (n.d.) reminded us that Bruner's constructivism situates the learner's environment in their culture. Learning in this context requires adaptation from the learner and the teacher to the new social situation of the girl and women. Creating lessons and a curriculum using constructivism as one of its pillars will allow the learner to solve challenges according to their culture, cognition, experience, age, and gender role in the community they live in. Jerome Bruner's constructivism is pertinent and vital under the context of redesigning education post-COVID-19 is the cultural aspect that influences how a learner will solve a challenge. Pacing and scaffolding are fundamental tenets of Bruner's constructivism (Pagán, n.d.), and precisely a different pace and scaffolding of concepts is what girls and women with and without disabilities who experienced trauma, learning loss need to learn and succeed. The new design requires a teacher who facilitates and listens to the learner. The assessment methods, the instructional strategies, and the integration of the culture and the student's experience in designing an educational program are the foundation of a program that encourages the learner to find and discover knowledge. Problem-solving is one of the most effective ways of instruction under this theory. Constructivism was applied in Brazil in the twentieth century due to high rates of failures in school. Students from rural and low-income areas were failing in urban schools. An educator in Brazil, Helena Antipoff, helped make education more inclusive for low-income students after putting many accommodations; in other words, she started differentiated instruction back then (Pagán, n.d.).

INDIVIDUALIZED EDUCATIONAL PROGRAMS (IEP) IN LOW-INCOME COUNTRIES AND INCLUSIVE EDUCATION

IEPs implementations require legislation, but more importantly, they require funding to access resources, train teachers, and build the capacity of special education programs. On the other hand, an IEP in a low-income country might look different because of financial constraints and insufficient funding for these programs. The 1979 Convention on the Elimination of All Forms of Discrimination against Women acknowledges the right to education for vulnerable groups, including people with disabilities and women, and the 2006 International Convention on the Rights of Persons with Disabilities requires IE (Juma, 2018). Mwabili et al. (2020) conducted a study in Kenya to identify students with learning disabilities under Bruner's constructivism learning theory. The study results showed that most teachers in Kenya used the learner's writing, reading, comprehension, speech, behavior, and academic performance to identify or determine a learning deficit. The study has a limitation in relation to the implementation of IEPs in low-income countries, and it is that it does not share the socioeconomic status and gender of the students and teachers involved in the study. The number of students with disabilities and the number of students with disabilities in need of special education in Kenya is growing (Mwabili et al., 2020). In the past, Kenya did not focus on dyslexia, dyscalculia, or other learning disabilities until in 2017 stories of mistreatment and teachers' lack of patience with students who learn differently were revealed. Juma (2018), in her report, said that inclusive pedagogy/ IE needs to be aligned with the culture and realities of the learner, an aspect that Bruner's constructivism made fundamental for the learning process.

MULTIPLE INTELLIGENCES THEORY AND INCLUSIVE EDUCATION

In light of all the inequities that COVID-19 aggravated and made evident, educational systems must make a paradigm shift in curriculum, instructional strategies, delivery of instruction, resources, assessments to create the conditions of best practices globally. "Therefore, educational systems should be able to contribute to creating a more equal, inclusive, and socially just world (Allan, 2020, p. 17). Inclusion in this chapter is aligned with five of the six categories of inclusion by Ainscow (as cited by Allan, 2020): 1) inclusion with disability and "special needs"; 2) inclusion after disciplinary consequences/measures; 3) inclusion of vulnerable and low-income groups;

4) inclusion for all (non-binary/gender); 5) inclusion as a social and moral commitment to society. These categories intersect, and many of the girls and women in low-income countries have at least three or four of those inclusive criteria or risk factors. Gardner's MI learning theory states that we all have different intelligences where ones are more enhanced than others. It targets the uniqueness and different abilities of human beings. The nine MI are:

1. Visual-Spatial Intelligence
2. Verbal-Linguistic Intelligence
3. Logical-Mathematical Intelligence
4. Bodily-Kinesthetic Intelligence
5. Musical-Rhythmic Intelligence
6. Intra-Personal Intelligence (reflection)
7. Inter-Personal Intelligence (communicating with others)
8. Naturalist Intelligence (related to biodiversity and the environment)
9. Spiritual Intelligence (related to assessing that one life path is more meaningful than another) (Gardner, 1999).

Allan (2020) added moral Intelligence is related to the ability to differentiate the good from the bad when practicing problem-solving. Allan's (2020) concern comes from the amount of highly successful individuals who show no empathy when making global decisions. Allan (2020) mentioned brain plasticity, "the ability and power of our brains to change with experience" (p. 22), and its ability to put into work areas of the brain in an individual with a disability that is not at a loss. This combination of brain plasticity or extraction and Gardner's theory of MI in a classroom (or outside a classroom) that looks like Bruner's constructivism will provide the activities, resources, and trained teachers to maximize and customize the learning experience of girls and women at risk of dropping out of school in low-income countries.

Allan (2020) proposes that students achieve higher levels when they understand how they learn and what teachers need to do to help them learn best. This statement is very empowering; it is crucial to help girls and women in low-income communities be aware of their abilities to monitor their progress and setbacks and create a path for success. According to this learning, theory inclusion is more than integration in a school system. Inclusion refers to the ability to address the needs of each learner more than having all demographics in the same facility and measuring their achievement on only one type of Intelligence when Gardner is telling us learners have different intelligences. For such different intelligences, different assessment methods should be used. Asrifan (2020) shared that a student's success or not in a class depends on the learning/teaching style of the teacher. Behavior and lack of achievement can result from a mismatch between the instruction and the learner's learning style. It is recommended to give the learners a survey or learning style inventory to determine how they learn best.

SOCIAL-EMOTIONAL INTELLIGENCE AND INCLUSIVE EDUCATION

Intelligence Quotient and Emotional Intelligence are both necessary to achieve success in life. Emotional Intelligence drives our decision-making and our interpersonal relations (Mwai & Runo, 2012). Mwai and Runo (2012) shared in their study that girls in Kisumu County in Kenya are already learning how to apply emotional intelligence within their communities with a bridal preparation ritual called "unyago." Uyango refers to the indigenous knowledge that a girl receives from puberty until marriage with a series of teachings to help her adopt her role in that community. In the form of storytelling and songs, the expected behaviors are transmitted from one generation to another. This practice is aligned with Gardner's MI theory and the social-emotional Intelligence the girls develop with uyango. Social-emotional learning (SEL) can be implemented according to UNICEF (2020, p. 10), if the following tenets are followed: the integration of SEL resources and materials into the academic and vocational curriculum; regular and ongoing professional development for teachers; a checklist of risk factors for the identification of girls who are struggling by the staff of an educational setting; and the creation of systems where educational settings can refer girls who experience violence to agencies for psychological, health, and legal support.

UNIVERSAL DESIGN FOR LEARNING AND INCLUSIVE EDUCATION

UDL approaches teaching and reaching all learners in every instructional episode by creating resources, instructional activities, and assessments that address different learning styles and intelligences. For the inclusion of marginalized populations, including girls and learners with special needs, into careers in technology and science, technology, engineering, arts, and mathematics (STEAM), UDL is beneficial. In their study, Tovar and Garg (2020) reported that using UDL to teach STEAM in an IE setting with learners with special needs, low-income students, and girls was effective. In their study, the implementation of UDL became the equalizer creating equity and inclusion in education by reducing accessibility barriers for learning. UDL seems to be one application of Gardner's theory of MI and Bruner's cultural and social constructivism in action. During the pandemic, some schools in Poland implemented UDL in the virtual setting. The ability of the students to contact their teachers at any time or send messages with questions help them pace and monitor their learning (Baran et al., 2021). UDL helped create collaboration among students and between teachers and students. The experience of implementing UDL in online classes in Poland samples a different population since the students had access to technological devices, broadband Internet, and parents engaged in the process. Students' experience in rural areas with limited internet access is not included in Baran et al.'s (2020) research.

BLENDED LEARNING AND INCLUSIVE EDUCATION

Access to Technology—Devices and Internet Access and Challenges during COVID-19

A common theme among many articles and studies is the benefits of online learning combined with brick-and-mortar instruction as the new normal after COVID-19. However, this ideal situation needs to investigate the difficulties of students who live in rural areas with limited or no access to broadband and the difficulties some students in low-income countries have to access a technological device. Asrifan (2020) reported data from the Ministry of Education in Indonesia where 30% of the students in rural areas had no internet access and limited availability to have devices like smartphones or laptops (computers) to support distance learning. In some municipalities, if the family had a TV, the lessons were provided by television. Allier et al. (2020) and Al-Shaya and Oyaid (2021) identified in their research the following barriers: "language, location, and cultural beliefs and limited leisure time prevent girls from benefiting from technology-based education interventions" (p. 12).

Inequity is a vital issue that impacts the access to technology for the girls in low-income communities. Household chores, forced marriage, pregnancy, and other risk factors limited access to community broadband and facilities with WiFi. Access and not lack of interest in learning seems to be the predominant risk factor according to Allier et al. (2020) after they reviewed the UNESCO report that women have a more positive attitude about reading and reading on technological devices than men. Al-Shaya and Oyaid (2020), in their study, proved that "neglecting women's access to ICT tools denies growth opportunities and increased income to them and their families, reduces communities' skill level and productivity and hinders a country's global competitiveness" (p. 88). Another evidence cited by Allier et al. (2020) is the experience of women with blended learning in Saudi Arabia, where they show achievement since blended learning allowed them to have a flexible schedule (these women have access to technological devices and training to access the online platforms before joining the online portion of their classes).

For low or limited technological options (laptops, PCs, Chromebooks), Allier et al. (2020) recommended mobile phones, radio, and television. Mobile phones have the capacity for texting, and free download apps like WhatsApp create learning communities for discussion and access to articles sent via attachments. Acceleration of the curriculum is another recommendation, and that implies covering a curriculum in a shorter time. Suppose the girls use online access to prepare for in-person instruction that helps to cover more material in a shorter period. Sharing technological devices per group or pair can help reach more girls with the virtual aspect of blended learning. Collaborative work among girls reduces the risk factor of violence if the community prepares safe spaces for these reunions.

Virtual learning empowers women to develop hands-on abilities and skills for future employment opportunities that give them the ability to compete for leadership positions and promotions (Al-Shaya & Oyaid, 2021). It also benefits them by creating a virtual learning network that connects them with professors, teachers, and classmates while simultaneously participating and providing their opinions and voices.

RESEARCH DESIGN AND METHODS

More than thirty articles about barriers for women and girls to access quality and IE during the pandemic were reviewed. The search engines and databases used were Google Scholar, ERIC, SAGE, and the terms used to research *were MI theory and girls' education, blended learning and girls' education, COVID-19 and girls' education, UDL and IE post-COVID-19, Bruner's and inclusive education for girls, technology access in schools in COVID-19, IE post-pandemic,* and *blended learning and girls' empowerment.* The studies and articles researched are from the United States, United Kingdom, Kenya, Arabia, Zimbabwe, Sierra Leone, the Philippines, Liberia, and China. The emerging themes found were *forced marriage, learning loss, exploitation of the girls, economic impact, women empowerment, and VAW.* The overarching themes found were IE and special needs education under Bruner's constructivism theory of learning, Gardner's theory of MI, the ability for girls and women in low-income countries to improve their communities if they have access to education, and the way culture would determine curriculum design with differentiated and scaffolded instruction and assessments.

ANALYSIS, DISCUSSION, AND FINDINGS

Prior to the pandemic, access to education for girls and women in low-income countries and individualized education to students with disabilities in the same countries was a struggle. The struggle became aggravated by the lockdown imposed due to COVID-19. There is some variety in the information, resulting from the purposeful sampling used in some of the studies and articles. There is a parallelism in the results of studies of low-income countries where violence, marriage, pregnancy, poverty, taking care of siblings, lack of teacher training for diverse learners (including learners with special needs) were risk factors that contributed to the learning loss of these vulnerable and marginalized populations.

CONCLUSION

Distance learning, access to broadband and technological devices, and teachers with updated skills in technology are still a challenge and barrier to girls and women, and it impacts more students with disabilities who live in poverty since some of the online platforms lack the features to accommodate for them. Distance learning is an area that needs further investigation and funding since education is moving into blended, hybrid, or full virtual learning. The application of UDL, MI, and the tenets of Bruner's cultural and social constructivism are recommended for creating learning environments of diversity and inclusion. Based on my research, these are the suggested solutions and recommendations concerning policy (legislation) and best practices in teachers' instruction.

1. The principle of the least restrictive environment (LRE) for students with disabilities to implement IE.
2. Capacity-building programs for educators and college students to learn and implement LRE, a curriculum with a gender perspective, MI, differentiated instruction.
3. Governments at the local, county, national levels should allocate more funding to IE in their annual budgets.
4. Funding from the government should be used to purchase specialized resources, equipment, and educators' professional development.
5. Varied models of IE should be created to address diverse disabilities (Asamoah et al., 2021).

6. To empower families and girls with disabilities to advocate for their right to access inclusive and equitable education, learning modules targeting self-advocacy as a skill should be developed.
7. A bottom-top approach where governments should create consultation mechanisms for the girls and women to request their input regularly about the process of schools' re-opening (UNICEF, 2020). It makes sense since the impacted girls and women know what they need and who is better than them to guide the decision-makers whose experiences are far and different from the experiences of the girls and women living in low-income households. Parents' input also should be considered.
8. Bringing all girls to school should be a priority, with focused-on equity by eliminating accessibility barriers for married or pregnant students. This action should include governmental participation in the creation of policies that eliminate discriminatory practices.
9. Blended learning, distance learning that includes messages of self-advocacy in case they are victims of violence, and messages about gender equality [SDG 4 and SDG 5].
10. The creation of back-to-school campaigns to reduce teenage pregnancy while schools are still closed.
11. The addition of the gender equality perspective in the academic curriculum includes teacher professional development to implement such a curriculum.
12. Global and local financial support from businesses, industries, and nonprofit organizations supports the limited budget some low-income countries have for education.
13. Access to technology via television, radio, smartphones, media facilities, laptops. This is essential to prepare girls for the 21st-century economy.
14. Professional training for teachers in the UDL, Gardner's theory of MI, and the principles of Bruner's social and cultural constructivist classroom to address the needs of diverse learners and students with special needs in the cultural contexts of their communities.

BIBLIOGRAPHY

Acosta, A. & Evans, D. (2020). COVID-19 and Girls' Education: What We Know So Far and What We Expect. *Center for Global Development.* www.cgdev.org /blog/COVID-19-and-girls-education-what-we-know-so-far-and-what-we-expect -happen

Allier-Gagneur, Z., Chuang, R., McBurnie, C., & Haßler, B. (2020). *Using Blended Learning to Support Marginalised Adolescent Girls' Education: A Review of the Evidence.* docs.edtechhub.org/lib/H3AI5F3C/download/DKG76ZCG/

Allier-Gagneur%20et%20al.%20-%202020%20-%20Using%20Blended%20 Learning%20to%20Support%20Marginalised%20Ado.pdf

Al-Shaya, H., & Oyaid, A. (2021). Effects of E-learning on Girls' Presence and Empowerment to Access Education. *International Journal of Information and Communication Technology Education (IJICTE)*, *17*(3), 86–104. www .igi-global.com/pdf.aspx?tid=277380&ptid=253935&ctid=4&oa=true&isxn =9781799859383

Altan, M. Z. (2020). Extrability and the Theory of Multiple Intelligences as a Phenomenon for an Inclusive Education Renewal. *European Journal of Special Education Research.*

Asamoah, E., Hau-lin Tam, C., & Abdullah, A. (2021). Implementation of Inclusive Education Policy in Ghana: Recommendations from Social Workers and Policy Makers. *International Journal of Disability, Development and Education*, 1–15.

Asrifan, A. (2020*). Pandemic, Humanity and Education.* https://osf.io/q2gpk

Bage, M. G., & Sethy, P. K. (2019). Education for Girls. *Mahila Pratishtha, 4*(3), 165.

Baran, J., Cierpiałowska, T., & Dyduch, E. (2021). The Use of the UDL Approach as a Factor in the Success of Inclusive Education despite the Pandemic Period. In *Improving Inclusive Education through Universal Design for Learning* (pp. 119–144). Springer, Cham. library.oapen.org/bitstream/han dle/20.500.12657/50729/978-3-030-80658-3.pdf?sequence=1#page=130

Burzynska, K., & Contreras, G. (2020). Gendered Effects of School Closures during the COVID-19 Pandemic. *The Lancet, 395*(10242), 1968. www.thelancet.com/ journals/lancet/article/PIIS0140-6736(20)31377-5/fulltext

Canetto, S. S. (2019). Teaching about Women and Gender from a Transnational and Intersectional Feminist Perspective. *International Perspectives in Psychology: Research, Practice, Consultation, 8*(3), 144–160. doi-org.ezp.waldenulibrary. org/10.1037/ipp0000111

Carew, M., Deluca, M., Groce, N., Fwaga, S., & Kett, M. (2020). The Impact of an Inclusive Education Intervention on Learning Outcomes for Girls with Disabilities within a Resource-poor Setting. *African Journal of Disability, 9*(0), e1–e8. doi-org. ezp.waldenulibrary.org/10.4102/ajod.v9i0.555

Corlatean, T. (2020). Risks, Discrimination and Opportunities for Education during the Times of COVID-19 Pandemic. *Proceedings of the 17th Research Association for Interdisciplinary Studies Conference* (pp. 37–46). papers.ssrn.com/sol3/papers. cfm?abstract_id=3794869#page=43

De Klerk, E. D., & Palmer, J. M. (2021). Resetting Education Priorities during COVID-19: Towards Equitable Learning Opportunities through Inclusion and Equity. *Perspectives in Education, 39*(1), 12–28. doi-org.ezp.waldenulibrary. org/10.18820/2519593X/pie.v39.i1.2

Desai, K. (2016). Teaching the Third World Girl: "Girl Rising" as a Precarious Curriculum of Empathy. *Curriculum Inquiry, 46*(3), 248–264.

Dube, B. (2020). Rural Online Learning in the Context of COVID-19 in South Africa: Evoking an Inclusive Education Approach. *REMIE—Multidisciplinary Journal of Educational Research, 10*(2), 135–157. doi-org.ezp.waldenulibrary.org/10.17583/ remie.2020.5607

Gardner, H. (1999). *Intelligence Reframed: Multiple Intelligences for the 21st Century*. New York: Basic Books.

Girls' Education is the Best Investment We Can Make to Grow the World's Economies. (2017, November 2). *Quartz*.

Global Partnership Summit. (2021). Gender Equality in and through Education. *Global Education Summit: Financing GPE 2021–2025*. www.globalpartnership.org/financing-2025/summit

Green, E. (2021). Prioritising Inclusive Education Post COVID-19. *Leonard Cheshire*. www.leonardcheshire.org/our-impact/stories/prioritising-inclusive-education-post-COVID-19

Hui, N., Vickery, E., Njelesani, J., & Cameron, D. (2018). Gendered Experiences of Inclusive Education for Children with Disabilities in West and East Africa. *International Journal of Inclusive Education*, 22(5), 457–474.

Jones, N., Sanchez Tapia, I., Baird, S., Guglielmi, S., Oakley, E., Yadete, W. A., Sultan, M., & Pincock, K. (2021). Intersecting Barriers to Adolescents' Educational access during COVID-19: Exploring the Role of Gender, Disability and Poverty. *International Journal of Educational Development*, 85, N.PAG. doi-org.ezp.waldenulibrary.org/10.1016/j.ijedudev.2021.102428

Juma, S. (2018). Developing Inclusive Education Policy and Practice in Zanzibar: Collaborative Action Research. *Jyväskylä Studies in Education, Psychology and Social Research*, (611). jyx.jyu.fi/bitstream/handle/123456789/57790/978-951-39-7424-4_vaitos12052018.pdf?sequence=1&isAllowed=y

Mwabili, J. W. M., Kathuri, N. J., & Owiti, B. (2020). Identification of Learning Disabilities for Implementation of Individualized Educational Programme in Taita-taveta County, Public Primary Schools. repository.kemu.ac.ke/bitstream/handle/123456789/969/Jeslinah%20Waleghwa%20Mwabili.pdf?sequence=1&isAllowed=y

Mwai, W., & Runo, D. M. N. (2012). Nurturing Multiple Intelligences through African Indigenous Education: A Case Study of Unyago a Swahili Girls to Women Nuptial Institution. *International Journal of Education and Research*, 1(2), pp. 1–17.

Ngulube, J. Y., Njelesani, D., & Njelesani, J. (2020). Implementation of Inclusive Education Policy in Secondary Schools in Zambia. *Zambia Interdisciplinary Journal of Education (ZIJE) Online-ISSN 2710–0715*, 1(1), 1–29.

Ord, K. (2020). Three Stories from Zimbabwe: How Communities Can Help Pregnant Girls and Adolescent Mothers Continue Their Education. *World Vision International*. www.globalpartnership.org/blog/3-stories-zimbabwe-how-communities-can-help-pregnant-girls-and-adolescent-mothers-continue

Pagán, B. (n.d.). *Positive Contributions of Constructivism to Educational Design*. ejop.psychopen.eu/index.php/ejop/article/view/318/html

Pfunye, A. & Ademola-Popoola, I. (2021). The Effects of the COVID-19 Pandemic on Girls' Education. *Global Partnership.org* www.globalpartnership.org/blog/effects-COVID-pandemic-girls-education

Tomar, G., & Garg, V. (2020). Making STEAM Accessible for Inclusive Classroom. *Global Journal of Enterprise Information System*, 12(4), 94–101.

Uleanya, C., Ezeji, I. N., & Uleanya, M. O. (2021). Inclusive Education in the Face of a Global Pandemic: Providing Support. *Multicultural Education*, 7(5), pp. 139–146.

UNICEF. (2020). *Building Back Equal Girls Back to School Guide.* www.unicef.org/media/75471/file/Building-back-equal-Girls-back-to-school-guide-2020.pdf

Wahyudin, U., Purnomo, P., & Yondri, S. (2018). Challenges of Community Education in the Digital Era. *Proceedings of the International Conference on Educational Sciences*, *214*, 194–199.

Chapter 8

Women's Political Inequality in the Arab World

An Exit Strategy

Ari Baghdassar Tatian

Women's political rights are controversial phenomenon in the Arab world,[1] where despite efforts to advance them, modest achievements were made. Such efforts were recently conducted in an environment of instability and armed conflicts, which greatly eroded many of the simple attainments made, and derailed existing developmental objectives and priorities. Historically and globally, women's political rights were prone to challenging variables of varying intensities. Such variables either fostered, or more importantly, hampered the maintenance of substantive political representation of women (SPRW), which was quite apparent in the Arab world that harbored certain contending (political, economic, social, religious) features, rendering SPRW's attainment an arduous task. There were serious difficulties in creating synergy among the variables that react with women's political rights, weakening the efforts that tended to garner positive drivers for the advancement of SPRW. Those threatened by such endeavors resorted to new strategies to contain and avert efforts made. One could sense a kind of (organized) resistance against the ventures made to ameliorate Arab women's political rights, a resistance that could be the result of domination exercised by certain (male) parties and elites, who deny women their political rights and aspirations.

Many Arab countries adopted strategies to further women's political rights and to increase their presence in public institutions. And among the ones applied, gender quotas are worthy of consideration. They tend to secure the descriptive political representation of women, hoping to lead to substantive representation at some point. Gender quotas were utilized as a strategy for political reform, and as a provisional measure to further women's political participation and representation in public institutions (political, legislative, administrative), despite the debate regarding their efficacy, especially in countries that already applied the strategy but there was dissatisfaction regarding the outcome.

The application of gender quotas was taking place in a time when the Arab region had a large democratic deficit, which raised questions regarding the feasibility of conducting pro-gender policies in environments that lacked appreciation and application of democratic principles, which could have created better chances for SPRW to emerge. In that respect, it is imperative to undertake a process of democracy building, to establish firm foundations for SPRW. The chapter bears importance in terms urging policymakers and SPRW proponents, whether domestic or foreign, to reconsider their various pro-women initiatives and strategies, and align them along with democratic principles, to render their efforts more productive.

The chapter analyzes the nexus between women's political (in)equality on one hand, and democratization on the other, by focusing on the Arab states, and especially on those who applied gender quotas to move women's political rights onward. It also dwells upon the various variables that affect women's political representation and participation, which need to be taken into consideration when adopting pro-women strategies. The basic statement that the chapter likes to make is that women's political representation and equality strategies could deliver better results if they are preceded (or accompanied) by the maintenance of democracy.

After the introductory part, including a brief assessment of the political status of women in the Arab world, the chapter undertakes a literature review of the main variables that intersect with women's political equality. Then it moves to a short discussion about the hypothesis. An explanation is provided about the methodology and data collection techniques. Later, there is an analysis and discussion of the findings. And the last part concludes.

LITERATURE REVIEW

Studying women's political rights and equality in the Arab world could not be done independently of the variables that affect their status and course. They need to be taken into consideration regardless of the strategies applied, where among which, democracy building occupies an important place in facilitating the attainment of SPRW. Following is a scholarly review of some of the concepts that are of direct relevance to the theme at hand.

Democracy and SPRW

Democracy provides a favorable setting that fosters women's political rights, including substantive political representation. It secures the space in which pro-women policies are nurtured and enhanced while confronting the challenges that compromise the attainment of gender political equality. Scholars noted the importance of democratic political systems in the provision of freedom and equality of opportunity to people, in addition to a conducive environment, for citizens to exercise their basic rights. Having the issue of the efficacy of representation in mind, scholars underscored the importance of maintaining a substantive representation of women, in addition to the descriptive one, while referring to gender equality as benchmarks for maintaining women's political rights.

The conducive democratic environments for producing favorable SPRW policies were the center of attention of many scholars and organizations. There was a stress on the importance of democratic institution-building,[2] although "the empirical evidence in support of a positive relationship between a democratic regime type and women's representation in politics is mixed" (Stockemer 2015, 400). Such a statement is an indicator of the controversial nexus between democracy and women's political rights, although democracy's role is generally cherished by scholars, since it creates favorable conditions for social development ventures to emerge.

Democratic political systems have the "advantage" of making periodic assessments of themselves, and thus have the opportunity to reconsider undertaken politics and policies, including those that are unfavorable to women's political rights. In that respect, political accountability and public oversight could play an important role in deterring abuse of power, which was exercised by the male political elites in many states (including Arab), to maximize their interests, preventing institutions from performing effectively, and thus compromising the political rights of the people, including those of women.

According to scholarly input, democracy furthered the freedom and equality of citizens, which are conducive to women's (political) rights. It is about power and will that are vested in people, who decide what the representatives do (Holmberg 2011; Karakamisheva-Jovanovska 2013). It also reconciled conflicting values of liberty and equality (Rosema 2011, Aarts, and Denters 2011), furthering stability in contending political settings. Moreover, political systems that harbored principles of democracy and liberalism accommodated a diverse span of views expressed by both genders (Hay 2006; Samet and Schmeidler 2003). Such statements signaled the important role that democracy played in providing ample space for various groups, to have their voices heard in their respective societies, and manage their relations with the competitors that seek to dominate the political landscape.

Like democratic ones, liberal political systems could enhance the maintenance of women's political rights, where democracy assigned the powers of decision making to majorities, while liberalism required that decisions on certain matters rest with the individual and not with society (Samet and Schmeidler 2003). In that respect, there will be many women who will have an independent vision of their own, which might not align with those of men; and even among women, there will be some who will try to differentiate themselves from the others. It is here where liberalism steps in, trying to protect the interests of certain groups in democratic societies, accommodating their needs and demands that would otherwise, get lost in the crowd.

Countries (including the non-democratic ones) can achieve numerical political representation of women. In this case, scholars raise the issue of substantive representation, i.e., the ability of women to pursue their own policies, represent their concerns and interests, set their agendas, and struggle for their interests, which are greatly facilitated in democratic political systems.

The scholarly input provided a concise picture of the important role that democracy plays in furthering women's political rights, where its lack could greatly compromise SPRW efforts, and would eventually increase the prospects of women's political underrepresentation.

Women's Political Representation as a Strategic Objective

Having spoken about democracy and its contribution to the maintenance of women's political rights, it is only natural to speak about one of the main functions of democratic political systems, which is the political representation and participation of citizens, ought to be carried out effectively, allowing all to express and exercise their (political) aspirations freely and without undue constraints. And as democracy allows the practice of political representation and participation unreservedly to all citizens, women, in their turn will be able to reap the rewards of that political system in favor of their political aspirations.[3]

The nexus between political representation and women's rights bears some significance. Scholars often discussed Hanna Pitkin's scholarly contribution to the notion of political representation,[4] which sketched the theoretical framework of the principles that furthered women's political inclusion. In the same manner, Williams (2003) stressed on the concept of citizenship, which provides a freedom that is bound only by laws to which one could rationally consent,[5] as the principal virtue of citizenship is its active participation in political activities, which is again of main concern to women and their political ventures.

Equality among citizens is the basis of political representation. "Modern political theory asserted the equal moral worth of all persons."[6] Although there is no direct reference to women, however, they can constitute an integral part of the description and they are entitled to enjoy the full benefits of citizenship like their male counterparts, free from any form of undue restrictions exercised by certain parties that tend to limit their political potential. There were some remarks regarding the political representation of women. It "takes place in settings that are not designed to serve that purpose. For example, the main lines of division that structure political representation are territory and ideology, not gender" (Celis and Lovenduski 2018, 151), which leaves less room for women's political rights to evolve. Women's political issues must be reconsidered within the legal infrastructure of the state and should receive the same attention as other public issues, mainly as far as electoral laws are concerned.

Despite the scholarly importance given SPRW, the concept is still liable to further shortcomings. Celis (2008a, 112) noted that "there exists no consensus about the content of the substantive representation of women," and women's "interests are as diverse as the acts involved in the substantive representation of women" (Celis 2008b, 18), as "those studying the substantive representation should walk away from assuming to know a priori what women's issues and interests are and, therefore, are in need of representation" (Celis and Childs 2012, 222). Such statements point out to the complications associated with defining the concepts related to the political interests of women, in addition to determining the nature of the efforts required to maintain women's political representation, the fact which compels the adoption of certain strategies that could further women's political orientations and aspirations.

Feminists had often strived to further their interests (political, economic, social), and to broaden their goals and scope of activities against diverse contenders. They aimed at different modes of representation (descriptive, substantive) to further their political inclusion. When deprived of such modes, women's political rights would greatly suffer. Women are a group, often unable to raise their voice against male domination and social marginalization. They are trapped in a vicious circle of chronic political underrepresentation in many countries, including Arab. Adequate measures should be taken at various levels to rectify matters and bring women's political issues to appropriate levels of representation, which could be done best in democratic political systems.

Achieving Gender Political Equality

Gender (political) inequality is a universal phenomenon, being especially apparent in developing countries and rural societies, which are particularly affected by conservative religious and cultural beliefs and practices. Phillips (2004) presented equality in terms of outcome—equalizing where people end up rather than where or how they begin. Gender inequality could refer to a societal imbalance of power between men and women (Morna et al. 2002, 6), where despite efforts for its eradication, it persists in many (Arab) societies, signaling instances of male domination.

Gender equality is on a challenging track, incorporating political, social, and cultural dimensions, where its achievement is a moral imperative and not just economic empowerment (OECD 2012). The "cultural practices and religious norms have been frequently invoked, in international and constitutional law contexts, as a form of defense to oppose gender equality claims" (Raday 2003, 665). Gender inequality is further "perpetuated through interlocking economic, political, and sociocultural mechanisms, creating inequality traps,"[7] being the case in Arab communities.

The importance of gender equality in legislatures was also stressed upon by scholars (Clark and Rodrigues 2009; Htun, Lacalle, and Micozzi 2013), pointing out to barriers in the form of electoral systems, quotas, socio-economic status, religion and party features (Caul 1999; Manning 2014), which prevent women from getting elected. Given such difficulties, women must enjoy certain privileges to start their careers (Rosenbluth, Kalla, and Teele 2015) while facing institutional (Bashevkin 2014) and societal (Norris 2009) challenges. Such variables, which are mostly a global phenomenon, are particularly apparent in the Arab world, leading to low figures of women's representation in the legislatures, as it would become apparent later in the chapter.

The Strategy of Gender Quotas

Among the strategies that were employed to foster women's political inclusion, gender quotas seemed to occupy an interesting place, both at academic and policy levels. They are a universal phenomenon, intended to treat women's political underrepresentation, especially in developing countries, or those in transition. They caught much attention and raised considerable controversy regarding their feasibility, notably in furthering women's political rights.

Gender quotas intended to further the descriptive representation of women. They were defined as "numerical targets that stipulate the number or percentage of women that must be included in a candidate list or the number of seats to be allocated to women in a legislature" (Dahlerup et al. 2013, 16). There were mixed reflections on their use:[8] some considered quotas to be a form of "discrimination and a violation of the principle of fairness, while others view them as compensation for structural barriers that prevent fair competition" (Dahlerup 2003, 5).

To be effective, gender quotas should be accompanied by certain supporting measures, like "changing the beliefs, institutions, and practices that structure women's opportunities to act effectively" (Htun, Piscopo, and von Bergen 2015, 41). In that respect, the "importance of the electoral system and the political parties' attitudes and positions towards gender equality and their readiness to change the situation with either internal or external rules" (Dahlerup and Gaber 2017, 312) should be taken into consideration during the application of gender quotas in the Arab world or elsewhere, although many Arab states lack multi-party political systems or internal party democracy.

It is important to examine how gender quotas may or may not alter some of the barriers, which prevent women's equal participation and representation (Darhour and Dahlerup 2013, 1), as they "do not remove all barriers for women in politics,"[9] and "their success has not been guaranteed; some quotas have been much more effective than others,"[10] while their "presence within the political sphere does not guarantee that the women's agenda will be pursued."[11] Furthermore, some resented their utilization, due to the allegation that they are against the principle of the political elite formation based on merit, since they rely on the principle of imposition based on gender, as "this imposition limits and denies voters' freedom of choice and is therefore undemocrati. (El-Makari 2009, 42). On the other hand, and in an effort to contain the application of gender quotas, and curtail any possible results in favor of women, Zetterberg (2008, 443–445) referred to some measures taken by male political leaders to subdue the presence of elected women.[12]

Based on the scholarly input, scholars were not able to give an unanimous and decisive answer regarding the feasibility of applying gender quotas, as there were both positive and negative views regarding them. Some advocated their application, considering them an interim act towards maintaining women's political rights, while others criticized their focus on increasing the number of women, without taking into consideration the quality of increased representation, in terms of the consolidation of women's political agendas. Their application is liable to the setting and circumstances in which women's political equality efforts are conducted, besides the reaction of the forces that oppose such a venture. Gender quotas must be supported with additional policies to increase the prospects of the maintenance of SPRW.

As such, gender quotas could be a quick remedy to women's political underrepresentation, provided they are supported by democratic practices that would enhance the maintenance of women's political rights. It could further the developmental prospects of the state, including gender political equality.

HYPOTHESIS

The literature review indicated that women's political rights and inclusion efforts are prone to different kinds of difficulties. Many states adopted gender quotas to further those rights. The applied strategies, however, could deliver better results, if they are conducted within the framework of democratic political institutions and policies that could effectively deal with the challenges faced, flanking SPRW strategies towards the envisaged goals, otherwise waged efforts could only have a cosmetic effect on the status of the political rights of women. The chapter will refer to the Arab world to verify the hypothesis made.

METHODOLOGY

To test the hypothesis, and to verify the supporting role of democracy in that respect, it is imperative to assess the performance and achievements of women's political equality in both democratic and non-democratic states, including the Arab. Information is retrieved from the input of international (development) organizations and scholarly community, to ascertain whether there is a positive correlation between democracy and gender political equality.

DATA COLLECTION

Women in Legislatures: A Comparative Perspective

Data is retrieved from a list of the Arab states that adopted gender quotas to advance women's political rights in their societies, which are being disclosed by the quota project.[13] The information included data available on the elections held at the level of the Arab parliaments, which would be an indicator of the status of Arab women's political representation and participation.[14] Women's political rights still fell behind—to say the least—in the Arab world, a fact which was also made apparent through the statements and figures produced by various scholars and organizations, which will be made evident. Also, and even with the application of gender quotas, the percentage of women parliamentarians in Arab legislatures is still low, ranging from 13% to 31% (UAE excluded).

Based on the data retrieved from the International Parliamentary Union (IPU), the average figure of women's representation in their case was 8.4% or approx. 1/12.[15]

One could realize that the average of women's political representation in Arab parliaments (with quotas: 23.3% and without quotas: 8.4%) equals 15.8% (or 2/12), against a global average[16] of 25.0% (or 3/12). Countries with democratic political systems, like those in Europe and North America, scored above the global average (25.0%), while countries with significant democracy deficits (Sub-Saharan Africa, Asia, Arab World and Pacific) scored less than the average.

Also, and as a further example, women's representation average reaches as high as 39.0% (or approx. 5/12), when the gender composition of the European Parliament is taken into account.

Table 8.2 provides a concise presentation of the data disclosed to facilitate their comparison.

Based on the data presented, it becomes apparent that democratic countries (North America and Europe) had a better performance in women's political representation as compared to non-democratic ones. It can be concluded that democracy played a favorable role regarding the political rights of women, although numbers are not a guarantee of the efficacy of the said representation. It was clear that Arab countries had a poorer performance concerning women's political representation. So, what democracy then has to do with it?

Democracy and Arab Women

After a comparative presentation of women's political representation and performance across legislatures globally, including the Arab world, the status of democracy in the Arab states is focused upon, together with its impact on the political rights of women. Information is retrieved from scholarly literature, periodic reports, and indicators published by the international and regional

Table 8.1. Gender composition of the European Parliament.

Source: Gender balance by country: 2019 Constitutive session, European Parliament[17]

States	% of women	States	% of women	States	% of women	states	% of women
Sweden	55	Netherlands	50	Italy	41	Estonia	33
Finland	54	Slovenia	50	Belgium	38	Bulgaria	29
Austria	50	Spain	47	Hungary	38	Lithuania	27
France	50	UK	47	Croatia	36	Greece	24
Latvia	50	Denmark	46	Germany	36	Romania	22
Luxembourg	50	Ireland	45	Poland	35	Slovakia	15
Malta	50	Portugal	43	Czechia	33	Cyprus	0

Table 8.2. A summary.

Percentages of women's repres. in lower houses			Percentages of women's repres. in lower houses		
Arab states with gender quotas	23.3	3/12	Americas	31.7	4/12
Arab states without gender quotas	8.4	1/12	Europe	30.1	4/12
Arab states' average	15.8	2/12	Global average	25.0	3/12
			European Parliament	39.0	5/12

organizations. As far as international organizations are concerned, they provided an unfavorable image about the status of democracy in the Arab world. Examples included Arab Barometer,[18] Arab Democracy Index[19] of the Arab Reform Initiative;[20] Governance Assessment Portal of UNDP;[21] rule of law indicators of the World Justice Project, World Bank;[22] rule of law indicators of the Freedom House;[23] governance indicators of Bertelsmann Stiftung;[24] corruption indicators of Transparency International;[25] Fragile States Index (on human rights and rule of law) of the Fund of Peace.[26] The substantiated lack or flawed practice of democracy in Arab states had its negative impact on a wide range of public issues, where among which, women's political rights occupied an important place.

Besides international organizations, scholars as well had their input regarding the status of democracy in the Arab world. Ottaway (2004), Perthes (2008), Diamond (2010), Chaney (2012), Jones (2016), Khanfar (2017), and others criticized its status, repercussions of which could be felt at the different levels and domains of public policies and political development ventures. Besides the impact of the flawed democratic practices in the Arab states, the contending settings of the Arab communities also furthered Arab women's political underrepresentation. They are manifested in terms of human rights (Abdelaal and Mura 2014; Norris 2009; Dudwick and Kuehnast 2016), and livelihood (Abdelaal and Mura 2014; World Bank 2004), along with other affecting variables like politics (Retta 2013; CARE 2013; Sabbagh 2005), religion (Salbi 2003; Dabbous-Sensenig 2002; Würth 2004), institutions (Rama 2013), laws (Abdelaal and Mura 2014), and civil society (Dabbous-Sensenig 2002). They harmed women's causes, affecting the course and mode of women's political participation (Abdelaal and Mura 2014; Blaydes and El Tarouty 2009) and inclusion, and thus the maintenance of gender political equality.

Among the various domains mentioned, which contributed to Arab women's political underrepresentation, the "social environment also play[ed] an important role in the disadvantaged position that Arab women have in the social and economic sectors" (Abdelaal and Mura 2014, 103). In that respect, and "despite the changes in the economic and social reality of Middle Eastern women [. . .] traditional/religious laws continued to regulate family codes that include marriage, divorce, inheritance, and other aspects directly affecting women" (Salbi 2003, 15–16), limiting women's political potential to a great extent.[27]

Islam, being the basic religion of the Arab world, received much criticism regarding its role in curtailing the (political) rights of women. It is stated that "religious leaders and scholars often justify discrimination by referring to Islamic sources, which are interpreted in a patriarchal way, with different interpretations by the jurisprudents" (GTZ 2009, 1), which would have a negative effect on a great number of public issues, including women's political rights. Moreover, Islamic religious laws are usually not flexible enough to accommodate and process gender values. The failure "to address the role, power and impact of the Islamic religion [. . .] in redefining gender roles and policies will make it very difficult to affect change in that area" (Dabbous-Sensenig 2002, 4), as harnessing religious practices is of utmost importance to create better space in the region for women's political rights to evolve.

The nexus between religion and Arab women's (political) rights received further scholarly attention. As an example of the negative impact of the first on the latter, Würth (2004, 14) explained that the "constitutions of all Arab countries (except Lebanon) declare the shari'a to be the main or sole source of legislation,"[28] granting religious institutions with powers which could be detrimental to women's interests. Being prone to the influence of shari'a (Islamic laws), Arab constitutions (and the legal infrastructure of the state) signal the extent of the difficulties that SPRW efforts would encounter, especially when religious teachings and gender values might not cohabitate with each other.

There were calls to treat the challenges that emanate from religious practices against women's political rights in the Arab world. In that respect, Dabbous-Sensenig (2002, 5) noted that the "failure to know the difference between what is traditional and what is religious or sacred, and failure to know that there are actually different interpretations of Islam [. . .] can doom any human rights effort seeking to change the status of Arab women,"[29] as such a trend is further influenced by notions like politics, customs, culture . . . being clashed, intermingled, reinforced, and fed on each other, creating an unfavorable environment for women's political rights to nurture, as laws and policies generally failed to immune themselves from their intrusion.

There were frequent external demands to foster women's political rights in the Arab world. The latter "falls considerably short [. . .] on indicators of women's economic participation and political empowerment" (World Bank 2004, 1), even though most governments in the Middle East pledged to establish women's rights, but the outcome was extremely modest.[30] In the Arab world, there was an "average of 5.68 per cent women in their parliaments in 2003, the lowest average any region of the globe, but in 2013, the proportion increased significantly to 13.62 per cent, but still remained the lowest across the globe" (GOPAC 2014, 2). It is equally stated that "despite the achievements in terms of the increased number of women in decision-making positions, [. . .] the proportion of Arab women participating in elected parliaments is still one of the lowest in the world" (Abdelaal and Mura 2014, 103). Arab states' policies and the resulting women's political underrepresentation are indicators of the magnitude of the problem that Arab women are facing.

Recently, women "played a prominent role in the Arab uprisings, but as the protests led to political transitions and societies entered a state of flux, the future of women's political empowerment became uncertain" (Retta 2013, 3). It could be inferred that there was some significant involvement by Arab women in pro-democracy movements, but they did not receive any tangible "rewards" in return.[31]

Women's (political) empowerment efforts were being carried out in a "region long characterized by political activity, whether in its anticolonial movements, its own regional and internal conflicts, or the various wars it has witnessed" (Sabbagh 2005, 52), and were intertwined with the agendas of Western donors and regional actors that were driven by geopolitical imperatives (CARE 2013, 29). Given such facts, and especially the prevailing regional political instability, efforts seeking to maintain Arab SPRW faced serious difficulties, which left Arab pro-gender efforts in a difficult situation, although one should consider that foreign agencies usually, work under difficult political conditions and are prone to restrictions by the host Arab states, besides theirs.

Speaking further about the external involvement, it should be noted that "donor commitment to women's participation in the region remains questionable [. . .] the proportion of funding allocated to women's programs is usually quite low [. . .] despite donors' insistence that women's participation is vital in their work" (CARE 2013, 24), which would have a negative impact on SPRW efforts in the Arab world.[32] However, allegations made against the nature of the foreign intervention should not be used as an excuse to hamper such endeavors, and to reject the assistance offered by external donors, as SPRW efforts should have been carried out regardless of foreign aid in the first place, especially when many Arab countries have the financial resources to undergo such a venture.

There were further contending variables that hampered the course of SPRW. Obstacles like legal discrimination against women, patriarchy,[33] and authoritarianism[34] were some of the hindrances that faced the efforts made. To deal with this issue, Rama (2013, 31) proposed to "critically evaluate barriers to reform and assist women in reclaiming their roles in leadership and politics in the Arab world,"[35] which requires a tremendous amount of work and effort, given the complexities entailed, which are quite varied and diversified.

Yet, and despite the barriers mentioned and challenges faced, there were some achievements, through certain institutional and administrative arrangements, which were carried out by pan-Arab (governmental) institutions.[36] However, the progress made was not enough to boost women's political rights, as scholars already gave an account of the hindrances that faced the efforts made.

ANALYSIS AND DISCUSSION OF THE FINDINGS

Based on the findings of the literature review, democracy provides a substantial contribution to the stability and advancement of states, enhancing their political, economic, and social potential, furthering equitable political representation, with the adoption of certain strategies (gender quotas, for instance) towards that end, while facing difficulties and barriers.

When considering the figures and indicators of women's political representation in the Arab world (as a result of with or without gender quotas), and after comparing them with the results achieved in democratic countries, it becomes apparent that women in the Arab world are suffering from political underachievement, as the international (development) organizations and scholarly literature often stated. Certain variables, which were dwelled upon, had their crucial impact on the strategies adopted and on the outcome emerged.

Arab countries implemented gender quotas to further women's political inclusion, as women's political rights were prone to prolonged challenges of political, economic, social, and religious nature, which led to criticisms from the international and donor community. Gender quotas, however, did not yield the aspired results, as Arab countries are still witnessing substantial women's political underrepresentation, and their marginalization in the political affairs of the state, including political decision making.

Due to the various difficulties that they are faced with, women's political rights are considered a challenging topic in the Arab world. Despite popular upheavals to overthrow dictatorships and to establish a democratic rule during the recent decade, no strong democratic political systems were established in the Arab world, which could have helped to establish a favorable environment for SPRW efforts. Many Arab states are lost in systemic mayhem, unable to find their way out of the prevailing instability and conflict. Given the present situation, achieving Arab gender political equality seems an arduous process.

But what about the Arab states that did not witness such conflicts? The picture is also quite discouraging. They were long characterized by the rule of one man (king, prince, or president), ruling for indefinite periods, lacking transparency in acts and policies, and being unaccountable to the public. Citizens lacked adequate mechanisms and literacy of oversight, and thus were unable to exercise their basic rights, as it was evident with women's insufficient exercise of their political rights. Even though there is some presence of women in parliaments, the effectiveness of that presence in terms of advancing women's political rights is not ascertained yet.

Democracy is not a guarantee that women's political rights are going to be necessarily respected or maintained in the Arab world or elsewhere. Yet, it does not mean that it has no role to play in the efforts to enhance the maintenance of women's political rights. The problem is that in many (Arab) countries, despite the existence of written laws and regulations, in addition to some limited democratic practices, the impact of culture (and other variables like religion and norms) is so strong that citizens would generally adhere to their own beliefs and practices, rather than abiding by the legal principles and regulations that could be the output of democratic political systems, which are sometimes considered odd to them, leaving a negative impact on women's political inclusion in many instances.

As the data showcased, democratic political systems were conducive to women's political rights and inclusion, as it was the case in Europe and North America. Most Arab states were either undemocratic or had weak democratic institutions. As a result, women's political inclusion efforts were often stranded and did not lead to SPRW, despite the application of gender quotas.

The primary reason for the inability of gender quotas to deliver results was not due to some of the negative features that it incorporated, but rather to the setting in which gender quota strategies were implemented, i.e., the political environment and other pertaining themes that intersected with it, which were already made evident, and which compromised the chances of producing credible results. The multitude of barriers noted was primarily associated with the democracy deficit prevailing in the Arab world that hindered vast developmental policies, including women's (political) rights, from evolving.

Indeed, Arab countries lacked the enabling (democratic) environment in which pro-gender policies and strategies could have been maintained, especially when democratic structures are key drivers for empowering social justice ventures. Given this fact, the application of gender quotas had a superficial impact in many instances, unable to deliver tangible results in terms of pro-women policies. There was no sense of applying such a strategy when it was deprived of the strong foundations, empowerment modes, means, and drivers that democracy could have provided, for women to be able to exercise their political rights effectively. Such findings have their leverage on SPRW attainment strategies (including gender quotas), whether conducted at the public policy level or the level of international development organizations and donor agencies.

Culture and religious beliefs and practices were often considered an obstacle that prevented (Arab) women from enjoying their basic (political) rights. Arab states had strong religious institutions that had their influence on public issues and decision making, along with their frequent alliance with the political elite, which rendered SPRW attainment efforts a difficult task. Although some religious leaders might play a lenient role, but it is too early to generalize it, in the time when the rewards of that leniency are still difficult to measure.

As such, the substantive political representation of Arab women is liable to various difficulties and challenges, due to the weak democratic structures and insufficient political space to accommodate it, along with strong social tension when discussing such topics. Women are a vulnerable group, subject to improper treatment, as a significant role is expected to be played by Arab governments and legislatures to maintain favorable political and policy settings, to further citizens' (and women's) various political aspirations. Therefore, and given democracy provides a credible contribution towards maintaining women's political representation and participation, and since Arab states mostly lack democratic political institutions and inherent women's political rights, it is imperative to consolidate democracy building efforts in the Arab world and embed SPRW efforts in it.

CONCLUSIONS

The chapter dealt with a highly controversial topic for an equally highly controversial region. In doing so, it reviewed concepts that intersected with women's political rights; addressed the status of women's political representation and participation in the Arab world; assessed the results obtained from the strategies applied (gender quotas); appraised the hypothesis posed, verifying its viability along the findings garnered. Women's political rights overlapped with variables like religion, customs, education, economy . . . leading to an uneasy environment that harmed efforts to further those rights. They do not function in isolation. They exist in a contending setting that hinders their advancement.

Women's political empowerment strategies (including quotas) excel in democracies, through freedom, rule of law, periodic fair and free elections, and equal opportunities, which are conducive to SPRW efforts, especially in instances when democracy and liberalism coexist harmoniously. The Arab states and legislatures failed to embody gender values in their policies, as they suffered from a serious democratic deficit, and failed to provide an enabling framework for their advancement and their eventual extension to other government branches.

The Arab religious institutions played a negative role in the attainment of women's (political) rights, either to further their doctrines/beliefs or to preserve existing powers—which are usually embedded in law. Harnessing religious practices and societal norms is a complicated challenge that gender equality efforts normally experience, in the face of the prolonged alliance of "political-religious" complex in the Arab countries.

As such, women's political representation and participation could be fostered in the Arab world, provided that gender political equality schemes, like quotas, are accompanied by a process of democratization, which would, inter alia, limit perpetuating economic and social disparities, further long-term growth, inhibit gender impaired institutional development, and predatory acts of certain elites, while preventing gender political inequality from reproducing itself across time. The outcome of strategies adopted depends on the fact whether they constitute an integral part of a process of democratization, which could deliver credible results at some point.

BIBLIOGRAPHY

Abdelaal, Doaa and Eleonora Mura. 2014. "The League of Arab States and Gender: Political Participation and the Arab Woman." In *Inclusive Political Participation and Representation: The Role of Regional Organizations*, 99–120. Stockholm: International Institute for Democracy and Electoral Assistance.

Arab Spring or Arab Autumn? Women's Political Participation in the Uprisings and Beyond: Implications for International Donor Policy. 2013. CARE International.

Bashevkin, Sylvia. 2014. "Numerical and Policy Representation on the International Stage: Women Foreign Policy Leaders in Western Industrialised Systems." *International Political Science Review,* vol. 35, no. 3, 409–429.

Blaydes, Lisa and Safinaz El Tarouty. 2009. "Women's Electoral Participation in Egypt: The Implications of Gender for Voter Recruitment and Mobilization." *Middle East Journal,* vol. 63, no. 3, 364–380.

Caul, Miki. 1999. "Women's Representation in Parliament: The Role of Political Parties." *Party Politics,* vol. 5, no. 1, 79–98.

Celis, Karen. 2008a. "Studying Women's Substantive Representation in Legislatures: When Representative Acts, Contexts and Women's Interests Become Important." *Representation,* vol. 44, no. 2, 111–123.

———. 2008b. "Substantive Representation of Women (and Improving it). What is and should it be about?" *Annual Meeting of the American Political Science Association* 1–24.

Celis, Karen and Sarah Childs. 2012. "The Substantive Representation of Women: What to Do with Conservative Claims?" *Political Studies,* vol. 60, 213–225.

Celis, Karen and Joni Lovenduski. 2018. "Power Struggles: Gender Equality in Political Representation." *European Journal of Politics and Gender,* vol. 1, no. 1–2, 149–166.

Chaney, Eric. 2012. "Democratic Change in the Arab World, Past and Present." *Brookings Papers on Economic Activity,* 363–414.

Clark, Lesley and Charmaine Rodrigues. 2009. *Utilising Temporary Measures to Promote Gender Balance in Pacific Legislatures: A Guide to Options.* Suva, Fiji: UNDP Pacific Centre.

Dabbous-Sensenig, Dima. 2002. *The Arab World and the Challenge of Introducing Gender-Sensitive Communication Policies.* Beirut: United Nations Division for the Advancement of Women (DAW).

Dahlerup, Drude. 2003. *Comparative Studies of Electoral Gender Quotas.* Stockholm: International Institute for Democracy and Electoral Assistance.

Dahlerup, Drude. 2005. "Increasing Women's Political Representation: New Trends in Gender Quotas." In *Women in Parliament: Beyond Numbers,* by Julie Ballington and Azza Karam (eds.), 141–153. Stockholm: International Institute for Democracy and Electoral Assistance.

Dahlerup, Drude and Milica Antić Gaber. 2017. "The Legitimacy and Effectiveness of Gender Quotas in Politics in CE Europe." *Teorija in Praksa let,* vol. 54, no. 2, 307–316.

Dahlerup, Drude et al. 2013. *Atlas of Electoral Gender Quotas.* Stockholm: International Institute for Democracy and Electoral Assistance.

Darhour, Hanane and Drude Dahlerup. 2013. "Sustainable Representation of Women through Gender Quotas: A Decade's Experience in Morocco." In *Women's Studies International Forum.*

Diamond, Larry. 2010. "Why Are there No Arab Democracies?" *Journal of Democracy,* vol. 21, no. 1, 93–104.

Dudwick, Nora and Kathleen Kuehnast. 2016. *Gender and Fragility: Ensuring a Golden Hour.* Fragility Study Group: Carnegie Endowment for International Peace, Center for a New American Security, United States Institute of Peace.

Effective Participation and Representation in Democratic Societies. 2007. Warsaw: OSCE Office for Democratic Institutions and Human Rights.

El-Makari, Mark. 2009. "The Proposed Gender Quota in Lebanon: Legal Crisis or Democratic Transformation?" *Al-Raida,* Issue 126–127, Institute for Women's Studies in the Arab World, Lebanese American University, 39–52.

Gender and Development in the Middle East and North Africa: Women in the Public Sphere. 2004. Washington, DC: MENA Development Report, International Bank for Reconstruction and Development, World Bank.

"Gender Equality in Education, Employment and Entrepreneurship." 2012. *Meeting of the OECD Council at Ministerial Level.* Paris: OECD.

Gender Equality in Parliaments and Political Corruption. 2014. Ontario: GOPAC.

Hay, William Anthony. 2006. "What Is Democracy? Liberal Institutions and Stability in Changing Societies." *Democracy* 1–18.

Helou, Marguerite. 2011. "Lebanese Women and Political Parties: History, Issues and Options for Reform." In *Emerging Voices: Young Women in Lebanese Politics*, 16–17. International Alert.

Holmberg, Soren. 2011. "Dynamic Representation from Above." In *How Democracy Works*, by Martin, Rosema, Bas Denters and Kees Aarts, 53–76. Amsterdam: Pallas Publications, Amsterdam University Press.

Htun, Mala, Marina Lacalle and Juan Pablo Micozzi. 2013. "Does Women's Presence Change Legislative Behavior? Evidence from Argentina, 1983–2007." *Journal of Politics in Latin America*, vol. 1, 95–125.

Htun, Mala, Jennifer M. Piscopo and Sophia von Bergen. 2015. "Women in Politics in Latin America." In *Women, Policy and Political Leadership: Regional Perspectives in Today's World*, by Wilhelm, Megha Sarmah and Dilpreet Kaur Hofmeister, 35–43. Singapore: Konrad-Adenauer-Stiftung.

Jones, Seth. 2016. "Democracy in the Arab World: Still a Mirage." *Foreign Affairs*. https://www.rand.org/blog/2016/03/democracy-in-the-arab-world-still-a-mirage.html

Karakamisheva-Jovanovska, Tanja. 2013. "Modern Democracy and the Limitation." *The 1st Human And Social Sciences at the Common Conference*. Zilina: HASSACC, 104–108.

Khanfar, Wadah. 2017. "Democracy Is still the Answer for Arab World." *The World Today,* Chatham House: The Royal Institute of International Affairs, 38–42.

Manning, Amy. 2014. "The Effects of Electoral Systems and Gender Quotas on Female Representation in National Legislatures." *Clocks & Clouds*, vol. 4, no. 2, 73–90.

Morna, Colleen Lowe et al. (eds). 2002. "Culture, Religion and Gender." Harare: Inter Press Service.

Norris, Pippa. 2009. *Why do Arab States Lag the World in Gender.* John F. Kennedy School of Government, Harvard University.

Ottaway, Marina. 2004. *Women's Rights and Democracy in the Arab World.* Washington, DC: Carnegie Endowment for International Peace.

Perthes, Volker. 2008. "Is the Arab World Immune to Democracy?" *Survival*, vol. 50, no. 6, 151–160.

Phillips, Anne. 2004. "Defending Equality of Outcome." *Journal of Political Philosophy*, vol. 12, no. 1, 1–19.

Raday, Frances. 2003. "Culture, Religion and Gender." *International Journal of Constitutional Law*, vol. 1, no. 4, 663–715.

Rama, Sevita. 2013. "Remembering Their Role: Keeping Women Involved Post-Arab Awakening." *Journal of Women and Human Rights in the Middle East*, vol. 1, Baker Institute, Rice University, 31–48. https://www.bakerinstitute.org/media/files/Research/dfe28b28/WHR-Pub-StudentJournal-101613.pdf

Retta, Julia. 2013. "Consequences of the Arab Spring for Women's Political Participation." *Journal of Women and Human Rights in the Middle East*, vol. 1, Baker Institute, Rice University, 3–19. https://www.bakerinstitute.org/media/files/Research/dfe28b28/WHR-Pub-StudentJournal-101613.pdf

Rosema, Martin, Kees Aarts and Martin Denters. 2011. "How Democracy Works: An Introduction." In *How Democracy Works*, by Martin, Rosema, Kees Aarts and Martin Denters (eds.), 9–17. Amsterdam: Pallas Publications, Amsterdam University Press.

Rosenbluth, Frances, Joshua Kalla and Dawn Teele. 2015. *Female Political Career.* Washington, DC: World Bank.

Sabbagh, Amal. 2005. "The Arab States: Enhancing Women's Political Participation." In *Women in Parliament: Beyond Numbers*, by Julie Ballington and Azza Karam, 52–71. Stockholm: International Institute for Democracy and Electoral Assistance.

Salbi, Zainab. 2003. "Why Might Women Support Religious Fundamentalism?" *The Impact of Religion on Women in the Development Process, Critical Half*, vol. 1, no. 1, 14–19.

Samet, Dov and David Schmeidler. 2003. "Between Liberalism and Democracy." *Journal of Economic Theory*, vol. 110, 213–233.

Schwindt-Bayer, Leslie A. 2009. "Making Quotas Work: The Effect of Gender Quota Laws on the Election of Women." *Legislative Studies Quarterly*, vol. 34, 5–28.

Sethi, Gabriella. 2013. *Increasing Women's Political Representation and Participation in Cambodia.* Cambodia: Heinrich Böll Foundation.

Stockemer, Daniel. 2015. "Women's Descriptive Representation." *International Political Science Review*, vol. 36, no. 4, 393–408.

Waring, Marilyn. 2010. *Women's Political Participation.* Department for International Development (DFID), International Development Research Centre (IDRC).

Williams, Melissa S. 2003. "Citizenship as Identity, Citizenship as Shared Fate, and the Functions of Multicultural Education." In *Citizenship and Education in Liberal-Democratic Societies: Teaching for Cosmopolitan Values and Collective Identities*, by Kevin McDonough and Walter Feinberg, 208–241. Oxford: Oxford University Press.

Women's Rights and Islam. 2009. Eschborn: Deutsche Gesellschaft für Technische Zusammenarbeit (GTZ) GmbH.

World Development Report 2006: Equity and Development. 2005. Washington, DC: World Bank.

Würth, Anna. 2004. *Women's Rights in the Arab World: Overview of the Status of Women in Family Law with Special Reference to the Influence of Islamic Factors.* Eschborn: Deutsche Gesellschaft für Technische Zusammenarbeit (GTZ) GmbH.

Young, Iris Marion. 1989. "Polity and Group Difference: A Critique of the Ideal of Universal Citizenship." *Ethics*, vol. 99, no. 2, 250–274.

Zetterberg, Par. 2008. "The Downside of Gender Quotas? Institutional Constraints on Women in Mexican State Legislatures." *Parliamentary Affairs*, vol. 61, no. 3, 442–460.

NOTES

1. The Arab world is comprised of the twenty-two states of the Arab League. It has a common language, culture, and religion, the majority being (Sunni) Islam, besides

other religious and ethnic groups and minorities. The region was subject to prolonged political instability and armed conflicts, whether with foreign powers, or among Arab states themselves, or even within them. Different forms of governments exist, ranging from monarchies (Bahrain, Jordan, Kuwait, Morocco, Oman, Qatar, Saudi Arabia, and the United Arab Emirates), to republics (the remaining countries). The Arab world has flawed and weak democratic practices and structures. It has developing economies and many of its countries rely on their export revenues from oil and gas, and other raw materials.

2. ODIHR, *Effective Participation and Representation in Democratic Societies*, OSCE Office for Democratic Institutions and Human Rights Democratization Department (Warsaw), 2007.

3. Like democracy, political representation and participation are important drivers that could bring citizens' interests to an appropriate level of treatment. Being a distinctive feature of democratic systems, they constitute an outlet through which diverse needs and demands are expressed and processed. And among the various political agendas that would traffic along the theme specified, women's political rights remain one of the many contenders that wander along the course, where the existing diversity in women's needs and aspirations leads into a debate over the nature of women's interests, as a proper understanding of those interests is vital to conduct women's political empowerment policies.

4. "The Concept of Representation," 1967.

5. The role of the citizen is defined by the activities of authorizing public decisions and holding government officials accountable through participation in the institutions established by the constitution.

6. "[A]nd the social movements of the oppressed took this seriously as implying the inclusion of all persons in full citizenship status under the equal protection of the law." Young, *Polity*, 250.

7. World Development Report (WDR 2006, 129), World Bank.

8. Various arguments have been put forward for and against the introduction of quotas as a means to increase the political presence of women. The pros: quotas for women do not discriminate, but compensate for actual barriers that prevent women from their fair share of the political seats; women have the right as citizens to equal representation; women's experience is needed in political life; only many women can represent the diversity of women; women are just as qualified as men, but women's qualifications are downgraded and minimized in a male-dominated political system; quota rules limit the tendency of political parties to nominate only men; several internationally recognized conventions on gender equality have set targets for women's political representation; how can it be justified that men occupy more than 80 per cent of the parliamentary seats in the world? The cons: quotas are against the principle of equal opportunity for all since women are given preference; political representation should be a choice between ideas and party platforms, not between social categories; quotas are undemocratic because voters should be able to decide who is elected; quotas imply that politicians are elected because of their gender, not because of their qualifications, and that better-qualified candidates have pushed aside; introducing quotas creates significant conflicts within the party organization, quotas for women

will be followed by demands for quotas for other groups, which will result in a politics of sheer group-interest representation (Dahlerup, *Increasing*, 144).

9. "Stigmatization of women politicians may even increase in quota systems. Difficulties combining family life, work-life and politics still remain a severe obstacle to women's full citizenship" (Ibid., 152).

10. It "is not simply having a quota but how the institution is designed that increases women's representation" (Schwindt-Bayer, *Making*, 22).

11. As other factors like political will, capacity support, re-shaping patriarchal structures, grassroots movements also matter (Sethi, *Increasing*, 41).

12. According to him, such measures render their presence ineffective in terms of political participation and policy-making, by furthering institutional constraints, restraining their activities and marginalizing them by depriving them their independence.

13. www.quotaproject.org of International IDEA, Inter-Parliamentary Union and Stockholm University.

14. It should be noted that political representation does not occur only in legislatures, but also in other public institutions, such as the government, with all its branches and agencies. However, parliaments are conventional targets of SPRW efforts and strategies, and a preliminary indicator of whether such strategies are delivering results.

15. There are no voluntary quotas adopted by the political parties in the Arab world.

16. IPU, global averages, June 1, 2020.

17. "MEPs' gender balance by country: 2019," https://europarl.europa.eu/election-results-2019/en/mep-gender-balance/2019-2024/

18. Arab Barometer, www.arabbarometer.org

19. Arab Democracy Index, www.arab-reform.net/project/arab-democracy-index/

20. Arab Reform Initiative, www.arab-reform.net

21. Lebanon, Sustainable Development Goals, www.lb.undp.org/content/lebanon/en/home.html

22. Lebanon Ranked 89 out of 126 Countries on Rule of Law, Rising Three Positions, worldjusticeproject.org/sites/default/files/documents/Lebanon_1.pdf

23. Freedom House, freedomhouse.org/country/lebanon/freedom-world/2020

24. Bertelsmann Stiftung, www.bertelsmann-stiftung.de/en/system/search-results?tx__%5Baction%5D=index&tx__%5Bcontroller%5D=Standard&cHash=066035b666091c9898f7b901dbd1e04b

25. The Lebanese Transparency Association, https://www.transparency.org/en/countries/lebanon

26. FFP, Fragile State Index, Annual Report 2019, https://fragilestatesindex.org/wp-content/uploads/2019/03/9511904-fragilestatesindex.pdf

27. Among the many examples that can be given regarding malpractices against Arab women, Blaydes and El Tarouty (2009, 380) referred to the issue of voter recruitment in Egyptian parliamentary elections in 2005, stating that "[c]lientelistically-based voter recruitment tends to empower women economically rather than politically as elections provide an opportunity for disadvantaged women to auction their voice to the highest bidder," a fact which would disorient Arab women's political

deeds, and have a negative impact on their political rights. Arab women and states have a great deal of work to do for the betterment of women's political rights.

28. In most countries, this article is in clear disagreement with the principle of equality between men and women and the ban on gender discrimination, according to her.

29. "However, a homegrown approach to gender equality, coupled with Western expertise can undermine the (often flawed) arguments used by the threatened patriarchal establishment and culture and can more effectively introduce change," according to her.

30. As efforts that were made were met by stiff resistance by those whose interests were threatened, since the said efforts were not carried out in good faith, or lacked adequate means and resources (Norris 2009).

31. Like Arab women during and after the Arab uprisings, the Lebanese women had the opportunity to boost their political rights after the end of the Lebanese civil war. During the war years, they "entered militias and participated in conflict. Unlike women in the West after the Second World War, however, Lebanese women did not continue to make gains because of increased empowerment linked to their wartime efforts" (Helou 2011, 16–17). Matters got more complicated when the "situation of women in politics in Lebanon in a post-war period reinforced their economic deprivation and the patriarchal nature of politics. While the war opened new space to participate in public life, this has not extended to full political citizenship" (Waring 2010, 21). Indeed, Lebanese women's political performance should have been upgraded, just like during the years of belligerency; however, such prospect faded away when the civil war was over.

32. Donors were accused of following covert political objectives, where "women were often as critical as men of the perceived motives behind international aid" (CARE 2013, 20), which indicates the need to reconsider some of those efforts against which certain claims were made.

33. "[D]espite the progress made in recent years, many Arab women continue to struggle for equal treatment. Many legal provisions, in particular, family and personal status laws, entail discrimination against women and give them lower status than men, especially when it comes to inheritance, custody of children, the right to divorce and property rights in general [. . .] the prevailing culture of a traditional patriarchal society hinders the application of the reformed legislation" (Abdelaal and Mura 2014, 102–103).

34. "[G]overnment decisions, traditional values, and dominant patriarchal interpretations of Islam [. . .] weakness, if not absence in some situations, of civil society in Arab countries. This weakness is mostly due to the predominantly authoritarian political systems, inexperience, and underdevelopment. In such an environment, local NGOs are left with little room for maneuvering, and indeed may face physical or legal persecution both from authorities and disgruntled, radical religious groups protecting the status quo" (Dabbous-Sensenig 2002, 1).

35. Besides discussing the institutional mechanisms that would support women's rights after the Arab uprising.

36. Among the achievements mentioned, Women's Committee, Women's Affairs Directorate, and Arab Women's Organization were established, along with Arab League's specialist agencies and program activities to enhance gender equality. (Abdelaal and Mura 2014, 104).

Chapter 9

Do Gender Quotas Reduce Gender Inequality in the Political Decision-making Process?

A Comparative Case of India and Bangladesh

Mahbub Alam Prodip and Helen Ware

Women's under-representation in politics is an eye-catching feature around the world. Women are often not considered in the assignment of posts as holders of power and authority, but they are widely used as objects and weapons for gaining political power. Their marginalization in the political sphere comes from their lack of access to and control over state resources as well as a lack of the exercise of authority in private life (Vetten, Makhunga, & Leisegang, 2012, 12). Women find themselves under-represented in political legislatures and far away from the decision-making processes in many socio-political domains. As women are excluded from decision-making practice, economic development and opportunities for entrenching the doctrines of democracy and the achievement of gender equality have remained difficult (Shvedova, 2005, 34).

Women's representation in politics can be enhanced by two distinct routes: the "incremental track" and the "fast track" (Dahlerup & Freidenvall 2005). The incremental track refers to the substantial growth in the levels of women's representation over a long period during which goals and party quotas are gradually accepted. The fast track reform refers to a trigger for instantaneous change through the introduction of constitutional or legislative quotas (Tripp & Kang 2008). Legislative gender quotas ensure that a certain number of women have their representation in candidate lists, in parliament itself and in committees, or even in the government. Their main objective is to enhance the participation of women at various levels of government, parliament, and local government (Dahlerup, 2005; Tajali & Hoodfar, 2011). In the context of *fast track* development, this chapter evaluates the ability and effectiveness of women members in influencing the political decision-making process in male-dominated political councils.

As of January 2021, women occupied 25.5% of seats in national parliaments worldwide. As agreed in the United Nations Economic and Social Council in 1990, 47 countries achieved a critical mass of 30% or promoted more women in their national legislatures. The majority of nations are yet to achieve critical mass: 84 countries have ensured women's representation of more than 15% up to 30%, whereas 64 countries have lower than 15% women parliamentarians in their lower house. In recent years, Rwanda leads the world having 61% of women in its lower house (World Economic Forum, 2020).

Similarly, local governments are yet to achieve gender parity in decision-making bodies (Ara, 2017, p. 18). Although several affirmative actions were introduced in different countries around the world, the advancement of women's participation in decision-making processes in local level politics has been slow since the late eighteenth century. Only 5% of women hold the positions of mayor and 20% of them occupy the places of councilors worldwide (UCLG, 2015, 3). Out of the 300 largest cities around the world, only twenty-five are headed by women (City Mayor Statistics, 2021). Moreover, only twenty-nine female mayors are witnessed in the 493 cities with more than one million peoples and of the twenty-seven megacities where more inhabitants are living than the total population of some countries, none were ruled by women until 2015 (UCLG, 2015, 3). In order to ensure equal gender representation in local government institutions, several countries have introduced gender quotas or affirmative action.

Like other countries worldwide, India and Bangladesh adopted a reservation policy in their local government institutions during the 1990s. In 1992, the Indian Parliament enacted the Constitutional Amendment Acts (no. 73 and 74). They provided for reserved seats for women in local governments. The 73rd Amendment Act made provision for the reservation for women of not less than 33% of the total seats, by direct election, in the Village Councils, (*Gram Panchayat*) (Priebe, 2017; Prodip, 2021a). In 1997, the government of Bangladesh introduced the Local Government (*Union Parishad*) (Second Amendment) Act of 1997, confirming that for direct elections the reserved seats for women should be not less than 25% in the *Union Parishad* (Prodip, 2021b). Scholars have found some positive impacts of gender quotas on women in local councils in both countries. Quota-elected women members in India have interests in offering public goods and services such as supplying pure drinking water and construction of roads (Chattopadhyay & Duflo, 2004; Deininger et al., 2011; Priebe, 2017), and dealing with practical gender needs (Jayal, 2006). Women members in Bangladesh have enhanced their voice and social legitimacy in contributing to certain women's issues, particularly in family disputes (Nazneen & Tasnim, 2010), and facilitated their voices to offer better services to their constituents (Panday, 2013). However, previous studies also found that quota-elected women members faced severe resistance from their male colleagues to their participation in day-to-day political affairs in local councils in both countries especially when the distribution of money and other resources was at stake. Thus, gender quotas have had limited impact on women in local councils in India and Bangladesh (Prodip, 2021b).

Previous academic studies have explored and compared the origin, actors, motivations, contexts, and implementation of gender quotas in developed and developing countries (Anderson & Swiss, 2014; Bush 2011; Dhalerup & Freidenvall, 2006, 2010; Krook, 2009). A handful of studies have examined the impact of gender quotas on political parties in Germany (Davidson-Schmich, 2006), plenary debates in the Ugandan Parliament (Clayton, Josefsson & Wang, 2014), candidate selection process in Belgium (Vandeleene, 2014), government expenditures in lower houses in one-hundred and three countries (Chen, 2010), electoral rules on the election of women to legislatures in nineteen countries in Latin America (Jones, 2009), women's political representation in more than one hundred countries (Paxton, Hughes, & Painter, 2009), women's political empowerment in India and Bangladesh (Prodip, 2021a, 2021b), women's descriptive representation in six African countries (Baur, 2008), women's substantive representation in Argentina (Franceschet & Piscopo, 2012), and six African countries (Baur, 2008), and symbolic representation in Rwandan society (Burnet, 2011) in national and local governments both in developed and developing nations. However, there has been little much less effort to examine the impact of gender quotas on reducing gender inequality in the political decision-making process (except Dimitrova-Grajzl & Obasanjo, 2019; Verge, 2012). Verge (2012) examined the impact of gender quotas on institutionalizing gender equality in political representation in Spain's parliament. Dimitrova-Grajzl and Obasanjo (2019) evaluated the effectiveness of gender quotas for improving gender equality in national parliaments in ten African countries. Thus, it is fair to claim that the relationship between gender quotas and reducing gender inequality in the political decision-making process is understudied. To bridge this research gap, this study aims to explain the impact of gender quotas on reducing gender inequality in the political decision-making process in local councils in India and Bangladesh. Thus this study has employed two research questions: 1) Do women who get positions in councils through quotas have the respect and support of their colleagues to argue for resources and services for women? 2) Do women in local councils through quotas affect the decision-making process enough to change the lives of local women? This study is important as it examines promoting gender equality in the political decision-making process through gender quotas from a comparative perspective which has not been done before. To our best knowledge, this is the first in-depth comparative study, which explores the impact of gender quotas (e.g., reserved seats) on reducing gender inequality in the political decision-making process in local level governments using the theory of women's substantive representation. The main argument of this study is that, despite facing strong resistance from their male colleagues, women members in reserved seats in both countries influenced the political decision-making process to improve the lives of women.

The remainder of the chapter is organized as follows. We first discuss the historical setting of women's reservation in India and Bangladesh followed by the theoretical arguments on gender quotas and reducing gender inequality. Then we describe the research design and methods. Finally, we present the discussions of our results.

GENDER QUOTAS IN LOCAL COUNCILS IN INDIA AND BANGLADESH: A HISTORICAL SETTING

The miracle of female politicians in India and Bangladesh has prevailed where women have held positions as Prime Minister, President, Chief Minister or opposition leaders several times. The most famous female politicians in India are Indira Gandhi, Sonia Gandhi, Pratibha Devisingh Patil, Sushma Swaraj, and Mamata Banerjee. The most popular female politicians in Bangladesh are Sheikh Hasina Wajed, Begum Khaleda Zia, and Rowshan Ershad. However, although some women have held vital political posts in India and Bangladesh, women in general in both countries are lagging behind men in nearly all spheres of development and democracy. In both countries, women have started to contest elections and have won seats or held political power at various levels of government, but their numbers are still low. Despite this, the lack of representation both countries have helped in mainstreaming women into local government systems, meaning that women's numbers are higher in local governments in comparison to national parliaments. Although women face different difficulties and challenges in India and Bangladesh, policies for reserved seats have increased their numbers in public life and enhanced the social legitimacy of their participation. The introduction and implementation of reserved seats policies in India and Bangladesh have a long tradition and history, which is discussed in the following section.

Historical Context of Reserved Seats in India

The principle of gender equality is enshrined in the India Constitution in its Preamble, Fundamental Duties and Directive Principles (Mathu, 2008, 80). In fact, the Constitution of India not only grants equality to women but also empowers the State to adopt measures of positive discrimination in favor of women. This is aimed at neutralizing the cumulative socio-economic, educational and political disadvantages faced by them (Bala, 2013; Mokta, 2014).

India has a long history of reserved seats for women. Initially, efforts for women's reservation in India emerged in the 1930s, when the country was still a part of the British Empire (Krook, 2009). Reserved seats emerged first in the 1935 Lothian Committee and Government of India Act, were abandoned in 1950 as per the principles of the new Constitution, and re-appeared again in 1988 as part of the government's National Perspective Plan for Women (Krook, 2009; Nugent, 2011). The Government of India Act of 1935 reserved seats for women in the Council of State, Federal Assembly, and various provincial legislatures, and the number of reserved seats were six, nine and forty-one respectively (Afzal, 1999). This Act of 1935 also reserved for fourteen other groups defined by race, religion, professions, and other minority positions (Clokie, 1936; Tinker & Walker 1956). As a result, forty-one women in reserved seats won in the 1937 election across the provincial bodies (Agnew, 1979). The new Constitution of independent India did not include any special provisions for women, it was argued that these were not necessary (Krook, 2009; Tejani, 2008).

However, in 1959, the government of India empowered local leaders to nominate some women for local councils if no female was elected directly. The majority of local councils exercised this right—but policies varied across the states—and co-opted one or two women if no women were directly elected. This system eventually became a critical and often the only, technique for the participation of women in local politics. For instance, there were 320 women in local government in the state of Maharashtra in 1978 but only six women were elected directly (d'Lima, 1993). Later in the 1980s, many states discarded this provision and introduced reserved seats for women in the various levels of local government. For example, the Janata Party government in Karnataka adopted a 25% women's reservation at the village and district level in 1983; the Telugu Desam Party in Andhra Pradesh increased from 9 to 25% reserved seats for women in the district councils in 1986; the Congress Party in Maharashtra declared 30% seats for women in urban corporations and district, block, and village councils in 1990; and the Communist Party government in Kerala reserved 30% of seats for women in district councils in 1991 (Balasu-Brahmayan, 1998; Lama-Rewal, 2001; Manikyamba, 1989).

When the Congress Party came to power in 1991, the newly elected government introduced the 73rd and 74th Amendment Bills to provide for decentralization and one-third reservations for women in rural and urban local government. More specifically, the 73rd Amendment adopted one-third women's reservation in all village, block, and district councils; the post of chairpersons and vice-chairpersons across all the bodies; and reserved seats for SCs and STs in each level of government according to their proportions of the inhabitants (Krook, 2009). The 74th Amendment extended these same measures to municipal corporations in large urban areas, municipal councils in smaller urban settlements, and local councils in changeover from rural to urban status. Under the conditions of both amendments, women in reserved seats would be elected by the voters and rotate across councils every five-year election cycle. The impact of the reservations was dramatic as more than one million women entered local politics after only one round of elections (Krook, 2009). In recent years, some states including Assam, Bihar, Chhattisgarh, Himachal Pradesh, Madhya Pradesh, Manipur, Rajasthan, Uttarakhand and West Bengal, have extended 33% to 50% reservation for women at all levels of local government (Prodip, 2021). Over the decades, India has offered quotas for women to enter local politics; however, a quota for women in the national parliament is still under debate.

Historical Perspective of Reserved Seats in Bangladesh

Bangladesh has a long practice of local government and it is detailed in the Constitution of the People's Republic of Bangladesh (GoB, 2020) which grounded an outline concerning local government bodies through 2 Acts, 59 and 60. Article 59 (1) states that: "Local Government in every administrative unit of the Republic shall be entrusted to bodies, composed of persons elected in accordance with law." Article 60 provides that: "For the purpose of giving full effect to the provisions of article 59, Parliament shall by law, confer powers on the local Government bodies referred to in that article, including power to impose taxes for local purposes, to prepare their budgets and to maintain funds" (Aminuzzaman, 2001, 4).

Since the Independence of Bangladesh in 1971, the first government (1972–1975) did not take any serious measures to ensure women's inclusion in local government institutions (Ali 1986; Alam, 1984). In 1976, the then government introduced the *Local Government Ordinance of 1976* and made a provision to reserve two seats for women at the *Union Parishad* level. The Local Government Ordinance of 1976 (Article 5) specified that: "The *Union Parishad* will comprise one elected chairman and nine elected members, two nominated women members and two peasant representative members" (Sheikh, 2012, 177). This was the first ordinance that made a provision for women's reservation in the *Union Parishad* in Bangladesh in comparison to India as early as 1935. However, the Local Government Ordinance of 1976 had a serious downside as this ordinance directed the government representative to nominate two women members and did not specify the working constituencies, which was different to the other, elected members of the *Parishad*. Women members were mainly dependent on the decision of the chairpersons on any issue in dispute (Ahmed et al., 2003). As a result, the presence of women in the *Union Parishad* was essentially a token representation (Sheikh, 2012, 178). The number of reserved seats for women was enhanced from two to three by *the Local Government Ordinance of 1983*. The Ordinance of 1983 kept the same rules and process of nomination of women in the *Union Parishad* (Khan & Ara, 2006). Thus, the chairperson did not consider women a driving force in taking any important decisions; women members were still viewed as token representative in the *Union Parishad* (Ahmed et al., 2003; Sheikh, 2012). *The Local Government Amendment Act of 1993* abolished the process of nomination by government representatives and made a provision for the selection of three women members by the Union councils. The Act of 1992 directed that the elected chairperson and members of the *Parishad* would appoint three women members. Yet, this act did not specify the working territory for women in reserved seats (Sheikh, 2012). As a result, the honor and prestige of women members remained the same as under the previous acts (Prodip, 2015).

The Local Government (*Union Parishad*) Second Amendment Act of 1997 is considered a landmark in the history of women's political participation and empowerment in Bangladesh (Begum, 2012; Khan & Ara, 2006; Panday, 2013; Prodip, 2014). This act of 1997 has directed that there would be a direct election for reserved seats for women in the *Union Parishad*. In other words, one woman would be directly elected from each of the three wards by the adult franchise. Besides, women could also stand for election for any of the general seats. One of the basic aims of this act was to generate more prospects for women to take part in local politics as well as to get rid of the disadvantages of previous acts. Some structural changes were brought to the *Union Parishad* by this act. Prior to the implementation of the act of 1997, each *Union Parishad* was divided into three wards. Now, each *Union Parishad* is divided into nine wards with general seats. These nine general seats are further allocated to three larger constituencies. Women could contest against other women only in these three larger constituencies and become members of the *Union Parishad*. As a result, women members represent three times larger constituencies than their male colleagues do (Panday, 2013). The Act of 1997 had further made some provisions to ensure women's effective participation in the political process in the *Union Parishad*. This Act has kept a provision directing that one-third of the positions of chair would be reserved for women in standing committees and project distribution and implementation committees in the *Union Parishad*. This Act, however, did not clarify the roles and responsibilities of the women members in the *Union Parishad*.

Due to some difficulties with the 1997 Act, the government of Bangladesh has further enacted the Local Government Act of 2009 in order to specify the roles and responsibilities of women members. Keeping the previous provisions, the Act of 2009 has brought two structural changes to the *Union Parishad*: in the *Ward Shava* and the Chairperson *Panel*. This Act directed that a woman member would be the advisor of the Ward *Shabah* and at least one woman member would be a member of the chairperson panel. Women have received better opportunities to represent their rights and issues in the decision-making process due to the introduction of different amendments, Acts, and provisions (Prodip, 2015, 2016).

Overall, both countries have a relatively long experience of local government and women's reserved seats in their political history. Women in both countries have been advanced in the political sphere through a series of different reforms. Both countries have used the same technique in enhancing women's visibility in local political systems using gender quotas.

GENDER QUOTAS AND GENDER INEQUALITY: A THEORETICAL ARGUMENT

This chapter aims to evaluate the impact of gender quotas on reducing gender inequality in the political decision-making process through using the theory of *substantive* representation—the capability of women to bring changes to women's lives in a society through political engagement (Swers, 2005). Women's substantive representation investigates whether women look for and are capable enough to advance women's interests once they are elected to the political office. A key aim is to figure out if women "make a difference," investigating whether women seek distinct political purposes from those of men (Franceschet, Krook & Piscopo, 2012, 8). Women's substantive representation is originally derived from Hanna Pitkin's (1967) classical work on the political theory of representation that perceived representation consists of formal, descriptive, substantive, and symbolic representation (Burnet, 2011, 304). Most scholars accept Pitkin's concept of representation as a starting point that representatives, who are descriptively analogous "stand for" their citizens and "act for" their constituents by advancing issues of interest to that group. Franceschet, Krook & Piscopo (2012) argued that some theorists make faulty assumptions that descriptive representation leads spontaneously to substantive representation.[1] Thus, Franceschet, Krook & Piscopo (2012) further debated whether substantive representation could be understood from two aspects of representation—process-oriented and outcome-oriented representation. Women's substantive representation as "process" appears when representatives initiate action on behalf of a few or many women. These activities comprise proposing and/or advocating agendas that focus on women's' issues, creating connections to same-minded colleagues or confirming networks with female voters, or placing women's issues on the plan in party platforms or committees. Therefore, women's substantive representation calls for representatives to have genuine perspectives and inclinations when acting as council members. These actions then enhance the prospect that transformative outcomes for organizations and practices arise. Transforming political actions and leading new practices are surely praiseworthy examples of substantive representation as "outcome."[2]

Most of the existing studies have reinforced the theory that women representatives tend to act for policies that promote the priorities of women. Dhalerup (2006) argued that female politicians are more concerned about the issue of equality policies than their male colleagues. Skjeie (1991) argued that female politicians behaved individually in terms of preferences and policy designs once their number are increased in political legislatures. Thomas and Welch (1991) uncovered that female representatives tend to give greater priority to health and welfare issue for women and children in state legislatures in the United States. Stevenson (1999) asserted that women in the Mexican parliament worked to endorse gendered policies for women. Wängnerud (2000) suggested that having more women in legislatures has made changes to policy issues including gender equality, social policy, and family policy in Sweden. Grey (2001) figured out that female parliamentarian pushed for parental leave and childcare policy in the parliament in New Zealand. Bauer and Britton (2006, 20) present a number of evidences of how African women representatives in national parliament have promoted gender issues and influenced legislative programs. Kittleson (2008) contended that women's representative played significant roles in influencing maternity and childcare policies in 19 OECD countries. Devlin and Elgie (2008) claimed that having more women in parliament changes the political program toward matters that are more important for women such as violence against women, and poverty alleviation. Burgos (2012) provided a number of examples from 102 developing countries of how female politicians influence on improving the child health outcomes over time. Duflo (2012) pointed out that women's participation in governing introduces policies that reflect women's priorities such as child health and nutrition as well as issues affecting the bargaining power of women within the household and access to labor markets. Although women representatives have influenced policy agendas, in most cases, they could not bring effective changes to policy outcomes (Devlin & Elgie, 2008). Previous research has shown that most women representatives have worked as proxies for men (Chattopadhyay & Duflo, 2004; Nanivadekar, 2006; Prodip, 2021a), and been loyal to their party leaders (Tripp, 2006; Prodip, 2021b).

The above evidence suggests that reservation policy at the national and local level has the potential to promote women's capabilities as well as to improve the gender balance in the political decision-making process. Therefore, this study aims to understand to what extent and how gender quotas reduce gender inequality in the political decision-making in local councils in India and Bangladesh. In other words, to what extent and how do quota-elected women members raise their voices to influence the decision-making process to bring public goods and resources for their women constituents.

RESEARCH DESIGN AND METHOD

This project applied a qualitative research approach. A qualitative research approach should provide researchers with well-grounded sources of rich data (Miles, Huberman, & Saldana 2014, cited in Austin & Sutton 2014, 436).

Selection of Study Sites and Respondents

The researchers selected *Nadia* district in India and *Rajshahi* district in Bangladesh as study locations. This is because these two study sites in India and Bangladesh have some strong similarities which embrace common culture and languages, as well as administrative evolution. Respondents were selected by purposive sampling. Purposive sampling is "used to select respondents that are most likely to yield appropriate and useful information" (Kelly, 2010, 317), and to choose respondents who are available and willing to provide an interview due to their expertise and relevant knowledge (Bernard, 2011; Spradley, 1999). The argument for selecting a purposive sampling technique is that types of individuals may carry various views about the ideas and concerns relating to the questions of a specific study, and thus, need to be included in the sample (Mason, 2002; Robinson, 2014; Trost, 1986).

This study selected seventy-two respondents (thirty-six each from India and Bangladesh) from different categories. A sample of eighteen elected women members from reserved seats in both countries was selected for interviews. Three elected women members from the reserved seats of each *Gram Panchayat* and three *Gram Panchayats* from each of the two *Panchayat Samiti*[3] of *Nadia* were selected for interviews. Similarly, three elected women members of each *Union Parishad* and three *Union Parishads* from each of the two *Upazilas*[4] of *Rajshahi* district were approached for interviews. In total, thirty-six participants were elected women members from *Nadia* and

Rajshahi districts. In addition, thirty-four key informant respondents were selected to elicit the informants' expert opinions *vis-à-vis* facilitating factors that influence quota women's activities in the *Gram Panchayat* and the *Union Parishad*. The sample size and sample technique are presented in table 9.1.

Data Analysis and Techniques

The data analysis is of a qualitative nature, but basic percentages were provided for respondents' profiling and descriptive purposes. Interviews were conducted in the *Bengali* language in both countries and the seventy-four interviews were translated into English. Data analysis was also accomplished through conversation analysis (Damico, Oelschlaeger, & Simmons-Mackie 1999). Conversation analysis assists researchers in catching responses as broadly as possible. It characterizes the data as authentically as possible, thus

Table 9.1. Sample Size and Technique

Respondents	Method of Data Collection	Number of Respondents Selected	Number of Respondents Interviewed	Sampling Technique	Nadia, West Bengal, India
Elected Women Members	Semi-Structured Interview	18	16	Purposive	Nadia, West Bengal, India
Elected Women Members	Semi-Structured Interview	18	17	Purposive	Rajshahi, Bangladesh
Elected Male Chairmen	Key Informant Interviews	10	9	Purposive	Nadia, West Bengal, India & Rajshahi, Bangladesh
Elected Female Chairmen	Key Informant Interviews	10	9	Purposive	Nadia, West Bengal, India & Rajshahi, Bangladesh
Elected Male Members	Key Informant Interviews	10	9	Purposive	Nadia, West Bengal, India & Rajshahi, Bangladesh
Academicians	Key Informant Interviews	4	4	Purposive	Nadia, West Bengal, India

Total selected respondents 70

Total interviewed respondents 66

enabling the researcher to realize the talk-in-interaction that lies at the heart of conversation analysis (Bloor & Wood 2011).

DISCUSSION OF RESULTS

Respect and Support of Male Colleagues

This study finds that quota-elected women in India, in most cases, do not have the respect and support of their colleagues (male) to their day-to-day affairs in the *Gram Panchayat*. Women members mentioned that although their numbers have been increased due to the introduction of the reservation policy, male representatives still do not consider them as colleagues and as capable to work effectively in the councils. In most cases, male members think that women should have contested against men in elections to prove their leadership qualities. An interview with an experienced woman member reveals how male members usually treat quota-elected women in the *Gram Panchayat*:

> I came to the *Gram Panchayat* in 1994 after the introduction of reservation policy for women. Male colleagues still cannot tolerate women members in the *Gram Panchayat* . . . They want to exclude us from each decision of the *Gram Panchayat*. Sometimes, they argued that we should have stood for elections in general seats and competed against male contestants before talking to the *Panchayat's* meeting. (WMIND05)

Interviews with male members also reveal that they do not want to accept quota-elected women cordially. The majority of male members argued that doing politics in local area is always a tough job. Local politicians need to perform many different tasks and meet different kinds of people for different issues. Local representatives even need to deal with police to solve many legal and social issues. Practically, performing these types of jobs are tough for women as they face some restrictions to come outside their homes at night. A senior male member said:

> In my view, women should stay at home and take care of their children, elders, and family members. They should not work in the public sphere. Politics is men's jobs. However, we do not have any option rather than obeying the rules and regulations of the central and state government. (MMIND01)

Quota-elected women in India have mentioned that male colleagues, especially those who have come to the *Gram Panchayat* from the *Panchayat Samiti*, known as ex-officio members, do not give them any space to work in the *Gram Panchayat*. They control the activities of the *Gram Panchayat* as they hold the top political positions in the party. An interview with a woman member revealed:

> Actually, members (male or female) of the *Gram Panchayat* are not able to work independently. The members who came to the *Gram Panchayat* from the *Panchayat Samiti* usually look after the plans and functions of the office. Personally, I cannot get enough support from them to talk to the meeting. (WMIND09)

The statement of a female *Pradhan* also supports the argument of the above-mentioned woman member:

> The ex-officio members are the *matha* (head) of the *Gram Panchayat*. They are the upper-level politicians and their understanding is better than any elected members of the *Gram Panchayat* have. In most cases, they direct us how to carry out our responsibilities. Thus, we often cannot consider the opinion of all members. (FCPIND03)

Similarly, in Bangladesh, this study finds that, in most cases, male members create severe obstacles to women members' work in the *Union Parishad*. Male members do not want to consider women members as their colleagues. They think that quota-elected women members came to the *Union Parishad* to take an equal share of the projects without having quality. A woman member says, "Male members consider women members as incapable and unqualified to carry out their duties and responsibilities effectively. They always show their traditional patriarchal norms, values, and behaviours to us." Another woman member argued:

> When the council calls for a meeting on how to distribute projects among the members, male members always try to create a fighting situation in the *Union Parishad*. We have received eighty maternal/pregnancy cards this financial year. There is also a legal direction that women members will distribute these cards among the beneficiaries. However, I have received only three cards for my three constituencies. If I would argue for my right, there would be serious fighting with male members. I keep myself calm and quiet to keep a good working environment in the *Union Parishad*. (WMBD08)

This study also reveals that male members have often shown extreme level of disrespect to women members. In some cases, male members have used slang words when women members claimed an equal share of development projects. Male members sometimes threaten women members if they continue to argue. Interviews with academics also revealed that male members still are not mentally ready to accept women members in local politics. They consider women members their opponents and not always competent in their political affairs. Academics argued that due to the absolute majority of male members in the *Union Parishad*, women members are sidelined in the decision-making process.

Affecting Decision-making Processes

Despite having strong male resistance, this study shows that women members in India and Bangladesh have actively participated in different meetings in order to argue for public goods and services for their female citizens. The findings further suggest that quota-elected women members in India are more active in offering core services to their women citizens than the quota-elected women in Bangladesh. The majority of women members in India said that they have worked to develop the quality of pure drinking water, and to improve hygienic toilet systems, whereas a few of them have worked to improve the quality of road connectivity. Indian women members argued that local citizens mostly suffer from the lack of pure drinking water as well as the scarcity of hygienic toilet systems. Lack of pure drinking water has further created extra burdens for girls and women, as they are primarily responsible to collect pure water for their family members. Women members said that they have worked to improve the quality of hygiene sanitation systems in the *Gram Panchayat*. They argued that although the state government implement the hygienic sanitation-related schemes, they initially select the beneficiaries. They encourage their citizens to raise their problems in the *Ward Sabha*. Only a few women members said that they have completed some projects related to road connectivity in the *Gram Panchayat*. They pointed out that doing projects related to road connectivity is very tough as male members usually prefer to do projects on repairing and constructing roads in the *Gram Panchayat*. A woman member explained how she has completed a project related to road's connectivity, "My husband was a member of the *Gram Panchayat*. He has a very good relationship with party leaders in block levels. Thus, *Pradhan* has offered me a project to repair . . . road in my ward" (WMIND05).

Unlike India, women members in Bangladesh have argued that they have much interest in implementing development projects such as the repairing and constructing of roads, bridges and culverts. However, only a few of them have received an equal share of development projects related to reforming and constructing of roads, bridges and culverts. A woman member explained how they have received development projects despite facing strong resistance from their male colleagues:

Male members usually do not want to give any space to women members to talk on the issue of development projects. In some cases, we however, receive an equal share of projects in the *Union Parishad*. Women members who have very good relationship with party leaders or the chairpersons get projects. In last year, I have argued for giving me a project of repairing roads in my wards. However, male members did not want to give me this project. Then, I have informed my party leaders and they talked to the chairperson. Finally, I have completed this project. (WMBD06)

Interviews with chairpersons also support the statement of quota-elected women members in Bangladesh. They mentioned that women members who have strong party affiliation or good personal connections with chairpersons, and come to the *Union Parishad* from strong political families, can influence the decision-making process in the *Union Parishad*. These women are particularly vocal on various issues in the *Union Parishad*.

In my view, most of the quota-elected women members are not capable to handle the issues of the *Union Parishad* due to their low level of education or lack of experience in politics . . . However, some of them have strong connection with political parties as well as chairpersons. A few of them came from a political family which means their husbands/fathers were the members of the *Union Parishad* previously. They usually argue for their equal shares. In such case, it is difficult to avoid them while we distribute different development projects among the members. (WMBD05)

This study also demonstrates that women members who have received training from NGOs can raise their voice strongly in the decision-making process. They are knowledgeable about the rules and regulations of the *Union Parishad*. Thus, the chairpersons and male members cannot avoid them while they distribute development projects among the members.

DISCUSSION AND CONCLUSION

This chapter aimed to evaluate to what extent and how gender quotas reduce gender inequality in the political decision-making process in local councils in India and Bangladesh using the theory of women's substantive representation. Swers (2005) argues that women's substantive representation refers to the capability of women to bring changes to women's lives in a society through political engagement.

This study finds that gender quotas have increased the number of women in local level politics in India and Bangladesh. However, quota-elected women members in both countries have faced serious resistance from their male colleagues. Male counterparts do not accept women members cordially, rather considering them as their competitors. In India, male members argued that quota-elected women members lack leadership qualities as well as the lack of physical mobility to work effectively in the *Gram Panchayat*. Male members, especially ex-officio members, have created strong obstacles to women's access to projects in the *Gram Panchayat*. The ex-officio members usually try to control the plans and functions of the *Gram Panchayat*. As a result, women members do not get enough opportunities to influence the decision-making process to bring resources for their constituents. Similarly, most quota-elected women members in Bangladesh also have limited influence in the decision-making process in the *Union Parishad*. Male members argued that women members are not capable enough and qualified to deal with political affairs in the *Union Parishad*. They sometimes show extreme levels of disrespect and use slang words when women members claim an equal share of development projects. In this regard, academics argued that male members sidelined women members in the decision-making process due to their absolute majority in the *Union Parishad*. The findings of this study support the arguments of previous studies that quota-elected women members encounter male domination in the political legislature (Prodip, 2021b).

Despite having met with strong male resistance, quota-elected women members in both countries have argued that they have influenced the decision-making process to provide public goods and services to their women constituents. They have tried to change the decisions by raising their voices and bringing governmental resources to offer to their women citizens. Women members in India have devoted their time and industry to ensure pure drinking water and hygienic sanitation system for people, particularly for the women. These women members argued that they have used their party affiliation to influence the decision-making process in the *Gram Panchayat*. Due to their good connection with party leaders, the *Pradhan* and male members cannot avoid women members' demands. It was also found that quota-elected women members encouraged their female citizens to raise their problems and issues in the *Ward Sabha*. Women members also talk to the meeting in the *Gram Panchayat* while they prioritize people's demands. A few women members also were keen to implement projects on road connectivity as their husbands help them to get these projects. The findings support the previous research as scholars argued that women members in India are interested in offering public goods and services (Chattopadhyay & Duflo, 2004; Deininger et al., 2011; Priebe, 2017).

Unlike India, women members in Bangladesh have more interest in implementing development projects related to construction of roads, culverts, and bridges. Women members who maintain very good relationships with party leaders and chairpersons have received an equal share of development projects with male members. It was also evident that some women members have come from political families and they have strong influence on the activities of the *Union Parishad*. Apart from this, NGO's interventions enhanced some women members' capability to deal with political matters in the *Union Parishad*. Women members are well briefed about the rules and regulations of the *Union Parishad*. As a result, the chairpersons and male members often cannot avoid women members during the project distribution process. Women members who have received training from the NGOs argued that they have tried to provide services such as offering blankets to elderly poor women in their constituencies. The findings are corroborated by previous studies that argued that gender quotas have enhanced women's voice and social legitimacy in contributing to certain women's issues (Nazneen & Tasnim, 2010; Panday, 2013).

It is interesting to see that quota-elected women members in both countries have used their party affiliations and personal relations with chairpersons to affect the decision-making process. Bangladeshi women also use their family power and tradition to influence the outcome of the decisions. It is also a manifest that NGO's interventions promoted women's capabilities to deal with political issues in the *Union Parishad* in Bangladesh. The empirical investigations of this chapter suggest that, despite facing strong resistance from their male colleagues, women members in reserved seats in both countries influenced the political decision-making process to improve the lives of women in society through offering public goods and services (Swers, 2005).

BIBLIOGRAPHY

Afzal, N. (1999). *Women and Parliament in Pakistan, 1947–1977*. Lahore: Pakistan Study Centre.

Agnew, V. (1979). *Elite Women in Indian Politics*. New Delhi: Vikas Publishing House.

Ahmed, S. et al. (2001). One decade of Bangladesh under women leadership. *Alochona Magazine*, October, p. 3.

Alam, B. A. (1984). Women's Participation in the Local Government in Bangladesh. *The Journal of Local Government*, 13(2), 44–52.

Ali, A. M. M. (1986). *Politics, Development and Upazila*. Dhaka: National Institute of Local Government.

Aminuzzaman, M. S. (2001). *Local Governance and Charland: An Overview*. Retrieved from, http://www.gsdrc.org/docs/open/PF11.pdf (accessed July 12, 2020).

Ara, F. (2017). *Women's Political Participation in the Context of Modernisation: A Comparative Study of Australia and Bangladesh* (PhD disser.). Perth: Murdoch University.

Bala, R. R. G. (2013). Policies and Programmes for the Advancement of Women. *International Journal of Economics, Commerce and Research*, 3(1), 95–106.

Balasubrahmanyan, V. (1998). *Who's Saying What on the Women's Reservation Bill.* Hyderabad: Asmita Resource Centre for Women.

Ban, R., & Rao, V. (2008). Tokenism or Agency? The Impact of Women's Reservation on Village Democracies in South India, *Economic Development and Cultural Change*, 56, 501–530.

Begum, A. (2012). Women's Participation in *Union Parishads*: A Quest for a Compassionate Legal Approach in Bangladesh from an International Perspective. *South Asia: Journal of South Asian Studies*, 35(3), 570–595. doi.10.1080/008564 01.2012.699885.

Bernard, H. R. (3rd Ed.). (2002). *Research Methods in Anthropology: Qualitative and Quantitative Approaches*. Walnut Creek, CA: Alta Mira Press.

Bloor, M. & Wood, F. (2006). Conversation Analysis. In M. Bloor & F. Wood (Ed.), *Keywords in Qualitative Methods* (pp. 39–43). London: SAGE Publications Ltd. doi: 10.4135/9781849209403.

Burnet, J. E. (2011). Women Have Found Respect: Gender Quotas, Symbolic Representation, and Female Empowerment in Rwanda. *Politics & Gender*, 7(3), 303–334.

City Mayor Statistics. (2021). *Largest Cities in the World and their Mayors: Largest Cities with Women Mayors*. Retrieved from http://www.citymayors.com/statistics/ largest-cities-women-mayors.html (accessed August 19, 2021).

Clokie, H. McD. (1936). *The New Constitution for India. American Political Science Review*, 30(6), 1152–65.

d'Lima, H. (1993). Participation of Women in Local Self-government. In S. Kaushik (Ed.), *Women's Participation in Politics*, (pp. 21–30). New Delhi: Vikas Publishing House.

Dahlerup, D. (2005). Increasing Women's Political Representations: New Trends in Gender Quotas. In J. Ballington and A. Karam (Ed.), *Women in Parliament: Beyond Number* (pp. 141–153). Stockholm: IDEA.

Dahlerup, D., & Freidenvall, L. (2005). Quotas as a "Fast Track" to Equal Representation for Women: Why Scandinavia is no Longer the Model. *International Feminist Journal of Politics*, 7(1), 26–48.

Damico, J. S., Oelschlaeger, M., & Simmons-Mackie, N. (1999). Qualitative Methods in Aphasia Research: Conversation Analysis. *Aphasiology*, 13(9–11), 667–679. doi:10.1080/026870399401777.

Franceschet, S., Krook, M. L., & Piscopo, J. M. (2012). *The Impact of Gender Quotas*. New York: Oxford University Press.

Government of Bangladesh [GoB] (2020). The Constitution of the People's Republic of Bangladesh (ACT NO. OF 1972). Retrieved from http://bdlaws.minlaw.gov.bd/ act-367.html (accessed June 30, 2021).

Kelly, S. (2010). Qualitative Interviewing Techniques and Styles. In: Bourgeault I, Dingwall R and de Vries R (Eds.), *The Sage Handbook of Qualitative Methods in Health Research* (pp. 307–326). Thousand Oaks: Sage Publications.

Khan, M. and Ara, F. (2006). Women, Participation and Empowerment in Local Government: Bangladesh Union Parishad Perspective. *Asian Affairs*, 1(29), 73–74.

Krook, M. L. (2009). *Quotas for Women in Politics: Gender and Candidate Selection Reform Worldwide*. New York: Oxford University Press.

Lama-Rewal, S. T. (2001). *Women in the Calcutta Municipal Corporation: A Study in the Context of the Debate on the Women's Reservation Bill*. New Delhi: French Research Institutes in India.

Manikyamba, P. (1989). *Women in Panchayati Raj Structures*. New Delhi: Gian Publishing House.

Mason, J. (2002). *Qualitative Researching*. 2nd Ed. London: Sage Publications Ltd.

Mathu, A. (2008). *Gender and Development in India: The Indian Scenario*. Delhi: Kalpaz Publications.

Mokta, M. (2014). Empowerment of Women in India: A Critical Analysis. *Indian Journal of Public Administration*, 60(3), 473–488.

Munshi, K., & Mark, R. (2010). The Efficacy of Parochial Politics: Caste, Commitment, and Competence in Indian Local Governments. NBER Working Paper No. 14335.

Nugent, A. (2011). *Panchayats, State Reservations and the Women's Question in India: A Historical Trajectory* (Honors disser.). South Hadley.

Panday, P. K. (2013) *Women's Political Participation in Bangladesh: Institutional Reforms, Actors and Outcomes*. New Delhi: Springer.

Pitkin, H. F. (1967). *The Concept of Representation*. Berkeley: University of California Press.

Prodip M. A. (2015). *Women's Participation and Decision-making Power after the Local Government Act of 2009: A Study of Local Government (Union Parishad) in Bangladesh* (Master's dissertation). Bangkok: Asian Institute of Technology, Thailand.

Prodip, M. A. (2014). Decentralization and Women Empowerment in Bangladesh: Union Parishad Perspectives. *International Journal of Scientific & Technology Research*, 3(12), 215–223.

Prodip, M. A. (2016). Gender Quotas in Politics and Empowerment of Women in Bangladesh: Symbolic or Real? *Jahangirnagar Journal of Administrative Studies*, July, 53–68.

Prodip, M. A. (2021). Exclusion through Inclusion: Institutional Constraints on Women's Political Empowerment in India and Bangladesh. *World Affairs*, 184(2), 213–244. doi: 10.1177/00438200211013017.

Robinson, O. C. (2014). Sampling in Interview-based Qualitative Research: A Theoretical and Practical Guide. *Qualitative Research in Psychology*, 11(1), 25–41. Doi: 10.1080/14780887.2013.801543.

Sheikh, S. A. (2012). *Women's Political Empowerment at National and Local Levels through Quotas: A Case Study of Pakistan and Bangladesh* (PhD disser.). Canberra: University of Canberra.

Shvedova, N. (2005). *Obstacles to Women's Participation in Parliament*. In J. Ballington and A. Karam (Ed.), *Women in Parliament: Beyond Number* (Rev. ed. pp. 33–50). Stockholm: IDEA.

Spradley, J. P. (1979). *The Ethnographic Interview*. New York: Holt, Rinehart & Winston.

Tajali, M., & Hoodfar, H. (2011). *Electoral Politics: Making Quotas Work for Women*. London: Women Living under Muslim Laws.

Tejani, S. (2021). *Indian Secularism: A Social and Intellectual History, 1890–1950*. Bloomington: Indiana University Press.

Tinker, I., and Mil, W. (1956). The First General Elections in India and Indonesia. *Far Eastern Survey*, 25(7), 97–110.

Tripp, A. M., & Kang, A. (2008). The Global Impact of Quotas: On the Fast Track to Increased Female Legislative Representation. *Comparative Political Studies*, 41(3), 338–361. doi 10.1177/0010414006297342.

Trost, J. A. (1986). Statistically Non-representative Stratified Sampling: A Sampling Technique for Qualitative Studies. *Qualitative Sociology*, 9(1): 54–57.

United Cities and Local Governments [UCLG]. (2015). *The Equality Agenda of United Cities and Local Governments*. Retrieved from http://issuu.com/uclgcglu/docs/uclg-women-en?e=5168798/2752455 (accessed April 30, 2018).

Vetten, L., Makhunga, L., & Leisegang, A. (2012). *Making Women's Representation in Parliament Count: The Case of Violence against Women*. Braamfontein: Womankind.

World Economic Forum. (2020). *Global Gender Gap Report 2020*. Geneva.

NOTES

1. Susan Franceschet, Mona Lena Krook, and Jennifer M. Piscopo, eds. *The Impact of Gender Quotas* (New York: Oxford University Press, 2012), 396.

2. Ibid., 397.

3. Panchayat Samiti is intermediate level of rural local government in India.

4. Upazilas is the lowest level of field administration in Bangladesh.

Conclusion

Elena V. Shabliy

The book provides an in-depth analysis of global perspectives on advancing public and social gender policy worldwide; it also examines women's political representation and participation (Chapters 8 & 9), their participation in peace processes (Chapter 3) in the context of their community emphasizing existing cultural norms with biases questioning societal prejudices toward women in STEM (Chapter 1) and their participation in creative economies (Chapter 2). The volume covers several domains presenting a wide range of important issues that demonstrate gender inequality, discussing a wide range of cultural and geographical realities. The volume also analyzes how female empowerment can benefit from changing the *status quo* and improving economic and collective action opportunities, as well as how the government can act and whether it should interfere with public policy to alter different norms and practices that hinder women's participation and active involvement globally. Other meaningful topics that are covered in the book are presentation of historic(al) case studies in the field of women in art (Chapter 5), and as political leaders (Chapter 4) while examining global gender dynamics and power hierarchies operating locally and internationally, posing challenges as well as opportunities, perpetuating gender gaps and economic stagnation.

Furthermore, the book concentrates on global policy development and advancing global social justice. The contributors focus on developed county parties (Chapters 1 & 4, and 5), upper-middle-income county parties (Chapters 2 & 8), also analyzing less developed economies (Chapters 3 & 6, 7, 8, and 9). There is a plethora of culturally sensitive aspects discussed by leading scholars on gender issues in low-and middle-income countries offering a global perspective. This book also provides a comparing policy paradigm offering global perspectives regarding gender equity at (inter) national and local levels. The realization of gender policies and advancing them in practice are interlinked with how stakeholders interpret gender equ(al)ity, as well as the effective monitoring of policy implementation. The key to advancing gender equ(al)ity is that the patent patterns of progress and persistence in gender equity do matter—for development outcomes and the policy making process. Gender equity is a core development objective of the nearest future. Greater gender equality also presupposes smart economies that enhance productivity and improve other development aspects, including intergenerational justice and the quality of societal wellbeing. Mere economic development is not sufficient for eradicating all gender disparities—effective policies that focus on persisting gender gaps are essential for the future sustainable society. Higher incomes do not to reduce gender gaps, but advancing gender policy can have a real impact, especially in less developed economies.

In conclusion, it is important to reflect on a place of global community today with regard to gender parity and in wellbeing and gender policy development. This book explores many other gender-related questions. There is growing acknowledgment that wellbeing is a multi-dimensional phenomenon going beyond income, educational attainment and health, considering self-realization, empowerment as well as subjective aspects. The given thematic framework is reflected in the gender analysis that considers gender differences in various key domains, such as agency, livelihood, and wellbeing. This book includes international cultural perspectives by leading scholars in gender studies across geographical regions—Africa, the Arab world, Bangladesh, India, Israel, Serbia, and the US. It aims at graduate students, researchers and professionals on gender policy design. The book may also have a possible impact on a wider audience—human right lawyers, educators, researchers, politicians, decision-makers, human resources managers, and other stakeholders.

Index

About the Editors and Contributors

EDITORS

Elena V. Shabliy graduated with honors from M. V. Lomonosov Moscow State University and received her interdisciplinary PhD from Tulane University in 2016. In 2009, she earned a master of liberal arts degree from Tulane. She was a visiting scholar at Harvard University in 2015–2017 and Columbia University in 2017–2019. She is the editor of *Representations of the Blessed Virgin Mary in World Literature and Art* (Lexington Books, 2017) and co-editor of *Emancipation Women's Writing at Fin de Siècle* (Routledge, 2018), *Renewable Energy: International Perspectives* (Palgrave Macmillan, 2019), *Global Perspectives on Women's Leadership and Gender (In) Equality* (Palgrave Macmillan, 2020), *Women's Human Rights in Nineteenth-Century Literature and Culture* (Lexington Books, 2020), and *Discourses on Sustainability: Climate Change, Clean Energy, and Justice* (Palgrave Macmillan, 2020).

Kimarie Engerman, PhD, is a full professor of psychology and dean of the College of Liberal Arts and Social Sciences at the University of the Virgin Islands.

Dmitry Kurochkin is a lecturer and researcher at Harvard University. He graduated *magna cum laude* from Lomonosov Moscow State University and earned his doctorate at Tulane University. Dmitry Kurochkin is an interdisciplinary scholar and holds master's degrees in a variety of fields, including mathematics and economic analysis and policy. He is the co-editor of *Emancipation Women's Writing at the Fin de Siècle* (Routledge, 2018), *Renewable Energy: International Perspectives* (Palgrave Macmillan, 2019), *Global Perspectives on Women's Leadership and Gender (In)*

Equality (Palgrave Macmillan, 2020), and *Women's Human Rights in Nineteenth-Century Literature and Culture* (Lexington Books, 2020).

CONTRIBUTORS

Melanie Barbini is a graduate of Northeastern University where she majored in behavioral neuroscience. She is planning to apply to medical school and dedicate a career to helping marginalized populations get the health care they deserve.

Moria Ran Ben Hai's research focuses on modern Orthodox feminism in Israel and the United States, from its inception to the present day. Her PhD dissertation sketched Professor Alice Shalvi's biography as a case study for changes in the status of women in Israel from the 1970s to 2000, focusing on the Pelech high school for religious girls and the Israel Women's Network organization. Her current study focuses on the religious feminist organizations JOFA and Kolech.

Dr. Fatou Janneh is an instructor at the University of The Gambia, political science unit. She studied history and international relations in Al-Hikmah and at the University of Ilorin and just completed graduate studies at Ohio University. Her research interests and writing are foreign policy, gender and politics, social justice, and human rights. She was supporting the ECOWAS Early Warning Directorate as field monitor for The Gambia from 2015 to 2019. Her role entailed the monitoring of peace and security indicators for the country, and she provided daily incident and weekly situation reports on the ECOWAS Warning and Response Network (ECOWARN) platform. Janneh also served as CSO coalition domestic observer and situation room analyst in the last presidential, parliamentary, and local government elections of The Gambia, and she has closely worked with local NGOs, mostly WANEP and GAMCOTRAP. She is enthusiastic about educating communities on harmful traditional practices such as FGMC, early marriage, and gender-based violence in The Gambia. Janneh is also a fellow at the study of US institute for Scholars (SUSI) on the US Foreign Policy, 2018 and Erasmus +, Las Palmas de Gran Canaria, 2019.

Dr. Orit Miller Katav teaches a variety of courses at the Middle East studies department. Her postdoctoral thesis was titled *U.S.-Mediated Talks, Overtures, and Agreements between Israel, Jordan, and the PLO 1977–1991*. Her PhD thesis was about U.S.–Israeli—Jordanian relations under the military administration in the occupied territories 1967–1974. She completed her master's degree in political science and Middle East history at Bar Ilan University. This year Dr. Orit Miller Katav graduated from the Weiss Livnat International M.A. Program in Haifa University for holocaust commemoration and education in the digital age. She is a researcher at the Institute for Middle Eastern Studies and Asian Studies in Ariel University and she also writes an opinion column in the daily Israeli newspaper *Maariv*.

Hristina Mikić is associate professor at the Metropolitan University in Belgrade and head of the Research Department in the Institute for Creative Entrepreneurship and Innovation. Ms. Mikić holds a PhD in economics from the Faculty of Economics, University in Belgrade in the field of creative economy. She has been engaged as a consultant and advisor in numerous national and international organizations in the area of cultural and creative industries. These include UNESCO Institute for Cultural Statistics, the Council of Europe, UNDP, World Bank, ministries of cultural affairs in Serbia, Macedonia and Montenegro, Serbian Chamber of Commerce and many others. She has been principal investigator on several regional and international research projects in the comparative cultural and creative industries statistics, developmental model and policy of creative industries (especially in rural and semi-periphery places). Her research interests include cultural and creative industries, female and ethnic creative entrepreneurship, interrelation of creative industries, cultural heritage, tourism, local development, and public policies.

Dr. Ana Belén Perianes Bermúdez is a Spanish political scientist. She completed a PhD in peace and international security and a University specialized degree in Mediterranean, Near, and Middle Eastern security at the University Institute General Gutiérrez Mellado-UNED in Madrid. At present, she works as a postdoctoral researcher on peace, security, and defense affairs at the same institution. Furthermore, she is an associate research fellow at the OSCE Academy in Bishkek, where she is developing research on women, peace, and security in Western and Central Asian countries, an overview of the current situation and implications for women and societies. She is also a member of the Institute for Economics & Peace's Ambassadors Program cohort of 2020. Regarding her fields of specialization, she is particularly focused on women, peace, and security; EU Security and Defense; EU-Central Asia relations and the Belt and Road Initiative; US Foreign Policy; Sahel; human security; and human rights and democratic governance.

Mahbub Alam Prodip is an associate professor in the Public Administration Department at the University of Rajshahi, Bangladesh. He is currently pursuing a PhD in peace studies at the University of New England, Australia. He received his master of science in gender and development studies from the Asian Institute of Technology in Thailand with excellence in research work. He also completed his master of social science and bachelor of social science in public administration from the University of Chittagong in Bangladesh. His research interests are gender, politics and empowerment, gender and violence, political violence and good governance, and health and education of refugee children. He has published a number of articles from peer-reviewed journals including *World Affairs, Asian Journal of Comparative Politics,* and *Policy Studies Yearbook.* He has also published book chapters and book reviews from renowned publishing companies. He (with Goutam Roy & Debasish Nandy) has recently published an edited book titled *Refugee Education in South Asia: Policies, Practices, and Implications* (Nova Science Publishers, 2021).

Maria Santiago-Valentín bas been a learning disabilities consultant and mindfulness educator, behavior analysis therapist, and case manager since 2014. Maria has twenty-nine years of experience as an educator. Prior to becoming an *LDT-C* she was a Spanish/French teacher and World Language Department Chair. Maria appeared listed as behavior analysis therapist in 2016, 2017, and 2018 in the Directory BA-eService of ABA French-Speaking providers published by the Université de Lille III of Nantes, France. Maria was the honorable speaker on July 9 and 10, 2018 at the Global Mental Health Congress in Paris, France, where she presented her paper "An Overview of the Neurological Base of Bipolar Disorder" published by the *Journal of Childhood and Development Disorders.* She is a doctoral candidate in education specializing in reading, literacy, and assessment at Walden University. Maria's eBook, *Bipolar Disorder Etiology and Treatment Overview: Mindfulness, Medication, Digital Psychiatry, and Classroom Accommodations,* won first place under the category special needs/disability awareness at the 2019 Royal Dragonfly Book Awards. She is a collaborating partner of the Organization of Battered and Abused Individuals founded in Trinidad Tobago by Sherna Alexander. Maria was appointed in 2018 as editorial board member of the *International Journal of Psychiatry Research* and education and research associate for the World Bank and the Global Research Network. She is a climate reality project mentor, trainer, and co-presenter. In her town, she is a member of the Franklin Township Environmental Commission. She is one of the contributing authors of *Climate Abandoned,* an anthology edited and compiled by the author Jill Cody. She is cofounder and director of New Jersey Affairs of the non-profit Atlantic Climate Justice Alliance. Maria was inducted by Walden University at their Kappa Delta Phi (International Honor Society of Education) chapter in 2021. Maria, of Puerto Rican origin, resides in New Jersey and has two adult daughters.

Eman Tadros is an assistant professor and the Marriage and Family Counseling Track leader at Governors State University in the Division of Psychology and Counseling. She received her PhD from the University of Akron's counselor education and supervision: marriage and family therapy program. She is a licensed marriage and family therapist, MBTI certified, and an AAMFT approved supervisor. Her research follows the trajectory of incarcerated coparenting, incorporating family therapy into incarcerated settings, and the utilization of family systems theories within these settings.

Ari Baghdassar Tatian is a doctoral researcher in political science at Vrije Universiteit Brussel, working on the theme of women's political representation and participation in Lebanon. He is as well head of Research & Studies Division in the Lebanese Parliament. He is engaged in extensive research activities, both at academic and professional levels. He has taken part in a variety of conferences, seminars, and courses, mainly in Europe and North America, conducted by universities, research centers, international organizations, and legislatures.

Professor Helen Ware, a former diplomat, is the inaugural professor of peace studies at the University of New England, Australia where peace studies has been taught for forty years. She is the author of *Women, Demography and Development*, a classic text on how responses to demography affect women's lives and their countries' development.

www.ingramcontent.com/pod-product-compliance
Lightning Source LLC
Chambersburg PA
CBHW062025270326
41929CB00014B/2318